BIBLIOGRAPHY OF GEOGRAPHY

PART II: REGIONAL
VOLUME 1. THE UNITED STATES OF AMERICA

by

Chauncy D. Harris

SAMUEL N. HARPER DISTINGUISHED SERVICE
PROFESSOR OF GEOGRAPHY
UNIVERSITY OF CHICAGO

THE UNIVERSITY OF CHICAGO
DEPARTMENT OF GEOGRAPHY
RESEARCH PAPER NO. 206

1984

Copyright 1984 by

Chauncy D. Harris

Library of Congress Catalog Card Number: 76-1910

International Standard Book No. 0-89065-112-4

Library of Congress Cataloging in Publication Data
(Revised for part 2, volume 1)

Harris, Chauncy Dennison, 1914-
  Bibliography of geography.

  (Research paper-The University of Chicago,
Department of Geography; no. 206)
  Includes index.
  CONTENTS: --pt. 2. Regional--v. 1. The United
States of America.

  1. Geography--Bibliography. 2. Bibliography--
Bibliography--Geography. I. Title. II. Series:
Chicago. University. Dept. of Geography. Research
paper; no. 206.
H31.C514 no. 179, etc.   910 s[016.91]   76-1910

[Z6001.G116]
ISBN 0-89065-112-4 (pt. 2, v. 1)

Bibliography of Geography: Part I. Introduction to General Aids,
1976, 276 p., Research paper no. 179, has been reprinted and is now available.

Published by the Department of Geography,
The University of Chicago

Research Papers are available from:

   Department of Geography
   The University of Chicago
   5828 University Avenue
   Chicago, Illinois 60637, U.S.A.

Price: $8.00; $6.00 series subscription

PREFACE

Part I of this <u>Bibliography of Geography</u> was published eight years ago. A longer time has elapsed between parts 1 and 2 than was originally anticipated. Work has been delayed by university administrative, teaching, and other obligations of the compiler, by time spent on the third edition of <u>International List of Geographical Serials</u>, the fourth edition of <u>Annotated World List of Selected Current Geographical Serials</u>, and the chapter "Geography" for the third edition of <u>Sources of Information in the Social Sciences</u>, by a period devoted to the study of urbanization in Japan, and by work on a number of articles or sections of books. With approaching retirement from university duties and completion of other projects, the compiler hopes to make more rapid progress on successive parts of this Bibliography.

Current plans envisage that Part II, Regional Geography, will consist of five segments. Two countries will be the subject of individual volumes: the United States, which comprises the present volume, and the Soviet Union, which is planned to be the next. Three later segments are projected to cover continental areas: the Americas (excluding the United States); Europe (excluding the Soviet Union); and Africa, Asia, Australia, and the Pacific. No schedule has been projected for the appearance of these segments.

A brief preliminary section in this volume is devoted to world-wide bibliographies and guides that generally cover all the major regions of the globe, and thus apply to all five of the projected regional segments of Part II.

The present volume, however, is almost entirely devoted to the United States. It is divided into four parts: general aids; physical geography and related earth science and environmental fields; human geography and related social sciences; and the regions, states, and cities of the United States.

This work is devoted to bibliographies, reference works, and sources of data. It is primarily a bibliography of bibliographies that are considered to be valuable for serious scholarly research in the diverse fields to which geographers have addressed their attention. In general it is limited to separately published bibliographies available through regular commercial publishers, university presses, government sources, or associations. Very few articles in periodicals, chapters in books, pamphlets, or fugitive items have been included. Although the emphasis is on bibliographies, a few textual volumes have been listed, which provide an orientation to specific fields, regions, states, or cities, or contain useful bibliographies.

Since this volume has been compiled to be of value in contemporary geographic research on the United States, it emphasizes recent works, particularly those published in the last fifteen years. It includes few items written more than forty years ago. For earlier publications one can turn to John K. Wright and Elizabeth T. Platt, Aids to Geographical Research, 2nd ed., 1947 [entry 10].

Because extensive bibliographies have been published for state and county atlases by E. Willard Miller, Maurice E. McGaugh, Richard W. Stephenson, Mary Galneder, David A. Cobb, and Peter B. Ives [entries 205-209], and for fire insurance maps of cities by the Library of Congress and the Western Association of Map Libraries [entries 203-204], state, county, and city atlases and maps are not separately listed here.

Dissertations and theses submitted in the United States and Canada, or devoted to this area, have been classified by Clyde E. Browning, Dean R. Hodson, Merrill M. Stuart, and the Comprehensive Dissertation Index [entries 229-234] and thus need not be repeated here. They typically contain extensive bibliographies.

Bibliographies in closely related fields have been listed if they provide comprehensive or geographically significant selections that cover the entire United States but not if limited to a part of the country. Thus the lists of publications of the United States Geological Survey are included [entries 186-188], but not state geological survey publications [listed by John B. Corbin, entry 260].

This Bibliography contains 1,257 entries, mostly annotated.

Some entries cover many references. Entry 195 for reports distributed by the National Technical Information Service lists 262 bibliographies or other reports arranged by 17 major subject categories. These reports have been kept separate since most of them are not generally available in libraries and require special procedures for identification and acquisition. They offer valuable leads for research on topics of great current interest, such as air, water, land, and noise pollution; water resources and flood control; energy; urban areas; or transportation. As far as the compiler is aware, this is the first time that a selection and inventory has been made of such bibliographies of potential geographic research value.

Some entries provide detailed information to assist in utilization of a particular source. Thus entry 66 for the Research Catalogue of the American Geographical Society, records in three parallel columns for the Catalogue and its two supplements the location by volume and page numbers of material on the United States classified by 69 topical or regional subdivisions.

The entries in this volume are overwhelmingly in English but a few relevant items in French, German, or Russian have been included.

Thanks are due to Miss Violet Milicevic, who patiently typed and retyped the manuscript and assisted in the compilation of the index.

January 31, 1984   CHAUNCY D. HARRIS

TABLE OF CONTENTS

	Entries	Page
PREFACE		iii

WORLD-WIDE BIBLIOGRAPHIES AND GUIDES   1- 52   1

	Entries	Page
1. Comprehensive Geographical Bibliographies	1- 7	1
2. Selective Guides to the Geographical Literature	8- 13	3
3. Guides to Geographical Serials	14- 15	4
4. Comprehensive General Bibliographies	16- 22	4
5. Selective General Guides to Reference Works and Bibliographies	23- 26	5
6. Statistics	27- 29	7
7. Other Government Publications	30- 32	7
8. Maps and Atlases	33- 41	8
9. Encyclopedias	42- 48	10
a. Geographical	42- 43	10
b. General	44- 48	10
10. Handbooks	49- 52	11

THE AMERICAS AS A WHOLE   53- 54   13
NORTH AMERICA AS A WHOLE   55- 65   13
THE UNITED STATES OF AMERICA   66-974   17

I. GENERAL AIDS   66-249   17

	Entries	Page
1. Comprehensive Geographical Bibliographies	66- 69	17
2. Selective Guides to the Geographical Literature	70- 73	19
3. Geographical Serials	74-129	20
a. Guides	74- 75	20
b. Major Geographical Periodicals	76- 79	20
c. Other Current Geographical Periodicals or Serials with frequent articles or monographs on the United States	80-110	21
d. Other University Series of Monographs with material on the United States	111-114	24
e. Other University Series with shorter articles or discussion papers	115-121	24
f. Other Geographic Periodicals with Regional and Local Focus	122-129	25
4. General Bibliographies and Reference Works	130-133	27
5. Statistics: Guides and Catalogues	134-149	27
6. Statistical Compilations	150-165	30
7. Government Publications	166-198	33
a. Comprehensive Inventories	166-174	33
b. Selective Guides	175-184	34
c. Publications in Special Areas or of Individual Departments or Bureaus	185-194	36
d. Reports distributed by the National Technical Information Service	195	37
e. Publications of State and Municipal Governments	196-198	53
8. Maps, Atlases, and Remote Sensing	199-223	53
a. Guides to Maps and Atlases	199-209	53
b. Atlases and Maps	210-219	55
c. Aerial Photographs and Remote Sensing	220-222	57
d. Map Collections	223	57
9. Encyclopedia	224	57
10. Gazetteers	225-226	57
11. Reviews	227-228	58
12. Dissertations and Theses	229-234	58
13. Directories	235-236	59
14. Textual Treatises of the Geography of the United States	237-249	60

v

		Entries	Page
II.	PHYSICAL GEOGRAPHY, RELATED EARTH SCIENCES, THE ENVIRONMENT, AND RESOURCES	250-389	63

    1. General Information Sources — 250-258 — 63
    2. Geomorphology and Geology — 259-262 — 64
    3. Energy and Minerals — 263-279 — 65
    4. Water Resources, Hydrology, Water Management and Floods — 280-307 — 67
    5. Coastal Resources and Management — 308-318 — 72
    6. Climate — 319-327 — 73
    7. Vegetation — 328-333 — 75
    8. Soils — 334-337 — 75
    9. Land Use — 338-347 — 76
    10. Conservation — 348-351 — 77
    11. Natural Landscapes and Open Space — 352-358 — 77
    12. Environment and Environmental Protection — 359-373 — 78
    13. Pollution — 374-383 — 80
    14. Hazards — 384-389 — 81

III. HUMAN GEOGRAPHY AND RELATED SOCIAL SCIENCES — 390-856 — 83

    1. Urban Geography and Related Studies — 390-513 — 83
        a. General — 390-417 — 83
        b. Urban Systems — 418-429 — 86
        c. Central Places and Capitals — 430-432 — 88
        d. Growth — 433-436 — 88
        e. City Classifications — 437-438 — 88
        f. Internal Structure — 439 — 88
        g. Urban Ecology and Neighborhoods — 440-441 — 89
        h. Land Use and Zoning — 442-445 — 89
        i. Commerce — 446-453 — 89
        j. Urban Transportation — 454 — 90
        k. Housing — 455-460 — 90
        l. Social Processes, Ethnic Neighborhoods and Ghettos — 461-465 — 91
        m. Urban Renewal — 466 — 91
        n. Urban Preservation — 467 — 91
        o. Governance and Services — 468-473 — 92
        p. City Planning — 474-480 — 92
        q. Suburbs — 481-489 — 93
        r. Small Towns — 490 — 94
        s. New Towns — 491-493 — 94
        t. Single Enterprise Communities — 494 — 94
        u. Problems — 495-496 — 94
        v. Urban Studies in Related Disciplines — 497-513 — 95

    2. Economic Geography — 514-615 — 97
        a. General Economic Geography of the United States — 514-517 — 97
        b. Industrial Location — 518-522 — 97
        c. Manufacturing — 523-528 — 98
        d. Mining — 529-530 — 98
        e. Agriculture — 531-551 — 99
        f. Trade — 552-554 — 101
        g. Transportation — 555-581 — 101
        h. Energy — 582-583 — 104
        i. Land Resources and Land Use — 584-597 — 104
        j. Housing — 598 — 106
        k. Regional Development and Economic Regions — 599-603 — 106
        l. Related Studies in Economics and Business — 604-615 — 106

			Entries	Page
3.	Social Geography		616-645	108
	a.	General	616-622	108
	b.	Elderly	623-628	109
	c.	Women	629	109
	d.	Poverty	630-632	109
	e.	Crime	633-640	110
	f.	Related Studies in Sociology	641-642	110
	g.	Related Studies in Psychology	643-645	111
4.	Studies of Ethnic Groups		646-701	111
	a.	General	646-664	111
	b.	Indians	665-669	113
	c.	European Immigrants	670-678	114
	d.	Afro-Americans	679-692	115
	e.	Hispanic Americans	693-699	116
	f.	Asian Americans	700-701	117
5.	Cultural Geography		702-720	117
	a.	General Studies	702-707	117
	b.	Settlements (excluding Cities)	708-709	118
	c.	Houses and Farm Buildings	710-714	118
	d.	Other Special Studies	715-717	118
	e.	Related Studies in Anthropology	718-720	119
6.	Population Geography		721-740	119
	a.	General Studies	721-729	119
	b.	Migration	730-738	120
	c.	Comprehensive Bibliography	739-740	121
7.	Medical Geography		741-752	121
	a.	General	741-744	121
	b.	Health Care Services	745-750	122
	c.	Spatial Aspects and Ecology of Disease	751-752	122
8.	Political Geography		753-767	122
	a.	General	753-755	122
	b.	Political Areal Organization	756-763	123
	c.	Other Special Studies	764-766	123
	d.	Related Studies in Political Science	767	124
9.	Historical Geography		768-827	124
	a.	Bibliographies and Guides	768-770	124
	b.	Surveys of Research in the Field	771-777	125
	c.	General Historical Geography of the United States	778-780	125
	d.	Studies in Topical Fields	781-796	126
		(1) Settlements and Frontiers	781-783	126
		(2) Immigration and Ethnicity	784	126
		(3) Cities	785-788	126
		(4) Agriculture	789-790	126
		(5) Land Survey	791-793	127
		(6) Historical Preservation	794-796	127
	e.	Regional Studies	797-824	128
		(1) The Northeast	797-804	128
		(2) The South	805-807	128
		(3) The Middle West	808-814	128
		(4) Texas and the Southwest	815-818	129
		(5) Exploration and Fur Trade of the West	819-821	129
		(6) The Pacific Northwest and Alaska	822-824	130
	f.	Related Studies in American History	825-827	130

		Entries	Page
10.	Geography of Recreation, Leisure, and Tourism	828-844	130
11.	Geographic Education	845	132
12.	Applied Geography	846	132
13.	Place Names	847	132
14.	General Guides to the Social Sciences	848-856	133

IV. REGIONS OF THE UNITED STATES — 857-974 — 135

    1. Regions and Regionalism in General — 857-858 — 135

    2. The Northeast — 859-880 — 135
        a. General — 859-861 — 135
        b. New England — 862-867 — 135
        c. The Middle Atlantic States — 868-876 — 136
        d. Border States — 877-880 — 136

    3. The South — 881-903 — 136
        a. General — 881-887 — 136
        b. South Atlantic States — 888-893 — 137
        c. Kentucky and Tennessee — 894-896 — 138
        d. Louisiana — 897-899 — 138
        e. Texas — 900-903 — 138

    4. The Middle West — 904-927 — 138
        a. General — 904-906 — 138
        b. East North Central States — 907-917 — 139
        c. West North Central States and The Great Plains — 918-927 — 140

    5. The West — 927a-974 — 141
        a. Mountain States — 928-939 — 141
        b. California — 940-958 — 142
        c. Pacific Northwest — 959-965 — 143
        d. Alaska — 966-971 — 144
        e. Hawaii — 972-974 — 144

INDEX OF SUBJECTS, AUTHORS, AND SHORT TITLES — 145

RESEARCH PAPERS, DEPARTMENT OF GEOGRAPHY, UNIVERSITY OF CHICAGO. COMPLETE LIST — At back of volume

WORLD-WIDE BIBLIOGRAPHIES AND GUIDES

1. COMPREHENSIVE GEOGRAPHICAL BIBLIOGRAPHIES

RESEARCH catalogue of the American Geographical Society.
Boston, Massachusetts: G. K. Hall, 1962. 15 v. v. 3-15 regional.   1

_____. First supplement [1962-1971]. Boston: G. K. Hall, 1972.
Regional part, 2 v.

_____. Second supplement [1972-1976]. Boston: G. K. Hall, 1978.
v. 2, Regional catalogue.

RESEARCH catalogue of the American Geographical Society Collection at the
University of Wisconsin-Milwaukee. Third supplement [1976-1980]. At the
end of 1983 the publication date had not yet been set.   1a

Covers principally the 60 years 1923-1982 but some earlier references
are included. For later years see Current geographical publications [2].
The most comprehensive cumulative bibliography of regional geography for
the years covered. International in scope but with fuller coverage of works
in English. The three supplements are much easier to use than the original
basic catalogue; they have better tables of contents, indexes, and headings
and more legible reproductions of cards. In utilizing the catalogue it is
well to remember that works with material on a particular country may be
listed either under the country or under a larger region which includes the
country.

Location of entries for regions and individual countries are listed
under each region or country in this Guide.

Cards for supplements 1976- are being accumulated in special
trays at the American Geographical Society Collection at the University of
Wisconsin-Milwaukee, and may be consulted there.

CURRENT geographical publications: additions to the Research Catalogue of the
American Geographical Society Collection of the University of Wisconsin-
Milwaukee Library. 1- (1938-). 10 nos. a year. Indexes. The American
Geographical Society Collection at the University of Wisconsin-Milwaukee
Library, P. O. Box 399, Milwaukee, Wisconsin 53201. v. 1-41, no. 2 (1938-
February 1978) published by the American Geographical Society, New York.   2

A major current geographic bibliography, organized both by region and
by systematic field. Since the entries for the period 1938 through 1976 have
been cumulated in the Research catalogue of the American Geographical Society
and its supplements [1], the monthly issue of Current geographical publications generally need be consulted only for the issues of 1977 and later. The
annual indexes, however, provide alphabetical topical index, author index,
and regional index, and thus are useful even for earlier years, since the
cumulated Research catalogue does not have such indexes.

GEO abstracts, 1960- . 7 separate series, each with 6 numbers a year. Geo
Abstracts, Ltd., University of East Anglia, Norwich NR4 7TJ, England.
1960-1965 as Geomorphological abstracts, 1966-1971 as Geographical abstracts
in 4 series A-D, 1972-1973 as Geo abstracts in 6 series, 1974- as Geo abstracts
in 7 series A-G.   3

cont.

In seven series: A. Landforms and the Quaternary; B. Climatology and hydrology; C. Economic geography; D. Social and historical geography; E. Sedimentology; F. Regional and community planning; G. Remote sensing, photogrammetry, and cartography.

Organization is by subdivisions of systematic fields not by regions. Works on particular regions or countries are therefore widely scattered. Annual indexes in no. 6 each year of each series provide a regional listing by entry numbers and an alphabetical author index. Since 1966 Annual separately published subject indexes (1966-1971 in one volume, 1972- in 2 volumes; v. 1 for series A, B, E, and G and v. 2 for series C, D, and F), in alphabetical order contains names of places, particularly if part of title, an author index and a list of journals. 5-year cumulative indexes for each series 1960-1965 (series A only), 1966-1970 (series A, B, C, and D), 1971-1975 (series A, B, C, and D), 1972-1976 (series E and F), 1974-1978 (series G).

BIBLIOGRAPHIE géographique internationale, v. 1-81 (1891-1976), annual; 1977- , quarterly, v. 1-60 (1891-1953) published by Librairie Armand Colin, 103 Boulevard Saint-Michel, 75005 Paris, France. v. 61-81 (1954-1976) published by Centre National de la Recherche Scientifique, 15, Quai Anatole France, 75700 Paris, France. 1977- published by Centre National de la Recherche Scientifique, Laboratoire d'Information et de Documentation en Géographie (INTERGÉO), 191, rue Saint-Jacques, 75005 Paris, France. v. 1-24 (1891-1914) as supplement to Annales de géographie. v. 23-24, 1913-1914; v. 25-29, 1915-1919; v. 30-31, 1920-1921, v. 50-54, 1940-1944; v. 55-56, 1945-1946; v. 59, 1949-1950; v. 60, 1951-1953; v. 61, 1954-1955; and v. 81, 1975-1976 (mislabeled 1975 on cover), include more than one year. 4

The most international and best balanced bibliography of regional geography, extending already over more than 90 years. In French with supplementary English table of contents and headings.

Under each region or country in this Guide the years are noted in which this area has a section in Bibliographie géographique internationale.

GEOGRAPHISCHES Jahrbuch. Gotha/Leipzig: VEB Hermann Haack Geographisch-Kartographische Anstalt. 1-12 (1866-1888), biennial; 13-58 no. 1 (1889-1944), annual (except in 1915-1925); 58, no. 2- (1948-), irregular and infrequent. 5

A great bibliographical enterprise, now largely of historical interest, but still of value in comprehensive retrospective bibliographies up to the mid-1930s. Extensive critical discussions in German.

GEOLIT: Rezensionen: Geographie, Raumwissenschaften. 1977- . 4 per annum (2 in 1977). 6

Recent books in geography, particularly in German (or English), noted and reviewed. Each issue has a section on regional geography. Some issues present broader reviews of works on specific regions.

REFERATIVNYI zhurnal: geografiia (Reference journal: geography). 1954- 12 numbers a year. Vsesoiuznyi Institut Nauchnoi i Tekhnicheskoi Informatsii, Baltiiskaia ulitsa 14, 125219 Moskva A-219, U.S.S.R. 7

Massive and detailed geographical bibliography. Especially strong in coverage of technical publications. Detailed coverage of works in Russian and other languages of the Soviet Union but includes publications in all languages. Abstracts in Russian.

In 1982 divided into two parts: part 1, systematic, and part 2, regional.

Regional sections are: E. Geography of the USSR; Zh. Geography of Europe outside the Soviet Union; I. Geography of Asia outside the Soviet Union and of Africa; K. Geography of the Americas and Australia, Oceania, and Antarctica.

Separately published annual subject and geographical index and author index.

2. SELECTIVE GUIDES TO THE GEOGRAPHICAL LITERATURE

HARRIS, Chauncy D. Bibliography of geography. Part I. Introduction to general aids. Chicago, Illinois: University of Chicago, Department of Geography, Research paper no. 179, 1976. 276 p. Index.

Covers bibliographies of bibliographies, comprehensive current bibliographies of geography, comprehensive retrospective bibliographies of geography, specialized bibliographies of geography, books, serials, government documents, dissertations, photographs, maps and atlases, gazetteers, place-name dictionaries, encyclopedias, statistics, and methodology in geography, with appendices listing gazetteers of the U. S. Board on Geographic Names and a small geographic reference collection. Comparative analysis of current and retrospective bibliographies of geography, pp. 25-86. 8

LEWTHWAITE, Gordon R., PRICE, Edward T., Jr., and WINTERS, Harold A., eds. A geographical bibliography for American college libraries. rev. ed., Washington, D. C.: Association of American Geographers, 1970. 214 p. (Commission on College Geography. Publication no. 9). Index. (1st ed. Robert E. Huke, Martha Church, and Wilbur Zelinsky, eds. A basic geographical library: a selected and annotated book list for American colleges, 1966. 153 p.). 9

Part IV, "Works Grouped by Region," p. 103-197, provides a list of 862 major geographical treatises, particularly in English, on major regions of the world, up to 1969.

WRIGHT, John Kirtland, and PLATT, Elizabeth T. Aids to geographical research: bibliographies, periodicals, atlases, gazetteers and other reference books. 2nd ed. completely revised. New York: published for the American Geographical Society by Columbia University Press, 1947. 331 p. Reprinted: Westport, Connecticut: Greenwood Press, 1971. (1st ed., 1923). 10

Part III, "Regional Aids and General Geographical Periodicals," p. 134-272, provides an overview of bibliographies and sources on the major regions, countries, and empires up to 1946, and is thus useful for historical studies and for works published between World War I and World War II.

BREWER, J. Gordon. The literature of geography: a guide to its organisation and use. 2nd ed. London: Clive Bingley; Hamden, Connecticut: Linnet Books, 1978. 264 p. (1st ed., 1973). 11

Chapter 13, "Regional geography," p. 219-240, provides a discussion of the principal substantive works on the geography of the major regions of the world.

BLOTEVOGEL, Hans H., and HEINEBERG, Heinz. Bibliographie zum Geographiestudium. Teil 3. Regionale Geographie: Deutschland, Europa, Sowjetunion. Paderborn: Ferdinand Schöningh, 1980. 304 p. Author index. Place and regional index. Teil 4. Regionale Geographie: Asien. Afrika. Nordamerika. Lateinamerika. Australien. Ozeanien. Ozeane. Polargebiete. Paderborn: Ferdinand Schöningh. 1981. 372 p. Author index. Place and regional index. 12

The most comprehensive, up-to-date, organized, and annotated (in German) listing of significant works in regional geography, by region and country. Annotations are signed. Particularly full in coverage of works in German and English, somewhat less so for works in French or other languages.

ARNIM, Helmuth. Bibliographie der geographischen Literatur in deutscher Sprache. Baden-Baden: Librairie Heitz, 1970. Reprinted: Baden-Baden: Koerner, 1980. 177 p. (Bibliotheca bibliographica Aureliana, 21). Author index. 13

cont.

Section 3, "Regionale Geographie," p. 87-132, lists 477 major works on regional geography in German, particularly for the period 1930-1970, arranged by regions.

NOH, Toshio. Bibliography of regional geography in western languages and regional bibliographies with emphasis on geography. Science reports of Tohoku University, 7th series, Geography, v. 19, no. 1 (1969). Appendix. 58 p. Author index. 13a

About 800 references arranged in two parts: regional geography in western languages; regional bibliographies with emphasis on geography. The larger first part is arranged by continent, then by country. The smaller second part is arranged by continent. Good coverage of works in English, French, and German.

3. GUIDES TO GEOGRAPHICAL SERIALS

HARRIS, Chauncy D., and FELLMANN, Jerome D. International list of geographical serials, third edition, 1980. Chicago: University of Chicago, Department of Geography, Research Paper no. 193, 1980. 457 p. 14

Comprehensive list of 3,445 geographical serials from 107 countries in 55 languages, by countries in alphabetical order. Includes both current and closed serials. Limited to geographical serials proper, although some entries, particularly in earlier years, include serials geographical in name but general in content. Notes dates and frequency of publication, listing in union catalogues, name changes, cumulative indexes, abstracts, and address of publication (if current).

HARRIS, Chauncy D. Annotated world list of selected current geographical serials, fourth edition, 1980. Chicago: University of Chicago, Department of Geography, Research paper no. 194, 1980. 165 p. 15

443 carefully selected current geographical serials considered to be of the greatest continuing scholarly geographic interest, usefulness, and accessibility. Entries from 72 countries arranged in alphabetical order. Annotations on nature of contents, editors, publishers, inclusion of abstracts, and language utilized.

Includes a study of serials most cited in geographical bibliographies.

4. COMPREHENSIVE GENERAL BIBLIOGRAPHIES.

SUBJECT guide to books in print, 1957- . Annual. New York: Bowker (Xerox). 16

Annual listing of books currently in print in English classified under subjects. For regional works see names of individual countries. [1983-1984, 1983. 3 v. 6,098 p.].

BESTERMAN, Theodore. A world bibliography of bibliographies and of bibliographical catalogues, calendars, abstracts, digests, indexes, and the like. 4th ed. Lausanne: Societas Bibliographica, 1965-1966. 5 v. 8,425 columns. Second printing: Totowa, New Jersey: Rowman and Littlefield, 1971. (1st ed., 1939-1940). 17

Regions and countries in alphabetical order, interspersed with other types of headings, with listing of bibliographies in chronological order down to 1963.

TOOMEY, Alice F. A World bibliography of bibliographies 1964-1974: a list of works represented by Library of Congress printed catalog cards. A decennial supplement to Theodore Besterman, A World bibliography of bibliographies. Totowa, New Jersey: Rowman and Littlefield, 1977. 2 v. 1166 p. 18

About 18,000 titles of bibliographies. Limited to separately published bibliographies represented by Library of Congress printed cards, reproduced photographically, in classed arrangement without notation of number of entries. Similar to U. S. Library of Congress catalogs. Subject catalog, cumulations for 1965-1969 and 1970-1974 [19], but restricted to bibliographies.

SUBJECT catalog. Library of Congress. 1950-1982. Quarterly with annual cumulations. Washington, D. C.: Library of Congress. Title 1950-1974: U. S. Library of Congress Catalog. Books: Subjects. Cover title: Library of Congress catalogs. Subject catalog. Closed 1982.

Quinquennial cumulations:
(a) 1950-1954. Ann Arbor, Michigan: J. W. Edwards, 1955. 20 v.
(b) 1955-1959. Paterson, New Jersey: Pageant Books, 1960. 22 v.
(c) 1960-1964. Ann Arbor, Michigan: J. W. Edwards, 1965. 25 v.
(d) 1965-1969. Ann Arbor, Michigan: J. W. Edwards, 1970. 42 v.
(e) 1970-1974. Totowa, New Jersey: Rowman and Littlefield, 1976. 100 v.   19

Includes books received and catalogued by the Library of Congress and other American libraries participating in its cooperative cataloging program. Entries by subject only. Subjects include names of continents, countries, regions, provinces, states, and cities. From 1983 a subject index is included in the National Union Catalog.

BRITISH Museum (now British Library). Department of Printed Books. Subject index of the modern works added to the Library, 1880- .   20

    1881-1900 (1902-1903), 3 v.   1931-1935 (1937), 2 v.
    1901-1905 (1906), 1 v.   1936-1940 (1944), 2 v.
    1906-1910 (1911), 1 v.   1941-1945 (1953), 1 v.
    1911-1915 (1918), 1 v.   1946-1950 (1961), 4 v.
    1916-1920 (1922), 1 v.   1951-1955 (1974), 6 v.
    1921-1925 (1927), 1 v.   1956-1960 (1965-1966), 6 v.
    1926-1930 (1933), 1 v.   1961-1970 (1982), 12 v.

See under name of country.

BIBLIOGRAPHIC index: a cumulative bibliography of bibliographies. 1937- . 3 issues a year, the last being an annual cumulation. Also multiyear cumulations. New York: H. W. Wilson.   21

Cumulations: 1937-1942 (1945); 1943-1946 (1948); 1947-1950 (1951); 1951-1955 (1956); 1956-1959 (1961); 1960-1962 (1963); 1963-1965 (1966); 1966-1968 (1969).

See under name of country.

BIBLIOGRAPHISCHE Berichte; bibliographical bulletin (BB); (Staatsbibliothek Preussischer Kulturbesitz). 1- (1959-). Frankfurt am Main: Vittorio Klostermann.   22

International classified list of recent bibliographies. See section 1.11 Regional bibliographies.

              5. SELECTIVE GENERAL GUIDES
         TO REFERENCE WORKS AND BIBLIOGRAPHIES

SHEEHY, Eugene P., with the assistance of Rita G. Keckeissen and Eileen McIlvaine. Guide to reference books. 9th ed. Chicago: American Library Association, 1976. 1,015 p.   23

cont.

    See especially the following sections, which are arranged by countries: Section AA, Bibliography: National and trade, p. 39-81; Section AG, Government publications, p. 191-203; Section CG, Statistics: Compendiums, p. 481-497; and Section D, History and area studies, p. 610-689.

_____. Supplement. 1980. 305 p.   23a

    See especially sections AA, Bibliography: National and trade, p. 8-15; AG, Government publications, p. 37-40; CG, Statistics: Compendiums, p. 131-134; D, History and area studies, p. 183-209.

_____. Second supplement. 1982. 243 p.   23b

    See particularly sections 2AA, Bibliography: National and trade, p. 6-11; 2AG, Government publications, p. 27-29; 2CG, Statistics, p. 109-112; and 2D, History and area studies, p. 151-169.

WALFORD, Albert John, with the assistance of Joan M. Harvey and L. J. Taylor. Guide to reference material. v. 2 Social and historical sciences, philosophy and religion. 4th ed. London: The Library Association, 1982. 812 p.   24

    Section 908. Area studies, p. 365-443, provides a carefully selected list of regional bibliographies, by continents, cultural realms, and countries, geographically arranged. See also v. 2, section 31. Statistics, p. 104-127; and in v. 3, Generalities, languages, the arts and literature (3rd ed, 1977), section 015. National bibliographies, p. 17-51; and section 087.7. Government publications, p. 181-192.

U. S. LIBRARY OF CONGRESS. The Library of Congress main reading room reference collection subject catalog. Compiled and edited by Katherine Ann Gardner. 2nd ed. Washington, D. C.: Library of Congress, 1980. 1,236 p.   25

    See under name of country or region.

AMERICAN Universities Field Staff. A select bibliography: Asia, Africa, Eastern Europe, Latin America, ed. by Phillips Talbot and Nelda S. Freeman. New York: American Universities Field Staff, Inc., 1960. 534 p. Indexes of authors, titles, journals, and bibliographies.   26

    7,544 entries organized by major geographical areas and by countries, and within countries, topically. Selected by specialists on each area. The more important items, especially recommended, are marked by the letters "A" (about 10 per cent of the entries) and "B" (another 20 per cent), and are annotated.

_____. _____. Cumulative supplement 1961-1971, ed. by Teg C. Grondahl, Janet E. Gregory, and Manon Spitzer. New York, and Hanover, New Hampshire: American Universities Field Staff, Inc., 1973. 357 p. Indexes of authors and of titles. 26a

    8,449 entries for the period 1961-1971 organized by major geographical areas and by countries and within countries by topics. Replaces and cumulates the supplements published in 1961, 1963, 1965, 1967, 1969, and 1972.

6. STATISTICS

(See also 5. Selective General Guides to Reference Works and Bibliographies and 7. Other Government Publications)

TEXAS. University. Population Research Center. *International population census bibliography*. Austin, Texas: Bureau of Business Research, 1965-1968, 7 v.   27

    World-wide coverage of population censuses. v. 1, Latin America and the Carribean; v. 2, Africa; v. 3, Oceania; v. 4, North America; v. 5, Asia; v. 6, Europe; v. 7, supplement 1968.

    Entries arranged alphabetically by area, then chronologically. Contents of multivolume reports are indicated.

GOYER, Doreen S. *International population census bibliography: revision and update, 1945-1977*. New York: Academic Press, 1980. 576 p. (Texas bibliography II).   27a

    Supplement to preceding entry. Extends coverage of national and territorial censuses through 1977. Entries arranged by country in alphabetical order. Includes original title and English-language title.

U. S. LIBRARY of Congress, Census Library Project. *Statistical yearbooks: an annotated bibliography of the general statistical yearbooks of the major political subdivisions of the world*. Prepared by Phyllis G. Carter. Washington, D. C.: Library of Congress, Card Division, 1953. 123 p.   28

    Detailed listing with full bibliographical notations of the statistical yearbooks of each country, arranged by continent and then by country or area (200 countries or areas).

STATISTICS *sources: a subject guide to data on industrial, business, social, educational, financial, and other topics for the United States and internationally*. Edited by Paul Wasserman and others. 7th ed. Detroit, Michigan: Gale Research Co., 1982. 1388 p. Bibliography.   29

    About 26,000 references arranged under 12,000 subject headings with finding guides to sources of statistical information. "Subject headings" include individual countries.

7. OTHER GOVERNMENT PUBLICATIONS

(See also 5. Selective General Guides to Reference Works and Bibliographies)

NEW YORK Public Library. Research Libraries. *Catalog of Government publications in the Research Libraries*. Boston, Massachusetts: G. K. Hall, 1972. 40 v. *Dictionary catalog of government publications: supplement 1974*. 1976. 2 v.   30

    Catalog of more than one million volumes of government publications or public documents, arranged by country, subdivided by departments, bureaus, and offices, and by political subdivisions such as states, provinces, or cities.

    Serials and monographs separately under each agency. Serials arranged alphabetically, monographs by date of publication.

    About 280,000 cards.

BIBLIOGRAPHIC guide to government publications--foreign. 1975 - . Annual. Boston, Massachusetts: G. K. Hall, 1976- .   31

   Based on publications cataloged each year by the Library of Congress and the Research Libraries of the New York Public Library. All entries integrated into one alphabetical sequence. Access is by main entry (corporate body or author) or added entries (titles, series titles, and subject headings). Thus though based on much the same material as that in the Subject catalog. Library of Congress [19], differs in being limited to government publications but in providing more access points to this material.

BUXTON, Elizabeth M. A guide to government and other official publications for social and economic geography. Thesis approved for fellowship, The Library Association, 1966. 557 p. Index. Typed. Reproduced by University Microfilms, Ltd., Tylers Green, High Wycombe, United Kingdom, LAT-43.   32

   See under region, continent, country, and sometimes under state or province. Mainly for the period 1950-1965 but series listed can be examined for publications of later date.

8. MAPS AND ATLASES

STATUS of world topographic mapping, World cartography, v. 14 (1976), p. 3-67.   33

   Covers topographic mapping at scale of or larger than 1:253,440, as of the end of 1974, based on questionnaire responses from 87 countries.

   Part I, Statistical summary, p. 4-21, notes total area covered and percentage of area covered for each country by topographic maps at four ranges of scale. Part II, Inventory of world topographic mapping, p. 22-63 lists for 87 countries, in alphabetical order, each topographic map series. Information for each series includes scale, title, number of sheets produced, relief, style, projection, and ellipsoid.

WINCH, Kenneth L., ed. International maps and atlases in print. 2nd ed. London and New York: Bowker, 1976. 866 p.   34

   Information on maps and atlases published throughout the world covering all countries including both official surveys and commercially produced maps, but excluding aeronautical and nautical navigation charts. Arranged by world region and country, and within each country by maps and atlases by subject matter.

   Includes about 400 map-index diagrams of multi-sheet series, with record of sheets published.

GEO-KATALOG. In two parts. Band 1. Touristische Veröffentlichungen. Landkarten, Reiseführer, Pläne, Atlanten, Globen aus aller Welt. Maps, plans, guides, atlases, globes. München: GeoCenter Verlagsbetrieb, 1972- . Annual. [1983. 612 p. plus Blattschnitt-Teil].

   Band 2. International. Amtliche geographisch-thematische Karten und Atlanten. Schnittübersichten von Kartenwerken. Official geographic-thematic maps and atlases. Indexes of map series. Stuttgart: GeoCenter Internationales Landkartenhaus, 1976. In two looseleaf volumes with distribution several times each year of groups of sheets to replace provisional or earlier indexes.   35

   The most comprehensive current world-wide inventory of available maps.

cont.

Map series both topographic and scientific-geographic thematic. Index sheets showing status of publication and availability of sheets in key topographic series and in thematic series, such as geological, hydrographic, or vegetation maps. Supplemented by Geo-Kartenbrief, 4-6 times a year, listing major new publications.

Supersedes Zumstein-Katalog. Landkarten, Reiseführer, Globen aus aller Welt, 1964-1971, editions 1-8, and RV-Katalog über deutsche und ausländische Landkarten, Reiseführer, Atlanten und Globen in systematischer geographischer Ordnung, für alle Teile der Welt, 1958-1971, looseleaf.

BRITISH Museum (from 1973 British Library). Catalogue of printed maps, charts, and plans. Photolithographic edition to 1964. London: British Museum, 1967. 15 v. Corrections and additions. 1968. 55 p. 36

A complete inventory of the great collection of printed maps, atlases, globes, and other cartographic material in the Map Room and other parts of the British Library at the end of 1964. About 225,000 entries. Alphabetical arrangement. See under names of country.

_____. _____. Ten-year supplement 1965-1974. London: Published for the British Library by the British Museum Publications Limited, 1978. 1,380 cols. 36a

NEW YORK Public Library. Research Libraries. Map Division. Dictionary catalog. Boston, Massachusetts: G. K. Hall, 1971. 10 v. 37

186,748 cards representing some 280,000 sheet maps, 6,000 atlases, and other cartographic publications, and 11,000 volumes other than atlases on the history of map making, bibliographies, and related topics in a single alphabetical order.

AMERICAN Geographical Society. Map Department. Index to maps in books and periodicals. Boston, Massachusetts: G. K. Hall, 1968. 10 v. 38

Comprehensive and unique bibliography of 164,338 cards of maps that appear in books or articles, not as separate publications. Alphabetical arrangement by subject, place, and author.

_____. First supplement. 1971. 603 p.

12,654 cards for the period 1968-1971.

_____. Second supplement. 1976. 568 p.

11,826 cards for the period 1972-1975.

AMERICAN Geographical Society Collection at the University of Wisconsin-Milwaukee. Index to maps in books and periodicals. Third supplement. Copy has been prepared for 1976-1982 but the work was not in press at the end of 1983. 38a

BIBLIOGRAPHIE cartographique internationale. 1936-1975. Annual. Closed 1975. Paris: Comité National français de géographie, 1938-1947; Armand Colin, 1949-1970; Librairie de Faculté de Sciences, 1972-1979 and Nendeln, Liechtenstein: Kraus-Thomson Organization, 1973-1979. 1936 as Bibliographie cartographique de la France; 1937-1945 as Bibliographie cartographique française; 1938-1945, 1946-1947, and 1951-1952 covered by single volumes. Indexes. 39

For the years covered a major source of information on maps published on all parts of the world. Edited in turn by Myriem Foncin, Pauline Sommer, and Christine Motsch.

U. S. LIBRARY OF CONGRESS. Map Division. A list of geographical atlases in the Library of Congress, with bibliographical notes. v. 1-4 by Philip Lee Phillips. v. 5-8 by Clara Egli LeGear. Washington, D. C.: Government Printing Office, 1909-1974. 8 v. indexes. v. 1-4 reprinted by Theatrum Orbis Terrarum Ltd., 1970, with bibliographical notes. 40

    v. 6 covers 2,647 atlases of Europe, Asia, Africa, Oceania, the polar regions, and the oceans acquired 1920-1960.

    v. 7 covers 8,181 atlases of the Western Hemisphere acquired 1920-1969.

ALEXANDER, Gerard L. Guide to atlases: world, regional, national, thematic: an international listing of atlases published since 1950. Methuchen, New Jersey: Scarecrow, 1971. 671 p. Index of authors, cartographers, and editors. 41

    Listing of 5,556 atlases published 1950-1970 with bibliographical details but no annotations.

_____. Supplement: An international listing of atlases published 1971 through 1975 with comprehensive indexes. 1977. 362 p.

    Listing of 2,993 atlases published 1971-1975.

9. ENCYCLOPEDIAS

a. Geographical

WESTERMANN Lexikon der Geographie. Ed. by Wolf Tietze. Braunschweig: Westermann, 1968-1972. 5 v. 42

    The most widely useful geographic encyclopedia with authoritative articles on major regions and countries of the world. Bibliographies written by 125 leading German geographers.

KRATKAIA geograficheskaia entsiklopediia (Short geographic encyclopedia). Moskva: Sovetskaia Entsiklopediia, 1960-1966. 5 v. 43

    Extensive articles on major world regions and countries. Bibliographies. Tables. Particularly useful for the Soviet Union and the countries of Eastern Europe.

b. General

NEW Encyclopaedia britannica in 30 volumes. 15th ed. Chicago, London, Toronto, etc.: Encyclopedia Britannica, Inc. 1974. 30 v. 44

    Micropaedia, 10 v. has short articles on about 14,000 places. The Macropaedia, 19 v., has long signed articles on continents, major regions, countries, large cities, and major physical features. Geographers from 60 countries contributed. The most international of the major encyclopedias.

    For some purposes the late printings (1970-1973) of the 14th edition, with extensive revisions and a detailed index volume are also valuable, or the original printings of editions 1-14 (1768-1929), especially the 9th ed., 1875-1889, the 11th ed., 1911, and the 14th ed., 1929.

LA GRANDE encyclopédie. Paris: Librairie Larousse, 1971-1978. 21 v. 45

    An entirely new encyclopedia at an advanced level. Articles on continents, countries, and cities. Emphasis on geography, history, society, economy, politics, art, and literature. Articles also on physical sciences and technology. Numerous colored maps, colored photographs, and tables. Bibliographies.

BROCKHAUS Enzyklopädie in 20 Bänden. 17th ed. Wiesbaden: F. A. Brockhaus, 1966-1974. 20 v. v. 21, Karten, 1975. Ergänzungen, v. 22, 1975, v. 23, 1976. (1st ed., 1796-1808). 46

Articles on continents, countries, and cities. Bibliographies.

MEYERS Enzyklopädisches Lexikon in 25 Bänden. 9th ed. Mannheim; Wien; Zürich: Bibliographisches Institut, Lexikonverlag, 1971-1979. 25 v. v. 26 Nachträge A-Z, 1980. v. 27. Weltatlas, 1979. 458 p. plus index 140 p. larger format (38 cm.). v. 28 Personenregister, 1981. v. 29 Bildwörterbuch Deutsch-English-Französisch, 1981. (1st ed., 1840-1855). 47

Many short articles but some longer ones. Articles on continents and countries have many tables, maps, charts, and illustrations (both in color and black-and-white). Bibliographies.

BOL'SHAIA sovetskaia entsiklopediia (Large Soviet encyclopedia). 3rd ed. Moskva: Izdatel'stvo "Sovetskaia Entsiklopediia, 1970-1978. 30 v. v. 24, part 2, USSR, 1977. Index, 1 v. 1981. (1st ed., 1927-1947. 2nd ed., 1949-1960). 48

World-wide in coverage but especially detailed on the Soviet Union and communist countries of East-Central and Southeast Europe.

Available also in English translation: Great Soviet encyclopedia. New York: Macmillan, and London: Collier Macmillan, v. 1-30, 1973-1982. v. 31, USSR, 1982. v. 32, Index.

10. HANDBOOKS

STATESMAN'S year-book: statistical and historical annual of the states of the world, for the year. 1864- . London: Macmillan; New York: St. Martin's Press, 1864- . v. 1- . Annual. Index. 49

Concise up-to-date information on each country of the world, revised annually. Arranged by countries in alphabetical order. Topics covered typically include history, area and population, constitution and government, defense, international relations, economy, energy and natural resources, industry and trade, communications, justice, religion, education, welfare, and diplomatic representatives. Section on international organizations. Bibliographies. [1982-83].

EUROPA yearbook: a world survey. 1959- . Ed. 1- . London: Europa Publications, 1959- . Annual. (Predecessors from 1926). 2 v. 50

Statistical tables for each country plus an introductory survey, government information, and directories of organizations in communications, trade and industry, transport, finance, and universities, revised annually. [1983. 2 v., 3600 p.].

WORLDMARK encyclopedia of the nations. Edited and published by Moshe Y. Sachs. 5th ed. New York: Worldmark Press, 1976. 5 v. v. 1, United Nations; v. 2, Africa; v. 3, Americas; v. 4, Asia; and v. 5, Europe. (1st ed., 1960). 51

Well-organized, brief, comparable data on 162 countries of the world arranged in a uniform outline of 50 topics including location, size, and extent; topography; climate; flora and fauna; population; ethnic groups; language; religion; transportation; communications; history; migration; international cooperation; economy; labor; agriculture; domestic trade; foreign trade; economic policy; and housing. Bibliographies.

MEYERS Kontinente und Meere in 8 Bände. Daten, Bilder, Karten. Werner Jopp, ed.
Mannheim, Wien, Zürich: Geographisch-Kartographisches Institut Meyer.
Bibliographisches Institut, 1968-1973. 8 v. 52

1. Afrika, 1968. 380 p.
2. Mittel- und Südamerika, 1969. 360 p.
3. Nordamerika, 1970. 400 p.
4-6. Europa, ed. by Werner Jopp and Adolf Hanle. 3 v. v. 1 A-F, 1971. 343 p.
   v. 2 G-O, 1972. 325 p. v. 3 P-Z, 1972. 328 p.
7. Sowjetunion, 1969. 340 p.
8. Asien (ohne Sowjetunion), Australien, Inseln und Meere, ed. by Adolf Hanle, 1973. 460 p.

Lengthy introductions to the continental areas as a whole, organized topically under geology, geomorphology, climate, vegetation, soil, peoples, population, economy, cultural landscape, history, bibliography (organization varies slightly from volume to volume), with numerous colored and black-and-white maps; major regions; alphabetically arranged articles on countries and places. Articles unsigned but many geographers contributed.

THE AMERICAS AS A WHOLE

See also   Latin America, North America, and South America.

RESEARCH catalogue of the AGS [1], "The Americas," v. 3, p. 1963-1995, 2445-2446. 707 entries for 1923-1961. First supplement, Regional, v. 1, pp. 1-2. 43 entries for 1962-1971. Second supplement, v. 2, Regional, pp. 1-2. 30 entries for 1972-1976.   53

780 references dealing with diverse aspects of the Americas as a whole including both North and South America.

BIBLIOGRAPHIE géographique internationale [4], "Amérique. Généralités," "Amérique. Ensemble," or "Amérique: ensemble et sous-continents," v. 1-57 (1891-1947), 59 (1949-1950), 62 (1956), 64 (1958), 65 (1959), 69 (1963), 71 (1965), and 76 (1970), annual, and v. 82- (1977-), quarterly.   54

NORTH AMERICA AS A WHOLE

Or Major Segments Covering More Than One Country. See also The Americas as a Whole, Latin America, the United States, Canada, Mexico, Central America, and the Caribbean.

RESEARCH catalogue of the AGS [1], "North America," v. 3, p. 1995-2022 and 2094-2098. 675 entries for 1923-1961. First supplement, Regional, v. 1, pp. 2-6, and 22. 128 entries for 1962-1971. Second supplement, v. 2, Regional, pp. 2-4, and 12-13. 70 entries for 1972-1976.   55

873 references on North America as a whole or on major segments extending over parts of two or more countries.

BIBLIOGRAPHIE géographique internationale [4], "Amérique du Nord: ensemble," v. 58-81 (1948-1975/1976), annual. See also "Amérique. Généralités," or "Amérique. Ensemble et sous-continents," 1891- [54].   56

GEOGRAPHISCHES Jahrbuch [5], "Nordamerika." or "Nordamerika. Der Erdteil."   57
a. 1931-1942, by Bruno Dietrich, v. 58, part 1 (1943), p. 88-109. Author index. 345 entries on the geography of North America as a whole, 1931-1942, arranged topically: American studies, bibliographies, geography as a discipline, regional geographies, travels, general geology, geomorphology, tectonics, stratigraphy, climate, waters, plants, animals, races and Indians, population, economy, fishing, trade, history of development, and history. Textual discussion of principal works for each systematic field.
b. 1916-1930, by Bruno Dietrich, v. 45 (1930), p. 243-261, 300.
315 entries, 1916-1930, arranged topically, with discussion.
c. 1914-1921, by Kurt Hassert, v. 39 (1919-23), p. 273-280.
148 bibliographical footnotes, with discussion.
d. 1900-1913, by Emil Deckert. 1908-1913, v. 37 (1914), p. 3-7; 1905-1907, v. 32 (1909), p. 389-392; 1902-1904, v. 27 (1904), p. 425-430; 1900-1901, v. 25 (1902), p. 91-98.
304 bibliographical footnotes, with discussion.
e. 1890-1899, by B. Weigand. 1897-1899, v. 22 (1899), p. 408-414; 1895-1896, v. 20 (1897), p. 175-177; 1893-1894, v. 18 (1895), p. 251-255; 1890-1892, v. 16 (1893), p. 447-449.
117 bibliographical footnotes, with discussion.
f. 1876-1889, by Franz Boas. 1887-1889, v. 14 (1890/91), p. 108-110; 1876-1886, v. 12 (1888), p. 73-74.
14 bibliographical footnotes, with discussion.

BIBLIOGRAPHY of North American geology, 1785-1970. Washingtin, D.C.:
Government Printing Office, 1923-1973. (U. S. Geological Survey Bulletins).
Closed 1970.   58

1785-1918. By John M. Nickles. U.S.G.S. Bulletins 746 and 747. 1923-1924.
    2 v. (Title: Geologic literature on North America, 1785-1918). Part 1,
    Bibliography, part 2, Index.
1919-1928. By John M. Nickles. U.S.G.S. Bulletin 823. 1931.
1929-1939. By Emma Mertins Thom. U.S.G.S. Bulletin 937. 1944. 2 v.
1940-1949. By Ruth Reece King and others. U.S.G.S. Bulletin 1049. 1957. 2 v.
1950-1959. By Ruth Reece King and others. U.S.G.S. Bulletin 1195. 1965. 4 v.
1960. U.S.G.S. Bulletin 1196. 1964.
1961. U.S.G.S. Bulletin 1197. 1965.
1962. U.S.G.S. Bulletin 1232. 1966.
1963. U.S.G.S. Bulletin 1233. 1968.
1964. U.S.G.S. Bulletin 1234. 1966.
1965. U.S.G.S. Bulletin 1235. 1969.
1966. U.S.G.S. Bulletin 1266. 1970.
1967. U.S.G.S. Bulletin 1267. 1970.
1968. U.S.G.S. Bulletin 1268. 1971.
1969. U.S.G.S. Bulletin 1269. 1972.
1970. U.S.G.S. Bulletin 1370. 1973.

    Covers the North American continent, Greenland, the West Indies and
adjacent islands, Hawaii, and Guam. Succeeded by Bibliography and index of
Geology, v. 33- , 1969- (Boulder, Colorado: Geological Society of America,
1969-1978; Falls Church, Virginia: American Geological Institute, 1979-   ).
Monthly with annual cumulations.

CLIMATES of North America. Reid A. Bryson and F. Kenneth Hare, eds. Amsterdam;
London; New York: Elsevier Scientific Publishing Co., 1974. 420 p. (World
survey of climatology, H. E. Landsberg, editor-in-chief, v. 11). Reference   59
index. Geographical index. Subject index.

    Text, maps and tables. 355 references, arranged by North America as a
whole, p. 46-47; Canada and Alaska, p. 188-192; conterminous United States,
p. 261-266; and Mexico, p. 389-390.

KÜCHLER, A. William, and McCORMICK, Jack. Vegetation maps of North America.
Lawrence, Kansas: University of Kansas Libraries, 1965. 453 p.
(International bibliography of vegetation maps, v. 1; University of Kansas
publications. Library series, no. 21).   60

    Lists about 1400 vegetation maps of North America, arranged regionally:
North America General, Canada (by provinces), United States (by regions and
states), Mexico, Central America (by countries), and the Caribbean (by countries), and within each area by date. Information includes title, colors,
scale, full legend, author, and standard bibliographical citation. Includes
both separately published maps and ones contained in books and articles.

    A shorter version (A. William Küchler and Jack McCormick, Bibliography of
vegetation maps of North America, Excerpta botanica, sectio B, sociologica,
v. 8, 1967, p. 145-289) omits the legends of the listed maps, add or drops a
few items, and has 987 numbered entries, arranged regionally.

KNAPP, Rüdiger. Die Vegetation von Nord- und Mittelamerika und der Hawaii-
    Inseln. The Vegetation of North and Central America and of the Hawaiian
    Islands. Stuttgart: G. Fischer, 1965. 373 p. Bibliography, p. 323-364.
(Vegetationsmonographie der einzelnen Grössräume, 1).   61

    About 1400 references listed in bibliography, arranged alphabetically by
author.

SHELFORD, Victor E. The ecology of North America. Urbana, Illinois: University of Illinois Press, 1963. 610 p. Locality index. Species index. Bibliography, p. 495-531. 62

Nearly 1000 references listed alphabetically by author.

VALE, Thomas R. Plants and people: vegetation change in North America. Washington, D. C.: Association of American Geographers, Resource Publications in Geography, 1982. 88 p. Bibliography, p. 68-88. 63

481 references.

MURDOCK, George P., and O'LEARY, Timothy J. Ethnographic bibliography of North America. 4th ed. New Haven, Connecticut: Human Relations Area Files Press, 1975. 5 v. v. 1, General North America. v. 2, Arctic and subarctic. v. 3, Far West and Pacific coast. v. 4, Eastern United States. v. 5, Plains and Southwest. Bibliographies. (1st ed. 1941). 64

About 40,000 entries on native ethnic groups of North America, arranged by regions with ethnic group subdivisions. The general introduction discusses sources of materials not included, such as government publications and dissertations.

HANDBOOK of North American Indians. Washington, D. C.: Smithsonian Institution; for sale by the Government Printing Office. 1978- . In progress. To be 20 vols. but volumes are not published in numerical order. Each vol. has index and bibliography. 65

v. 6. Subarctic. June Helm, ed. 1981. 837 p. Index. Bibliography.
v. 8. California, Robert F. Heizer, ed. 1978. 800 p. Index. Bibliography.
v. 9. Southwest. Alfonso Ortiz, ed. 1979. 700 p. Index. Bibliography.
v. 10. Southwest. Alfonso Ortiz, ed. 1983. 868 p. Index. Bibliography.
v. 15. Northeast. Bruce G. Trigger, ed. 1978. 924 p. Index. Bibliography.

Volumes still be be published: 1. Introduction; 2. Indians in contemporary society; 3. Environment, origins, and population; 4. History of Indian-White relations; 5. Arctic; 7. Northwest Coast; 11. Great Basin; 12. Plateau; 13. Plains; 14. Southeast; 16. Technology and visual arts; 17. Languages; 18, 19. Biographical dictionary; 20. Index.

United States:
Comprehensive Geographical Bibliographies

THE UNITED STATES OF AMERICA

I. GENERAL AIDS

1. COMPREHENSIVE GEOGRAPHICAL BIBLIOGRAPHIES

RESEARCH catalogue of the AGS [1], "United States," v. 3, pp. 2446-2782, v. 4, 2783-3569, and v. 5, pp. 3571-4157. 35,884 entries for 1923-1961. First supplement, Regional, v. 1, pp. 78-340. About 8,100 entries for 1962-1971. Second supplement, Regional, v. 2, pp. 47-195. About 4,450 entries for 1972-1976.   66

Topic or Area (AGS Classification)	Research Catalogue 1923-1961 v. 3, p.	First Supplement 1962-1971 Regional v. 1, p.	Second Supplement 1972-1976 v. 2, Regional p.
THE UNITED STATES AS A WHOLE	2446-2782	78-134	47-96
General geography (1)	2449-2454	78- 79	47-48
Travel and exploration (2)	2454-2456	79	48
Mathematical geography (3)	2456-2467	79- 81	48-50
Positions, surveying, remote sensing (34)	2456-2463	79- 80	48-49
Theoretical geography (36)	-	80	49
Cartography (39)	2463-2467	80- 81	49-50
Physical geography (4)	2468-2517	81- 90	50
Geology (42)	2469-2471	81- 82	50-56
Geomorphology (43)	2471-2485	82- 84	50-52
Hydrology (44)	2485-2496	84- 87	52-53
Oceanography (45)	2497-2498	87- 88	53-54
Meteorology and climatology (46)	2498-2513	88- 90	54-55
Biogeography (47)	2514-2517	90	55-56
Human geography (5)	2517-2769	91-130	56-95
Statistics (5001)	2520-2526	91- 92	57
Population geography (52)	2529-2589	95-110	61-75
Urban geography (5252)	2572-2589	101-110	69-75
Economic geography (53)	2589-2744	110-127	75-91
Natural resources and related industries (531)	2597-2695	111-122	76-85
Mineral resources; mining...(5311)	2621-2641	117-118	80-82
Agriculture...(5312)	2641-2672	118-121	82-83
Forests and forestry (5313)	2672-2685	121	83-84
Animal industries (5314)	2685-2693	121-122	84-85
Products of water bodies (5315)	2693-2695	122	85
Industrial geography (532)	2695-2706	122-123	85-88
Transportation communication (533)	2706-2726	123-125	88-90
Commerce; trade (534)	2726-2739	125-126	90
Labor (535)	2739-2741	126	90-91
Political geography (54)	2744-2756	127-128	91-92
Social and cultural geography (55)	2756-2767	128-130	92-95
Historical geography (6); History of Geography	2769	-	95
Geographical teaching and institutions (7)	2769-2776	130-133	95-96
Teaching of geography (71)	2771-2772	131-132	95
Geographical institutions (75)	2772-2776	132-133	95-96
Aids to geographical study (8)	2776-2778	133-134	96
Bibliographies (81)	2776-2777	133	96
Gazetteers (82)	2777	133	-
Atlases (83)	2777	133	96
Periodicals (85)	2777	-	-
Biographies (86)	2777-2778	134	96
History (9)	2778-2782	134	96

cont.

United States: 18
Comprehensive Geographical Bibliographies

	Research Catalogue 1923-1961	First Supplement 1962-1971 Regional	Second Supplement 1972-1976 Regional
REGIONS IN THE UNITED STATES	vols. 4-5	v. 1, p.	p.
	vol. 4		
Eastern United States (6-9, 6-7)	2783-2795	134-136	96- 98
Northeastern United States (6, 6.7a)	2795-2809	136-141	98-101
New York (6a)	2809-2889	141-154	101-111
New England (6b)	2889-2993	154-166	111-117
New Jersey, Pennsylvania (6c)	2993-3055	167-176	117-123
Southern United States (7.9)	3055-3078	176-178	123-125
Southeastern United States (7)	3078-3080	178-179	125-126
Delaware, D. C., Maryland, Virginia, West Virginia (7a)	3080-3137	179-189	126-131
Georgia, North Carolina, South Carolina (7b)	3137-3191	189-198	131-134
Florida (7c)	3191-3231	198-205	135-137
Mississippi Valley and the West (8-10)	3233-3256	205-207	138-139
North Central States, Great Plains (8)	3256-3281	207-211	139-140
Minnesota, North Dakota, South Dakota (8a)	3281-3337	211-220	140-144
Michigan, Wisconsin (8b)	3337-3396	220-228	145-148
Kansas, Nebraska (8c)	3396-3437	228-234	148-151
Illinois, Iowa, Missouri (8d)	3437-3516	234-244	151-156
Indiana, Ohio (8e)	3516-2569	244-251	156-159
	vol. 5		
Oklahoma, Texas (9a)	3571-3649	251-261	160-164
Alabama, Arkansas, Louisiana, Mississippi (9b)	3649-3717	261-271	164-168
Kentucky, Tennessee (9c)	3717-3752	271-276	168-170
Western United States (10)	3752-3780	276-279	170-172
Oregon, Washington (10a)	3780-3845	279-289	172-176
Idaho, Montana, Wyoming (10b)	3845-3901	290-297	176-179
California (10c)	3901-4030	298-316	179-188
Arizona, Nevada, Utah (10d)	4030-4108	316-331	188-192
Colorado, New Mexico (10e)	4108-4157	331-340	192-195
Alaska (1)	vol. 3, p. 2023-2094	5- 21	4- 12
Hawaii (46b1)	vol. 14, p. 9939-9967	v2:616-621	580-582

A <u>Third supplement</u>, 1976-1980, has been prepared but was not yet in press at the end of 1983.

BIBLIOGRAPHIE géographique internationale [4], "États-Unis," 1891-1976, annual; 1977- , quarterly.

Organization varies over the years. Since 1947 entries have generally been grouped into three main sections: physical geography, human geography, and regional studies.

GEOGRAPHISCHES Jahrbuch [5], "Vereinigte Staaten von Amerika."

1931-1942, by Bruno Dietrich, v. 58, part 1 (1943), p. 109-232, and v. 59, part 2 (1948), p. 285-428. Author indexes.

4,095 entries, of which 2,008 in systematic arrangement and 2,087 regional. Textual discussion.

1916-1930, by Bruno Dietrich, v. 45 (1930), p. 300-390 and v. 46 (1931), p. 227-340.

    1,662 entries on the United States as a whole in systematic arrangement and 1,810 entries on individual regions or states.

1914-1921, by Kurt Hassert, v. 39 (1919-1923), p. 290-322.

    Discussion of literature 1914-1921, with 709 bibliographical footnotes.

1900-1901, by Emil Deckert, v. 25 (1902), p. 102-114, 1902-1904, v. 27 (1904), p. 434-445, 1905-1907, v. 32 (1909), p. 397-408, 1908-1913, v. 37 (1914), p. 14-26.

    Discussion of literature 1900-1913, with 1,050 bibliographical footnotes.

1890-1892, by B. Weigand, v. 16 (1893), p. 452-459, 1893-1894, v. 18 (1895), p. 358-367, 1895-1896, v. 20 (1897), p. 183-192, 1897-1899, v. 22 (1899), p. 421-432.

    References 1890-1899, with 700 bibliographical footnotes.

1876-1886, by Franz Boas, v. 12 (1888), p. 83-104, and 1887-1889, v. 14 (1890/91), p. 113-122.

    Literature 1876-1889 on geography and ethnography, with 173 bibliographical footnotes.

    In aggregate some 9,490 references on the geography of the United States and related fields over the period 1876-1942 with textual discussion of the principal work by systematic fields and regions for given periods.

REFERATIVNYI zhurnal: geografiia [7], K "S.Sh.A." 1954- . Monthly. About a thousand entries a year for the United States, with abstracts in Russian.   69

2. SELECTIVE GUIDES TO THE GEOGRAPHICAL LITERATURE

WHEELER, Jesse H. "U.S.A.," Chapter 8, in A Guide to information sources in the geographical sciences, edited by Stephen Goddard. London: Croom Held; Totowa, New Jersey: Barnes and Noble, 1983, p. 131-178.   70

    The most detailed and up-to-date discussion of the geographical literature on the United States and its regions. Sections devoted to international sources that include material on the United States, works devoted to the United States as a whole and its historical, physical, political, cultural, social, economic, and urban geography, and to its regions: the Northeast, the South, the Middle West, and the West, and their states and localities.

LEWTHWAITE, Gordon R., PRICE, Edward T., Jr., and WINTERS, Harold A., eds. A geographical bibliography for American college libraries. rev. ed. Washington, D. C.: Association of American Geographers, 1970. 214. [9]   71

    "Anglo-American," entries 909-1090, p. 104-123, covers bibliographies, serials, atlases, statistical sources, general, historical geography, physical geography, human geography, economic geography, and regions: Northeastern states, Southeastern states, North Central states and the Great Plains, and the West.

BLOTEVOGEL, Hans H., and HEINEBERG, Heinz, eds. Bibliographie zum Geographiestudium. Teil 4. Regionale Geographie: Asien, Afrika, Nordamerika, Lateinamerika, Australien, Ozeanien, Ozeane, Polargebiete. Paderborn: Ferdinand
Schöningh, 1981. 372 p. [12]. 72

6.1, "Nordamerika insgesamt," p. 230-235, 40 annotated references, and 6.3
"USA," p. 246-268, 179 annotated references. Works on the United States as a
whole, and on its systematic and regional geography. Annotations by Heinz
Heineberg, Norbert de Lange, Hans Blotevogel, and Günter Tiggesbäumker.

DURRENBERGER, Robert W. "Regional--United States," in his Geographical research
and writing, p. 152-156. Entries 379-435. 73

57 references listed alphabetically by author.

3. GEOGRAPHICAL SERIALS

a. Guides

HARRIS, Chauncy D., and FELLMANN, Jerome D. International list of geographical
serials, third edition, 1980 [14]. "United States of America," p. 361-386,
entries 2989-3298. 74

List of 321 geographical serials, both current and closed, published at some
time in the United States.

HARRIS, Chauncy D. Annotated world list of selected current geographical serials,
fourth edition, 1980 [15], "United States," p. 129-137, entries 378-424. 75

47 selected current geographical serials published in the United States,
with annotations. A substantial fraction of the geographical literature on the
United States is published in these serials.

b. Major Geographical Periodicals

ASSOCIATION of American geographers. Annals. Washington, D. C. 1- (1911-).
Quarterly. Cumulative indexes: v. 1-25 (1911-1935), 26-55 (1936-1965), and
56-65 (1966-1975). 76

The leading scholarly geographical periodical of the United States with long
and short articles and book reviews.

GEOGRAPHICAL review (American Geographical Society of New York). New York.
1- (1916-). Quarterly. Cumulative indexes: v. 1-15 (1916-1925), 16-25
(1926-1935), 26-35 (1936-1945), 36-45 (1946-1955), 46-55 (1956-1965). 77

Includes original articles, extensive signed notes, and critical reviews.
Annual and cumulative indexes provide one of the best entries into the corpus
of geographical work on the United States.

ECONOMIC geography (Clark University). Worcester, Massachusetts. 1- (1925-).
Quarterly. Cumulative indexes: v. 1-25 (1925-1949), 26-41 (1950-1965). 78

A major journal devoted entirely to the field of economic geography, particularly of the United States, with original articles and book reviews.

Snipe's index to Annals of the Association of American Geographers, issues
1 through 1978, Snipe's index to the Geographical Review, issues origin (1916)
through 1978, and Snipe's index to Economic Geography, issues 1 through 1978
(all 3rd ed. Manitou Springs, Colorado: Snipe International, 1979 or 1980)
index by broad regions and subjects and by author these three leading geographical periocials. Also Snipe's index to the Professional geographer. 7

c. Other Current Geographical Periodicals or Serials
with frequent articles or monographs on the United States

AMERICAN cartographer (American Congress on Surveying and Mapping). Falls Church, Virginia. 1- (1974-). 2 per annum. 80

Articles on all aspects of cartography. Reviews. Recent literature. Cartographic news.

ANTIPODE: a radical journal of geography. Worcester, Massachusetts. 1- (1969-). 3 nos. a year. 81

Articles and essays with a radical viewpoint on social, economic, environmental, and spatial problems, and with attempts to formulate a Marxist approach to the study of geographical problems.

ASSOCIATION of American Geographers. Resource publications in geography, Washington, D. C. 1981- . Four each year, but not numbered. 82

Short monographs. Many with extensive bibliographies. Preceded by Commission on College geography. Resource papers 1-23 (1968-1974) and by Resource papers for college geography. 75, 1-4; 76, 1-4; 77, 1-4; and 78, 1-4. Not published 1979-1980.

ASSOCIATION of Pacific Coast Geographers. Yearbook. Corvallis, Oregon. 1- . (1935-). Annual. Indexes: 1-27 (1935-1965) in v. 27; 28-35 (1966-1973) in v. 35; 36-40 (1974-1978) in v. 40. 83

Focus on the Pacific Coast region of the United States (Washington, Oregon, and California). Reports on annual meetings and selected abstracts of papers presented.

CALIFORNIA geographer (California Council for Geographic Education). Los Angeles, California. 1- . (1960-). Annual. 84

Articles on California. Reports on annual meetings.

CHICAGO. University. Department of Geography. Research papers. Chicago, Illinois. 1- (1948-). Irregular. 85

Research monographs.

CURRENT geographical publications: additions to the Research Catalogue of the American Geographical Society Collection of the University of Wisconsin-Milwaukee Library. Milwaukee, Wisconsin. 1- (1938-). 10 per annum. 86

The regional section on the United States provides the best general coverage of geographic publications on this country and its regions.

EAST Lakes geographer. Bowling Green, Ohio. 1- (1964-). Annual. 87

Articles based on papers read at annual meetings of the East Lakes Division of the Association of American Geographers.

ECUMENE (East Texas State University). Commerce, Texas. 1- (1968-). Annual. 88

Diverse articles.

GEOGRAPHICAL perspectives. (University of Northern Iowa. Department of Geography). Cedar Falls, Iowa. 33- (1974-). 2 nos. a year. Continues Iowa geographer, 1-32 (1963-1974). Cumulative index 1-47 (1963- spring 1981) in v. 49 (spring 1982). 89

Articles; commentaries, reports, and research notes; and book reviews.

GREAT PLAINS-Rocky Mountain geographical journal (Association of American Geographers. Great Plains-Rocky Mountain Division). Laramie, Wyoming. 1- (1972-). Annual.

    Articles especially on the Rocky Mountains and the Great Plains. Abstracts of papers presented at annual meetings.

HISTORICAL geography. A Newsletter for historical geographers. Northridge, California. 1- (1971-). 2 per year.

    Articles on historical geography. Reports and announcements. Book reviews. Dissertation abstracts. Conference programs and abstracts.

ILLINOIS Geographical Society. Bulletin. DeKalb, Illinois. nsv 1- (1955-). 2 per annum.

    Short articles on Illinois or by Illinois geographers.

JOURNAL of cultural geography (Bowling Green State University in cooperation with the Popular Culture Association and the American Culture Association). Bowling Green, Ohio. 1- (fall/winter 1980-). 2 nos. a year.

    Articles on cultural geography.

JOURNAL of geography (National Council for Geographic Education). Macomb, Illinois. 1- (1902-). 7 per annum.

    Particularly for teachers of elementary, secondary, and college geography in the United States. Contains both methodological and substantive articles.

JOURNAL of historical geography (Academic Press), London, England. 1- (1975-). Quarterly.

    Contains some articles and reviews on the historical geography of the United States.

LANDSCAPE. Berkeley, California. 1-18 (1951-1968); 19- (1975-). 3 per annum.

    Articles on the landscape and culture.

NORTH CAROLINA. University. Chapel Hill. Department of Geography. Studies in Geography. Chapel Hill, North Carolina. 1- (1970-). Irregular.

    Research monographs, collected papers, and proceedings of symposia.

PENNSYLVANIA geographer (Pennsylvania Geographical Society). Kutztown, Pennsylvania. 1- (1963-). 4 per annum.

    Short articles especially on Pennsylvania.

PHYSICAL geography. (V. H. Winston and Sons). Silver Spring, Maryland. 1- (1980-). 2 per annum.

    Articles on physical geography, geomorphology, climatology, hydrology, soils, or vegetation.

POLITICAL geography quarterly. (Butterworth Scientific). Guildford, Surrey, England 1- (1982-). Quarterly.

    Articles and book reviews, including many on the United States.

PROFESSIONAL geographer. Forum and journal of the Association of American Geographers. Washington, D. C. n.s. v. 1- , 1949- . Quarterly. Index for 1946-1966 in v. 19, no. 2 (1967). 101

Short articles, views and opinions, commentary and reply, reports on major conferences, applied geography, contents of major foreign journals, large number of concise book reviews.

PROGRESS in human geography. (Edward Arnold). London, England. [Cambridge University Press, New York]. 1- (1977-). 4 numbers a year (v. 1-2, 1977-1978, each had 3 numbers only). 102

Articles, progress reports on major fields of human geography, book review essays, and book reviews. Many of the review articles contain references to the United States and some are devoted mainly to work on the United States.

PROGRESS in physical geography. (Edward Arnold). London, England. [Cambridge University Press, New York). 1- (1977-). 4 numbers a year (v. 1-2, 1977-1978, each had 3 numbers only). 103

Articles, progress reports on major fields of physical geography, book reviews. Many of the review articles contain references to work in or on the United States.

SOUTHEASTERN geographer (Association of American Geographers. Southeastern Division). Columbia, South Carolina. 1- (1961-). 2 nos. a year. 104

Focus on the American South or on studies by geographers from this area. Reports of annual meetings.

SPECIAL Libraries Association. Geography and Map Division. Bulletin. Bethesda, Maryland. 1- (1947-). 4 per annum. 105

Articles on maps, map bibliographies, map libraries, and United States government programs and publications. News. Reference aids. New atlases, maps, and books. Reviews.

URBAN geography. (V. H. Winston and Sons). Silver Spring, Maryland. 1- (1980-). 4 per annum. 106

Articles and book reviews on urban studies.

WESTERN Association of Map Libraries. Information bulletin. Santa Cruz, California. 1- (S 1969-). 3 nos. a year. Index v. 1-10 (1969-). 3 nos. a year. Index v. 1-10 (1969-1979). 107

Atlas and book reviews. New mapping of Western North America. News notes. Feature articles. Association news.

GEOGRAPHICAL bulletin. (Gamma Theta Upsilon). Ypsilanti, Michigan. Semiannual. Index v. 1-22 (1970-1982) in v. 23 (May, 1983). 108

Short articles. News from chapters of Gamma Theta Upsilon.

NEW YORK (State). State University, Binghamton. Department of Geography. Research in contemporary and applied geography: a discussion series. Binghamton, New York. 1- (1977-). Quarterly. 109

TRANSITION. (Socially and ecologically responsible geographers. Journal). Cincinnati, Ohio. 1- (1971-). Quarterly. 110

United States: Geographical Serials

d. Other University Series of Monographs with material on the United States

CALIFORNIA. University. <u>Publications in geography</u>. Berkeley and Los Angeles, California. 1- (1915-). Irregular.   11

    Research monographs on diverse topics and regions, including some on the United States (as in v. 1-3, 5-11, 13, 15, 16, 17, and 20).

GEOSCIENCE and man (Louisiana State University. School of Geosciences). Baton Rouge, Louisiana. 1- (1970-). Irregular.   11

    Symposia, monographic studies, and collections of papers in geography, anthropology, archaeology, geology, meteorology, paleontology, and other geosciences. Of particular interest are studies on the Mississippi delta and coastal environments (v. 2, 14, 18, 19) and on cultural geography in the United States (v. 5).

MICHIGAN geographical publications. (University of Michigan. Department of Geography). Ann Arbor, Michigan. 1-28 (1970-1982).   11

    Diverse monographs and collected works, some on Michigan or other parts of the United States (v. 5, 7, 9, 12, 13, 18, 20, 21, 22, 24, 25).

NORTHWESTERN University studies in geography (Northwestern University. Department of Geography). Evanston, Illinois. 1-25 (1952-1978). Irregular.   11

    Research monographs, collections of articles on a common theme, reports of symposia. Some monographs are on the Chicago area (v. 9, 10, 12).

e. Other University Series with shorter articles or discussion papers

    Note: For a list of the titles of papers in individual numbers of the various series of discussion papers see:

YOUNG, Bruce. <u>Bibliography and review of geography department discussion papers</u>. Waterloo, Ontario, Canada: Wilfrid Laurier University, v. 4 (June 1980). 166 p. United States, p. 102-145.   1

ILLINOIS. University at Urbana-Champaign. Department of Geography. <u>Occasional publication</u>. 1- (1972-). Irregular.   1

INDIANA State University, Terre Haute. Department of Geography and Geology. <u>Professional paper</u>. Terre Haute, Indiana. 1- (1968-). Irregular.   1

INDIANA University. Department of geography. <u>Geographic monograph series</u>. Bloomington, Indiana. v1- (1966-). Irregular.   1

IOWA. University. Department of Geography. <u>Discussion paper series</u>, Iowa City, Iowa. 1- (1966-). Irregular.   1

PENNSYLVANIA State University. Department of Geography. <u>Papers in geography</u>. University Park, Pennsylvania. 1- (1969-). Irregular.   1

SYRACUSE University. Department of Geography. <u>Discussion paper</u>. Syracuse, New York. 1- (1975-). Irregular.   1

f. Other Geographic Periodicals with Regional and Local Focus

ALASKA geographic (Alaska Geographic Society). Anchorage, Alaska. 1- (1972-). Quarterly. 122

    Beautifully illustrated articles on regions, economic activities, physical features, natural resources, and wilderness areas of Alaska.

ASSOCIATION of American Geographers. Middle States Division. Proceedings. Newark, Delaware: University of Delaware. Department of Geography. 1- (1966-). Annual. Papers presented at annual meetings. 123

ASSOCIATION of North Dakota Geographers. Bulletin. Grand Forks, North Dakota. 1- (1947). Annual. 124

FLORIDA geographer. (Florida Society of Geographers. Florida Atlantic University. Department of Geography). Boca Raton, Florida. 1- (1964-). Annual. Not published 1974-1975. 125

    1-2 (1964-1965) as Florida Society of Geographers. Newsletter.

KANSAS geographer (Kansas Council for Geographic Education and Kansas State University, Department of Geography). Manhattan, Kansas. 1-3 (1958-1961); 4- (1968/1969-). Annual. Not published 1962-1967. 126

MISSISSIPPI geographer (Mississippi Council for Geographic Education and University of Southern Mississippi, Department of Geography). Hattiesburgh, Mississippi. 1- (1973-). Annual. 127

    Short articles mainly on Mississippi.

OHIO geographers: recent research themes (University of Akron. Department of Geography). Akron, Ohio. 1- (1973-). Annual. 128

    Short papers by geographers of Ohio, mainly presented at meetings of the Geography Section of the Ohio Academy of Sciences. Papers focus on, but are not limited to, Ohio.

VIRGINIA geographer (Journal of the Virginia Geographical Society. Published in conjunction with the Department of Public Affairs and the Division of Continuing Education, George Mason University). Fairfax, Virginia. 1- (1966-). Semiannual. 129

    Short articles mainly on Virginia.

4. GENERAL BIBLIOGRAPHIES AND REFERENCE WORKS

U. S. LIBRARY OF CONGRESS. General References and Bibliography Division. A guide to the study of the United States of America; representative books reflecting the development of American life and thought. Prepared under the direction of Roy P. Basler, by Donald H. Mugridge and Blanche P. McCrum. Washington, D. C.: Government Printing Office, 1960. 1,193 p. 130

Excellent survey of 6,487 publications on the United States. Of special value are chapter 6, Geography, p. 269-281, entries 2933-2981, and Chapter 12, Local history: regions, states, cities, p. 466-528.

_____. _____. _____. Supplement, 1956-1965; prepared under the direction of Roy P. Basler by Oliver H. Orr, Jr., and the staff of the Bibliography and Reference Correspondence Section. Washington, D. C.: Library of Congress. 1976. 526 p. The geography section is a routine compilation. 131

U. S. LIBRARY OF CONGRESS. The Library of Congress main reading room reference collection subject catalog. 2nd ed, 1980 [25]. 132

"The United States," p. 1086-1184, provides a well-balanced up-to-date comprehensive list of the more important works and bibliographies on the United States selected for inclusion in the reference collection of the Main Reading Room of the Library of Congress, as of August 15, 1980.

HERSTEIN, Sheila, and ROBBINS, Naomi C. United States of America. Oxford, England; Santa Barbara, California: Clio Press, 1982. 307 p. Index. (World bibliographical series, v. 16). 133

1126 annotated entries arranged by subject fields, such as geography, (mainly maps and atlases and exploration and travel), history (the fullest section), nationalities and minorities, social conditions, politics, economics, commerce, business and industry, agriculture, transport, environment, city planning, and reference works, among others. Useful annotations.

5. STATISTICS: GUIDES AND CATALOGUES

AMERICAN statistics index: a comprehensive guide and index to statistical publications of the U. S. government. 1973- . Washington, D. C.: Congressional Information Service. 1973- . Annual, with monthly supplements. 134

The most useful and comprehensive guide to the vast statistical publications of the government of the United States. Separate index and abstract volumes each year. Indexes by subject and names, categories, titles, and agency report numbers. Abstracts of each statistical publication arranged by agency and series are particularly useful. The 1974 edition (3 v.) was a retrospective edition covering publications as of January 1, 1974. It superseded the more limited 1973 edition. Annual supplements, 1974- , covers only publications of stated period or years.

GUIDE to U. S. government statistics. By John L. Andriot. 4th ed. McLean, Virginia: Documents Index, 1973. 431 p. (1st ed., 1956). 135

Consists of two parts. Part 1 is a reproduction of Statistical services of the United States government (rev. ed. Washington, D. C.: Bureau of the Budget, 1968). Part 2 is a detailed guide to statistical series issued by the United States government, arranged by department and agency, often with notes on beginning date, frequency, and coverage. Lists more than 1700 published statistical series. Provides a useful background for and supplement to American statistics index [134], which is more detailed and covers the period since 1973.

Statistics: Guides and Catalogues   28

U. S. BUREAU OF THE CENSUS. Bureau of the Census catalog of publications
1790-1972. Washington, D. C.: Government Printing Office, 1974. 320 plus
591 p. Indexes.   136

    Two separately paged segments: (1) reprint of U. S. Library of Congress.
Census Library Project. Catalog of United States census publications, 1790-
1945, prepared by Henry J. Dubester. (Washington, D. C.: Government Printing
Office, 1950). 320 p. (2) Bureau of Census Catalog of publications 1946-1972,
prepared by Statistical compendia staff, Data user services office. 591 p.
Based on annual issues of U. S. Bureau of the Census. Catalog of United States
census publications, 1946-1972.

U. S. BUREAU OF THE CENSUS. Bureau of the Census catalog. Washington, D. C.:
Government Printing Office, 1946- . Quarterly and cumulative catalog and
subject guide, 1946-1951; Catalog of United States census publications, 1952-
1962; Bureau of Census catalog of publications, 1963; Bureau of Census catalog,
1964- .   137

    List of publications of the Bureau of the Census. From 1964 includes
also unpublished material available on tapes or punched cards. The years 1946
to 1972 are cumulated in U. S. Bureau of the Census. Bureau of the Census
catalog of publications 1790-1972 [136]. Therefore the annual and quarterly
numbers of this guide need be consulted only for 1973 and later.

U. S. BUREAU OF THE CENSUS. Bureau of the Census guide to programs and publications: subjects and areas, 1973. Washington, D. C.: Government Printing Office,
1974. 227 p.   138

    Description and inventory of the statistical programs of the Bureau of the
Census in the 1960's and early 1970's.

STATISTICAL sources: a subject guide to data on industrial, business, social
educational, financial, and other topics for the United States and internationally. Edited by Paul Wasserman and others. 7th ed. Detroit, Michigan:
Gale Research Co., 1982. 1388 p. Bibliography.   139

    About 26,000 references arranged under 12,000 subject headings with find-
ing guides to sources of statistical information. Extensive coverage of references in the United States. Alphabetical subject headings. See also under
names of each individual state and under "State data (for individual states)"
and "State and local government (combined data)."

STATISTICAL reference index: a selective guide to American statistical publications from private organizations and state government sources. Washington,
D. C.: Congressional Information Service, 1980- . Monthly with quarterly and
annual cumulations. Separate volumes for index and for abstracts.   140

    Index by subjects and names. Abstracts by issuing agencies, associations,
business organizations, commercial publishers, independent research organizations, state governments, universities. Covers a wide range of types of data.

U. S. BUREAU OF THE CENSUS. Directory of federal statistics for states: a guide
to sources, 1967. Washington, D. C.: Government Printing Office, 1967. 372 p.   141

    "A comprehensive finding guide to available published sources of Federal
statistics on social, political, and economic subjects." - Introduction.

U. S. BUREAU OF THE CENSUS. Directory of non-Federal statistics for states and local areas: a guide to sources 1969. Washington, D. C.: Government Printing Office, 1970. 678 p.

142

Lists non-Federal primary sources of statistics on population, vital statistics and health, education, public welfare, housing, labor and employment, finance, commerce, transportation and utilities, agriculture and conservation, government and finance, and law enforcement for the 50 states listed in alphabetical order, and for 3 outlying areas. Section on publications by private organizations. Appendix: Bibliography of supplementary sources.

BALACHANDRAN, M., ed. Regional statistics: a guide to information sources. Detroit, Michigan: Gale Research Co., 1980. 257 p. (Economics information guide series, v. 13). Geographic and author indexes.

143

Annotated guide to statistical data for individual regions, states, cities, and other small-area units in the United States arranged by eight subject chapters: general socioeconomic data sources; housing and construction; population and vital statistics; labor and industrial relations; industrial statistics; business directories; financial data; energy and transportation. Within each chapter arrangement is by author, usually a state or city agency, but for references on a particular area one should utilize also the geographic index and look under United States agencies for publications which provide data for all local areas in the country.

U. S. LIBRARY OF CONGRESS. Census Library Project. State censuses: an annotated bibliography of censuses of population taken after the year 1790 by states and territories of the United States. Prepared by Henry J. Dubester. Washington, D. C.: Government Printing Office, 1948. 73 p.

144

U. S. BUREAU OF THE CENSUS. Directory of federal statistics for local areas: a guide to sources, 1976. Washington, D. C.: Government Printing Office, 1978. 359 p. (earlier ed., 1966. 156 p.).

145

"Provides table-by-table descriptions of statistical reports on areas smaller than states...for the entire United States." Alphabetical arrangements by subject fields, such as agriculture. For each item includes subject; data items included; area to which data apply; frequency; and bibliographical source. Bibliography. Subject index.

_____. _____. Urban update 1977-1978. 1980. 138 p. [p. 361-490]. Cumulative index.

145a

MARTINSON, Tom L. "Statistics sources," chapter 5 in his Introduction to library research in geography; an instruction manual and short bibliography. Metuchen, New Jersey: The Scarecrow Press, Inc., 1972. p. 55-68.

146

The section, General statistics on the United States and/or its major subdivisions, p. 58-68, includes 97 entries for statistical publications of the United States government and its major departments and agencies, such as Agriculture; Commerce; Defense; Health, Education, and Welfare; Interior; Labor; Post Office; State; Treasury; and major independent government agencies; general handbooks; on the National Archives.

DURRENBERGER, Robert W. "Major sources of statistical information," chapter 7, in his Geographical research and writing. New York: Thomas Y. Crowell, 1971. p. 169-172. Entries 565-622.

147

58 sources of statistical data of interest to geographers, mostly for the United States, arranged alphabetically.

BALACHANDRAN, M. Basic economic statistics. Council of Planning Librarians. Exchange bibliography, no. 971. 1976. 37 p.   148

  112 references to sources published in the United States and information available in each.

BALACHANDRAN, M. Manpower statistics and related data for planners. Monticello, Illinois: Council of Planning Librarians. Exchange bibliography, no. 1063, 1976. 33 p.   149

  130 references to sources of information in the United States.

6. STATISTICAL COMPILATIONS

U. S. BUREAU OF THE CENSUS. Statistical abstract of the United States, 1878- . Washington, D. C.: Government Printing Office, 1879- . Annual.   150

  The basic one-volume summary statistical source for data on the United States. Each volume has data for the latest available year and for recent years. Sources for each table provide a lead to more detailed information. Index.

U. S. BUREAU OF THE CENSUS. County and city data book, 1949- . A Statistical abstract supplement. Washington, D. C.: Government Printing Office, 1952- . Every few years. Issued for 1949, 1952, 1956, 1962, 1967, 1972, and 1977.   151

  A geographic supplement to the Statistical abstract of the United States [150]. It provides important data areally disaggregated. The 1977 edition (1978. 956 p.) provides statistical data on 195 items for each of 4 regions, 9 census divisions, 10 standard federal administrative regions, 50 states, and 3,143 countries (or comparable units); statistical data on 161 items for 277 standard metropolitan statistical areas; and 190 statistical items for 910 incorporated cities with more than 25,000 inhabitants. Predecessor volumes provide data for 1940 and 1947 and later years.

U. S. BUREAU OF THE CENSUS. State and metropolitan area data book 1982: a statistical abstract supplement. Metropolitan areas (SMSA's), Central cities of SMSA's, Regions, divisions, states. Washington, D. C.: Government Printing Office, 1982. 611 p. Index. (Earlier ed. 1979 [1980], 562 p.).   152

  Statistics for 320 items for 318 standard metropolitan statistical areas (SMSA's), as designated on June 19, 1981, and for each county within these areas; 73 items for the 429 central cities in these metropolitan areas; and 2,018 items for the United States as a whole, for 4 major regions, 9 smaller regions, 50 states, and the District of Columbia. Data from the 1980 census of population are included.

U. S. BUREAU OF THE CENSUS. Historical statistics of the United States, colonial times to 1970. Bicentennial edition. Washington, D. C.: Government Printing Office, 1975. 2 vols. (U. S. Department of Commerce; also House document, 93d Congress, 1st session, no. 93-78).   153

  An historical supplement to Statistical abstract of the United States providing detailed data from the earliest date on which statistics were gathered for each series up to 1970.

  More than 12,500 time series, mainly annual, on social and economic development of the United States from 1610 to 1970.

  Replaces and substantially expands earlier editions: Historical statistics of the United States, 1789-1945 (1949) and Historical statistics of the United States, colonial times to 1957 (1960).

ANDRIOT, John L. Population abstract of the United States. McLean, Virginia:
Andriot Associates, 1983. 2 v. 1,316 p. (earlier ed., 1980. 925 p.). 154

    Provides available historical totals for 50 states, 3,064 counties, and
2,217 incorporated places with a 1980 population of 10,000 or more, from 1980
back to the earliest census for which data are available for each unit.
Includes a comparative table showing the 1970 and 1980 population for all
minor civil divisions for each county. v. 2 contains the index of more than
70,000 entries. Companion to Township atlas of the United States [217].

U. S. BUREAU OF THE CENSUS. Census of population. Washington, D. C.: Government
Printing Office. 155

    The basic census enumeration of the United States taken decennially: 1790,
1800, 1810, 1820, 1830, 1840, 1850, 1860, 1870, 1880, 1890, 1900, 1910, 1920,
1930, 1940, 1950, 1960, 1970, and 1980.

U. S. BUREAU OF THE CENSUS. Census of housing. Washington, D. C.: Government
Printing Office. 156

    Taken in conjunction with the decennial Census of population [155], 1940,
1950, 1960, 1970, and 1980.

U. S. BUREAU OF THE CENSUS. Census of agriculture. Washington, D. C.: Government
Printing Office. 157

    Taken with each decennial Census of population [155] from 1840 to 1950, in
mid-decade years 1925, 1935, and 1945, and thereafter in 1954, 1959, 1964, 1969,
1974, and 1978. Scheduled in future each 5 years, in years ending in 2 and 7.

U. S. BUREAU OF THE CENSUS. Census of business. Washington, D. C.: Government
Printing Office. 158

    Censuses in 1929, 1933, 1935, 1939, 1948, 1954, 1958, 1963, and 1967, and
every 5 years thereafter in years ending in 2 and 7:

    (a) Census of wholesale trade, 1972, 1977...
    (b) Census of retail trade, 1972, 1977...
    (c) Census of (selected) service industries, 1972, 1977...

U. S. BUREAU OF THE CENSUS. Census of manufactures. Washington, D. C.: Government Printing Office. 159

    Censuses taken every 10 years 1810-1900 (except 1830), every 5 years
1904-1919, biennial 1921-1939, then in 1947, 1954, 1958, 1963, 1967, 1972, 1977,
and scheduled for every 5 years, for years ending in 2 and 7.

U. S. BUREAU OF THE CENSUS. Census of transportation. Washington, D. C.:
Government Printing Office. 160

    Censuses taken in 1963, 1967, 1972, 1977, and scheduled for every 5 years,
for years ending in 2 and 7.

U. S. BUREAU OF THE CENSUS. Census of mineral industries. Washington, D. C.:
Government Printing Office. 161

    Censuses taken as part of decennial census 1840-1950, then in 1954, 1958,
1963, and 1967, and thereafter each 5 years, for years ending in 2 and 7: 1972,
1977...

Statistical Compilations

Note: The 1977 Economic censuses included the following individual economic censuses: Census of retail trade [158b]; Census of wholesale trade [158a]; Census of service industries [158c]; Census of construction industries; Census of manufactures [159]; Census of mineral industries [161]; Census of transportation [160]; Economic censuses of outlying areas [Puerto Rico, Virgin Islands, Guam]; Enterprise statistics; Survey of minority-owned business enterprises; and Women-owned businesses (See U.S. Bureau of the Census. Mini-guide to the 1977 economic censuses. Revised edition, prepared by Lawrence Hugg. Washington, D. C.: U.S. Bureau of the Census, revised December 1979. Reprinted July 1982. 38 p. See also 1982 economic censuses: geographic reference manual. Washington, D.C. Bureau of the Census, 1982. 343 p. 161a

U. S. BUREAU OF THE CENSUS. Foreign commerce and navigation of the United States, 1821- . Washington, D. C.: Government Printing Office, annual (irregular). 162

Not published 1947-1962. Volume for 1946/1963 contains summary data for this period. Before 1865 published by the Registrar of Treasury.

U. S. DEPARTMENT OF AGRICULTURE. Agricultural statistics, 1936- . Washington, D. C.: Government Printing Office, Annual. Index. 163

Annual statistics systematically organized. Major sections cover grains; cotton, tobacco, sugar crops, and honey; oilseeds, fats, and oils; vegetables and melons; fruits, tree nuts, and horticultural specialties; hay, seeds, and minor field crops; cattle, hogs, and sheep; dairy and poultry products; farm resources, income, and expenses; taxes, insurance, cooperatives, and credit; stabilization and price-support programs; agricultural conservation and forestry statistics; consumption and family living; and miscellaneous statistics. Tables typically include figures for several recent years for the United States as a whole, for individual states of the United States, and for principal producing countries of the world.

U. S. BUREAU OF MINES. Minerals yearbook, 1932/33- . Washington, D. C.: Government Printing Office, Annual. Index. 164

Detailed annual review of mineral industry. 1978/79 published in three volumes: Volume 1, Metals and Minerals (1980, 1,063 p.), contains chapters on individual metallic and nonmetallic mineral commodities important to the economy of the United States, and a chapter on mining and quarrying trends; Volume 2, Area Reports: Domestic (1981, 596 p.), contains separate reviews of each of the 50 states, of possessions, and trust territories; Volume 3, Area Reports: International (1981, 1,250 p.), contains chapters of individual countries plus a review of minerals in the world economy and of ocean minerals. Extensive text and abundant statistics.

Predecessor volumes from 1880: 1880-1923 in U. S. Geological Survey. Annual report of the director; 1924-1931 as Mineral resources of the United States.

U. S. BUREAU OF THE CENSUS. Annual survey of manufacturers: statistics for states, standard metropolitan statistical areas, large industrial counties, and selected cities: 1949/50- . Annual. Washington, D. C.: Government Printing Office. 165

Annual figures on employment, value added, cost of materials, value of shipments, capital expenditures, and inventories by selected industry groups, by state, and by standard metropolitan statistical areas, and for total industry for large industrial counties (with more than 5,000 employees) and for cities with 20,000 or more employees.

Other volumes for the United States as a whole cover statistics for industry groups and industries, fuel and electric energy consumes, and value of products shipped.

7. GOVERNMENT PUBLICATIONS

a. Comprehensive Inventories

U. S. SUPERINTENDENT OF DOCUMENTS. Monthly catalog of United States Government publications. 1- , Jan. 1895- . Monthly. Washington, D. C.: Government Printing Office. 166

The basic current list of United States government publications of all types. Annual alphabetical index in December issue includes subject, author, and title indexes. The February issue contains a directory of government periodicals and subscription publications. Decennial indexes 1941-1950 (1953), and 1951-1960 (1968), 2 v. Quinquennial indexes 1961-1965 (1976), 2 v.; 1966-1970 (1978), 2 v.; 1971-1976 (1981), 2 v.

Format changed with July 1976 issue to MARC format, with full cataloging according to Anglo-American cataloging rules for each entry. Subjects derived from Library of Congress Subject Headings. Extensive annual indexes: author, title, subject, series/report, stock number, classification number, and title-keyword. Beginning 1977 the directory of government periodicals no longer appears in February issue but as a separate "Serial supplement" with independent indexes.

CUMULATIVE subject index to the Monthly catalog of United States government publications, 1900-1971. Compiled by William W. Buchanan and Edna M. Kanely. Washington, D. C.: Carrollton Press, 1973. 15 v. 167

Merges the numerous annual and cumulative indexes to the Monthly catalog of United States Government publications and fills in some gaps, providing a subject index to more than 800,000 government publications for the period 1900-1971 in a single alphabetical sequence.

BIBLIOGRAPHIC guide to government publication--U. S. 1975- . Annual. Boston, Massachusetts: G. K. Hall, 1976- . 168

Based on publications cataloged each year by the Library of Congress and the Research Libraries of the New York Public Library. Entries integrated into one alphabetical sequence. Access is by main entry (author, corporate body), added entries (co-authors, editors, compilers), titles, series titles, and subject headings.

GUIDE to U. S. government publications. 1981 edition. Edited by John L. Andriot. McLean, Virginia: Documents Index. 1981. 3 v. Microfiche. 169

Primarily a listing of titles of government series, by Superintendent of Documents classification numbers. v. 1 covers all agencies currently in existence as well as those agencies abolished subsequent to January 1, 1975. v. 2 covers agencies abolished prior to end of 1974. v. 3 contains a detailed description to the Superintendent of Documents classification scheme, and agency class chronology, agency and title indexes to all entries in v. 1-2.

Previous editions (1959-1972) as Guide to U. S. government serials and periodicals. Present title as looseleaf service 1973-1976; 1976/78 edition in 4 v.; 1978/79 edition in 3 v.; 1980 edition in 2 v. (v. 1, 1063 p. v. 2, 589 p.).

GOVERNMENT reference books. A biennial guide to U. S. government publications, 1968/69. Littleton, Colorado: Libraries Unlimited, 1970- . Biennial. Indexes. 170

    Each volume covers publications over a 2-year period arranged by broad subject fields. Contains an extensive section "Area studies and geography" (entries 146-295, p. 42-68 in the 7th biennial edition, 1980/81). See also: economics and commerce, housing and urban development, recreation, statistics and demography, agricultural sciences, biological sciences, earth and environmental sciences, energy and transportation. 1968/69-1972/73 compiled by Sally Wynkoop, 1974/75-1976/77 compiled by Alan Edward Schorr, 1978/79- (1980-) compiled by Walter L. Newsome. 7th ed. 1980/81 (1982, 413 p.), has 1,433 entries.

BODY, Alexander C. Annotated bibliography of bibliographies on selected government publications and supplementary guides to the Superintendent of Documents classification system. Kalamazoo, Michigan: Western Michigan University, 1967. 181 p. 1st supplement, 1968. 115 p. 2nd supplement, 1970. 138 p. 3rd supplement, 1972. 143 p. 4th supplement, 1974. 142 p. 5th supplement, compiled by Gabor Kovacs, 1977. Greeley, Colorado: Gabor Kovacs, 1979. 177 p. 6th supplement, 1980. Greeley, Colorado: University of Northern Colorado, 1980. 202 p. 7th supplement, 1980, 1982. 166 p. Cumulative index, 1967-1980, microfiche, is enclosed inside back cover. 17?

    Annotated bibliographies arranged by the classification of the Superintendent of Documents.

SCULL, Roberta A. A bibliography of United States government bibliographies, 1968-1973. Ann Arbor, Michigan: Pierian Press, 1975. 353 p. Subject index. 172

_____. _____. 1974-1976. 1979. 310 p. Subject index. 17

    1,200 bibliographies, mostly annotated, for 1968-1973, and 1,560 for 1974-1976, arranged by broad subject categories, then by specific topics, and within topics by government agency.

FEDERAL information sources and systems: a directory issued by the Comptroller general. 1976- . Washington, D. C.: Comptroller General; for sale by Superintendent of Documents, Government Printing Office. (1980 edition: 1980 Congressional sourcebook series, PAD-80-50, 1980, 1,178 p.). Indexes. 17

    Description of authorization prupose and availability of federal information series.

b. Selective Guides

PALIC, Vladimir M. Government publications: a guide to bibliographic tools. 4th ed. Washington, D. C.: Library of Congress, 1975. 441 p. (3rd ed., as James B. Childs, Government document bibliography in the United States and elsewhere. Washington, D. C.: Government Printing Office, 1942. 78 p.). [Also reproduced by Pergamon Press, Oxford, and New York, 1977]. 17

    "The United States of America," p. 9-149, divided into two parts, Federal government, p. 11-80, and States, territories, and local governments, p. 81-149.

WYNKOOP, Sally. Subject guide to government reference books. Littleton, Colorado: Libraries Unlimited, 1972. 276 p. 1°

    Introduction to reference books published by government in classed arrangement with annotations and index. For continuation see Government reference books [170]. Geography, p. 99-104. See also: economics and business, history and area studies, recreation, statistics and demography, urbanology, agriculture, earth sciences, environmental sciences, and transportation.

MOREHEAD, Joe. Introduction to United States public documents. 3rd ed. Littleton, Colorado: Libraries Unlimited, 1983. 309 p. Selected title/series index. Subject/name index. Reference at the end of each chapter. 177

   Textual analysis of characteristics and problems of the whole range of United States public documents, particularly from the viewpoint of a documents librarian. Appendix A, p. 283-287. Selected online data bases for federal government information. See also 2nd ed., 1978, Appendix A. Special problems in documents librarianship: I. Federal mapping and charting activities, p. 295-308; II. Census Bureau information, p. 309-324; and III. Computer-based bibliographic services, p. 324-331.

MASON, John Brown. Research resources: annotated guide to the social sciences. v. 2. Official publications: U. S. Government, United Nations, international organizations, and statistical sources. Santa Barbara, California: American Bibliographical Center-Clio Press, 1971. 273 p. 178

   Discussion of official publications of the United States government by departments, bureaus, and agencies. Includes also a chapter on statistical sources. Indexes of subjects, titles, and names.

SCHMECKEBIER, Laurence F., and EASTIN, Roy B. Government publications and their use. 2nd rev. ed. Washington, D. C.: Brookings Institution, 1969. 502 p. (1st ed., 1936; rev. ed., 1961). 179

   A basic guide. Chapter 16, "Maps," p. 406-440, is especially useful.

BOYD, Anne Morris, and Rips, Rae Elizabeth. United States Government publications. 3rd ed. rev. New York: H. W. Wilson, 1949 (reprinted with corrections 1952). (1st ed. 1931). 627 p. 180

   Well-organized guide to major government agencies and their publications. Arranged by government agencies. Lists and describes typical publications of each unit of government. Now dated but still useful for the period up to 1948.

LEIDY, William Philip. A popular guide to government publications. 4th ed. New York: Columbia University Press, 1976. 440 p. (1st ed. 1953). Index. 181

   About 3,000 items, mainly 1967-1975, arranged by broad subjects. Earlier publications were covered in earlier editions: 1940 to 1950 in 1st ed. (1953); 1951-1960 in 2nd ed. (1963), and 1961-1966 in 3rd ed. (1968). See especially sections on agriculture, climatology and weather, conservation, economic and political geography, economics, energy and power resources, environmental and and ecology, ethnic groups in the United States, farming, fish and fishing, forage crops, forestry, geology, housing and urban planning, livestock, maps and mapping, mining, national parks, oceanography, pollution, recreation, soil conservation, surveying, transportation, United States: geography, United States: population, United States: statistics, and water resources and supply.

VINGE, Clarence L. and VINGE, Ada G. U. S. government publications for research and teaching in geography and related social and natural sciences. Totowa, New Jersey: Littlefield, Adams, 1967. 360 p. (Littlefield quality paperback, No. 225). 182

   Identifies out of more than a half million documents issued by the Federal Government of the United States in the period 1945-1966 about 3,500 considered to be of value to geographers. Arranged by departments and bureaus. Reference to entries in the Monthly catalog of United States government publications and to the code of the Government Printing Office. Price. Detailed subject index. Bibliographies, p. 241-263.

MARTINSON, Tom L. "Reference to government publications," chapter 4 in his
Introduction to library research in geography; an instruction manual and short
bibliography. Metuchen, New Jersey: The Scarecrow Press, Inc., 1972. p. 44-54.

    56 entries on guides to governmental publications, mainly of the United
States, of its states, and its local governments.

DURRENBERGER, Robert W. "Government documents and their use," in his Geographical
research and writing. New York: Thomas Y. Crowell, 1971, p. 124-127.

    Lists 33 guides to government publications, mainly of the United States.

        c. Publications in Special Areas or
          of Individual Departments or Bureaus

U. S. SUPERINTENDENT of DOCUMENTS. Subject bibliographies.
Washington, D. C.: Government Printing Office. 1975- . Frequently revised.

    Among the bibliographies of currently available government publications
of particular geographic interest are the following: 6, Minorities; 9, Solar
energy; 31, Department of Agriculture yearbooks; 32, Oceanography; 40, Shipping
and transportation; 46, Air pollution; 50, Water pollution and water resources;
55, Mass transit; 88, Environmental education and protection; 95, Solid waste
management; 97, National and world economy; 99, Minerals yearbooks; 102, Maps
and atlases; 123, Foreign trade and tariff; 146, Census of manufactures; 149,
Census of transportation; 150, Libraries and library collections; 151, Minerals
and mining; 152, Census of business; 157, Census of construction; 160, Earth
sciences; 162, Agricultural research, statistics, and economic reports; 166,
Foreign area studies; 181, Census of population; 183, Surveying and mapping;
234, Weather; 238, Conservation; 242, Census of housing; 273, Statistical
publications; 277, Census of agriculture; 280, Housing, urban and rural development; 298, Public and private utilities; 304, Energy supplies, prices and consumption; 305, Energy policy, ussues and programs; 306, Energy conservation
and research technology; and 310, Census of mineral industries.

U. S. GEOLOGICAL SURVEY. Publications of the Geological Survey, 1879-1961.
Washington, C. D.: Government Printing Office, 1964. 457 p.

    "A permanent catalog of books, maps, and charts issued by the Geological
Survey through December 1961." Replaces all earlier issues. Maps and charts,
p. 190-257. Indexes of subjects, areas, and authors.

    _____. _____. 1962-1970. 1972. 586 p.

    Maps and charts, p. 196-358. Indexes of subjects, areas, geological
survey research, and authors.

    _____. New publications of the Geological Survey. Monthly.
Cummulates annually, 1971- , to supplement the above catalogs.

U. S. BUREAU OF MINES. List of publications, July 1, 1910, to January 1, 1960,
with subject and author index. By Hazel J. Stratton. Washington, D. C.:
Government Printing Office. 1960. 826 p.

    _____. List of publications and articles. With author and subject.
Index. 1960-1964. Washington, D. C.: Bureau of Mines, 1966. 297 p.
1965-1969 (1970). 437 p. 1970-1974 (1975). 557 p. 1975-1979. (1981. 568 p.).
Washington, D. C.: Government Printing Office.

U. S. DEPARTMENT OF COMMERCE. United States Department of Commerce publications. Compiled under the direction of Wanda Mae Johnson, librarian. Washington, D. C.: Government Printing Office, 1952. 795 p. 191

　　　Publications up to 1950.

_____. _____. Supplements (Catalogs). 1951/52- . Annual. Title varies. 192

U. S. LIBRARY OF CONGRESS. Library of Congress publications in print. 1897- . Annual. Washington, D. C.: Library of Congress. 193

U. S. DEPARTMENT OF AGRICULTURE. Index to publications of the U. S. Department of Agriculture, 1901-1940, edited by Mary A. Bradley. Washington, D. C.: Government Printing Office, 1932-1943, 4 vols. 1901-1925, 2,689 p.; 1926-1930, 694 p.; 1931-1935, 518 p.; 1936-1940, 763 p. 194

d. Reports distributed by the
National Technical Information Service 195

262 reports distributed by the NTIS are listed on the following pages arranged by 17 broad categories with a separate numbering system within entry 195.

		No.
(1)	Environment in general	(1- 3)
(2)	Geology, geomorphology, soil erosion, earthquakes	(4- 11)
(3)	Water resources, hydrology, floods, and snow	(12- 55)
(4)	Meteorology and climatology	(56- 63)
(5)	Coastal zone	(64- 70)
(6)	Ecosystems	(71- 74)
(7)	Energy	(75- 94)
(8)	Oceanography	(95-104)
(9)	Air, water, and noise pollution and waste disposal	(105-186)
(10)	Regional economics	(187-188)
(11)	Population	(189-193)
(12)	Ethnic groups	(194-202)
(13)	Urban areas	(202-223)
(14)	Housing	(224-230)
(15)	Transportation	(231-255)
(16)	Agricultural resources	(256-257)
(17)	Tourism and recreation	(258-262)

GOVERNMENT reports. Announcements and index. v. 1- (1946-). Biweekly (26 issues a year). Springfield, Virginia: U. S. Department of Commerce. National Technical Information Service, 1946- . Keyword (subject), personal author, corporate author, contract/grant number, and NTIS order/report number indexes in each issue. Indexes also cumulate in separate annual volumes. Title varies: Bibliography of scientific and industrial reports, Bibliography of technical reports, U. S. government research reports, U. S. government research and development reports, Government reports announcements. Issuing agency and frequency vary.

195

About 70,000 reports annually arranged by 22 broad subject categories and 178 subcategories. Categories of major geographic interest are: 2, agriculture; 4, atmospheric sciences (especially 4B, meteorology); 5, behavioral and social sciences (especially 5C, economics, and 5K, sociology); 6, biological and medical sciences (especially 6F, environmental biology); 8, earth sciences and oceanography (especially 8F, geography, 8B, cartography, 8G, geology and mineralogy, 8L, snow, ice, and permafrost, 8H, hydrology and limnology, 8A, biological oceanography, 8C, dynamic oceanography, and 8J, physical oceanography); and 13B, civil engineering (a large and diverse class including many reports on pollution, environmental management, transportation, and urban planning).

The National Technical Information Service, a self-supporting agency of the U. S. Department of Commerce, is the central source for the public sale of United States Government-sponsored research, development, and engineering reports, by contractors and grantees. The NTIS makes available to the public reproductions of these reports, many of which are issued in very limited numbers, are not otherwise available, and are in few libraries. The NTIS also maintains a computerized data base of about 1.2 million titles and published bibliographies from this NTIS data base; these are listed in its Current published searches, 1981, or later editions. Bibliographies based on other data bases are also included. For example, bibliographies on acid precipitation [195 (numbers 126-133)] include bibliographies based on Pollution abstracts (126), the Engineering index data base (127), the International aerospace abstracts data base (128), the Selected water resources abstracts data base (129), and the Energy data base (130-133).

The following are some of these bibliographies and collections of abstracts of potential interest in geographic research on the United States. These particular bibliographies and abstracts are generally limited to reports on U. S. government research contracts with non-governmental agencies and do not report regular publications by U. S. government agencies or departments published by the Government Printing Office nor research or publications not funded by the government. In some fields of applied geographic research these reports may be useful sources of information on recent work on topics of current public concern such as pollution and environmental degradation. The identification of titles of geographic interest was greatly aided by the listings in Geo abstracts [3], all series, which provides the best current selection of such titles. The following bibliographies with abstracts were the latest that could conveniently be identified at the time of the compilation of this list (March, 1983). This listing is based not on personal examination of each bibliography but on information reported in Government reports. Announcements and index (up to 1983, no. 25), later issues of which should be consulted for subsequent editions of these and similar bibliographies, reported after December, 1983, when this listing was updated.

These reports are not regularly published works nor printed. They are therefore here listed together rather than under their diverse subject categories. Copies of these bibliographies, and of the reports abstracted in them, are available, at prices which cover the costs of reproduction and distribution, from The National Technical Information Service, Springfield, Virginia 22161. The order number is indicated in parentheses after each title.

Reports distributed by NTIS

(1) Environment in General

Areawide environmental assessment: annotated bibliography. Skidmore, Owings, and Merrill. Washington, D. C.: Skidmore, Owings, and Merrill, 1981. 108 p. (HUD-0002385). (PB83-123711). More than 800 annotated references arranged in topical sections, each with subdivisions: general; geology and soils; water; plant and animal life; air and climatic features; urban services; health and safety; community values; and case examples. (1)

Preparation and evaluation of environmental impact statements. 1970-March, 1982 (citations from the NTIS data base). 1982. 187 p. (PB82-807074). 180 abstracts of research on (1) effectiveness of environmental impact statements on deterring environmental degradation and (2) guidelines in preparation of statements. (2)

Remote sensing for natural resources, environmental, and regional planning (a bibliography with abstracts). Report for 1974-June, 1976. Audrey S. Hundemann. 1976. 273 p. (NTIS/PS-76/0500). 268 abstracts on use of LANDSAT satellites (formerly Earth Resources Technology Satellite [ERTS]) for environmental, coastal, forestry, regional, urban planning applications, highway engineering, recreational land, and open space. After 1976 divided into several separate bibliographies. (3)

(2) Geology, Geomorphology, Soil Erosion, and Earthquakes

Remote sensing applied to geology and mineralogy. 1973-January, 1983 (citations from NTIS data base). 1983. 240 p. (PB83-803866). 231 abstracts. (4)

Remote sensing applied to geology. 1977-July, 1980 (citations from the International Aerospace Abstracts data base). Gerald F. Zollars. Albuquerque, New Mexico: University of New Mexico. Technology Applications Center. 1980. 94 p. (PB80-813587). 393 entries. (5)

Landslides. 1970- July, 1983 (citations from the NTIS data base). 1983. 217 p. (PB83-868901). 174 abstracts on landslides and their causes, including earthquakes, soil erosion, rock blasting, glaciers, and flooding, and on landslide prevention. (6)

Soil erosion control. 1964-June, 1979 (a bibliography with abstracts). Guy E. Habercom, Jr. 1980. 295 p. (PB80-811813). 288 abstracts. (7)

_____. July, 1979-October, 1982 (citations from the NTIS data base. 1982. 231 p. (PB83-801241). 223 abstracts. (8)

Soil erosion control. 1977-September, 1983 (citations from the Selected water resources abstracts data base). 1983. 169 p. (PB83-871590). Prepared in cooperation with Office of Water Research and Technology. Washington, D.C. 140 abstracts fully indexed with a title list. (9)

Earthquake prediction. 1970-1981 (citations from the Engineering Index data base). 1982. 91 p. (PB82-804097). 84 abstracts. (10)

_____. January, 1975-November, 1981 (citations from the International Information Service for the Physics and Engineering Communities data base). 1981. 292 p. (PB82-857459). 270 abstracts. (11)

(3) Water Resources, Hydrology, Floods, and Snow

Hydrology. 1977-June, 1982 (citations from the Selected water resources abstracts data base). 1982. 259 p. (PB82-868654). Prepared in cooperation with Office of Water Research and Technology, Washington, D. C. 175 abstracts fully indexed with a list of titles. (12)

Water supplies: potential. 1976-August, 1982 (citations from the Selected water resources abstracts data base). 1982. 124 p. (PB82-873290). Prepared in cooperation with Office of Water Research and Technolody, Washington, D. C. 2 abstracts fully indexed and with a list of titles. (13)

Water resources planning 1977-May, 1982 (citations from the Selected water resources abstracts data base). 1982. 153 p. (PB82-866518). Prepared in cooperation with Office of Water Research and Technology, Washington, D. C. 98 abstracts fully indexed with a title list. (14)

Reports distributed by NTIS

    Planning and management of water resource programs. Robena J. Brown. v. 1. 1964-1974 (a bibliography with abstracts). 1977. 185 p. (NTIS/PS-77/0487). 180 abstracts. (15)

    _____. v. 2. 1975-May, 1977. 1978. 307 p. (NTIS/PS-78/0463). 301 abstracts. (16)

    _____. June, 1977-May, 1980 (citations from the NTIS data base). 1980. 308 p. (PB80-812670). 170 abstracts on water resource programs and projects at the local, regional, state, and national level, on water quality, drinking water, irrigation water, and industrial water studies. (17)

    _____. June, 1980-January, 1983. 1983. 156 p. (PB83-803825). 147 abstracts. (18)

    Economic factors in regional water supply management. v. 1. 1964-1973 (a bibliography with abstracts). Robena J. Brown. Springfield, Virginia: National Technical Information Service. 1976. 204 p. (NTIS/PS-76/0242). 199 abstracts on economics of supplying water for industrial, residential, agricultural, and recreational needs. (19)

    _____. 1974-July, 1981 (citations from the NTIS data base). 1982. 285 p. (PB83-800557). 277 abstracts. (20)

    _____. August, 1981-September, 1982. 1982. 46 p. (PB83-800565). 40 abstracts. (21)

    Public opinion and sociology of water resource development. 1970-July, 1981 (citations from the NTIS data base). 1981. 251 p. (PB82-800111). 244 abstracts on attitudes toward water resource programs and on effects of water resource development on the social conditions of a region or community. (22)

    Remote sensing applied to hydrology. 1964-January, 1983 (citations from the NTIS data base). 1983. 277 p. (PB83-803676). 270 abstracts. (23)

    Flood control. Robena J. Brown. v. 1. 1964-1974 (a bibliography with abstracts). NTIS/PS-76/0593). 224 abstracts. (24)

    _____. v. 2. 1975-July, 1977 (a bibliography with abstracts). 1978. 255 p. (NTIS/PS-78/0773). 248 abstracts. (25)

    _____. August, 1977-August, 1980 (citations from the NTIS data base). 1980. 229 p. (PB80-816069). 223 abstracts on floods in relation to control, forecasting, urban planning, prevention, zoning, urbanization, and land use management. (26)

    _____. September, 1980-January, 1982. 1982. 81 p. (PB82-804600). 74 abstracts. (27)

    Flood history and flood plain management. 1977-April, 1983 (citations from the Selected water resources abstracts data base). 1983. 483 p. (PB83-863761). Prepared in cooperation with Office of Water Research and Technology, Washington, D. C. 340 abstracts fully indexed and with a title list. (28)

    Forest watersheds. 1964-January, 1981 (citations from the NTIS data base). 1981. 317 p. (PB81-804338). 301 abstracts on water balance management practices, water supply augmentation, and influence of lumbering or land use on drainage, soil erosion, runoff, forest fires, flooding, and ground water pollution. (29)

    _____. February, 1981-April, 1982. 1982. 68 p. (PB82-808288). 61 abstracts. (30)

    _____. 1977-1982 (citations from the Selected water resource abstracts data base). 1982. 262 p. (PB83-857771). Prepared in cooperation with Office of Water Research and Technology, Washington, D. C. 183 abstracts fully indexed and with a list of titles. (31)

    Agricultural watersheds. 1977-March, 1983 (citations from the Selected water resource abstracts data base). 1983. 260 p. (PB83-862391). Prepared in cooperation with Office of Water Research and Technology, Washington, D. C. 176 abstracts. (32)

Reports distributed by NTIS

Reservoir and lake sedimentation. 1964-April, 1982 (citations from the NTIS data base). 1982. 100 p. (PB82-808106). 93 abstracts. (33)

Sediment transport in rivers. v. 1. 1964-December, 1977 (a bibliography with abstracts). Robena J. Brown. 1979. 206 p. (PB80-803349). 206 abstracts on stream erosion, scouring, particle size, water quality, flow rate, river mouth processes, and streambed degradation. (34)

_____. 1978-March, 1982 (citations from the NTIS data base). 1982. 105 p. (PB82-807520). 105 abstracts. (35)

Sediment transport and erosion in waterways, 1977-March, 1983 (citation from the Selected water resources abstracts data base). 1983. 154 p. (PB83-861856). Prepared in cooperation with Office of Water Research and Technology, Washington, D. C. 105 abstracts. (36)

Sediment water interaction and its effect upon water quality. 1964-1978 (citations from the NTIS data base). 1981. 200 p. (PB81-803793). 192 abstracts on the release and absorption of chemicals by sediments as they pertain to water quality. (37)

_____. 1979-March, 1982. 1982. 270 p. (PB82-807892). 263 abstracts. (38)

Stream erosion and scouring processes. 1964-June, 1981 (citations from the NTIS data base). 1981. 165 p. (PB81-807232). 158 abstracts on erosion of stream banks, bridge supports levees, and other hydraulic structures. (39)

Water resources in arid and semiarid regions. 1964-December, 1981 (citations from the NTIS data base). 1981. 274 p. (PB81-805632). 267 abstracts on water quality resource management, potable water, consumption, and irrigation in arid and semiarid regions, especially the western parts of the United States. (40)

_____. January, 1982-June, 1982. 1982. 98 p. (PB82-810474). 90 abstracts. (41)

Arizona Water Resources Research Center, Tucson. Bibliography on groundwater recharge in arid and semiarid areas. Susan J. Keith, Patricia Paylore, K. J. De Cooke, and L. G. Wilson. July, 1982. 158 p. (PB83-182055). (42)

River basin development. 1977-June, 1982 (citations from the Selected water resources abstracts data base). 1982. 339 p. (PB82-869454). Prepared in cooperation with Office of Water Research and Technology, Washington, D. C. 231 abstracts fully indexed and with a list of titles. (43)

Desalination of water. June, 1976-September, 1982 (citations from the Energy data base). 1982. 248 p. (PB82-874983). Prepared in cooperation with the Department of Energy, Washington, D. C. 246 abstracts. (44)

Desalination of water. 1977-May, 1982 (citations from the Selected water resources abstracts data base). 1982. 225 p. (PB82-866237). Prepared in cooperation with Office of Water Research and Technology, Washington, D. C. 154 abstracts fully indexed and with a title list. (45)

Desalination of water. June, 1970-December, 1982 (citations from the Engineering index data base). 1982. 299 p. (PB83-857326). 309 abstracts. (46)

Urban surface runoff: a bibliography with abstracts. Edward J. Lehmann. Springfield, Virginia: U. S. National Technical Information Service. Report for 1964-May, 1973. 1973. 99 p. (COM-73-11387/0). 95 abstracts on urban hydrology and its modelling: storm water runoff problems and abatement: and combined sewer overflows and their control. (47)

Water quality modelling. Hydrological and limnological systems. v. 1, 1964-1974 (a bibliography with abstracts). Edward J. Lehmann. 1976. 197 p. (NTIS/PS-76/0443). 192 abstracts of federally-sponsored research on models of water quality and the chemical, physical, biological, and hydrological processes important to water quality. Topics covered include euthrophication, nutrient removal, pollutant dispersion, stream flow, heat dissipation, limnological factors, aquifer water quality, and water run-off quality. (48)

Reports distributed by NTIS   42

_____. v. 2, 1975-June, 1977. 1978. 191 p. (NTIS/PS-78/0649). 185
abstracts.   (49)

_____. v. 3, July, 1977-September, 1981. 1981. 236 p. (PB82-801119).
249 abstracts.   (50)

_____. October, 1981-January, 1983 (a bibliography with abstracts). 1983.
27 p. (PB83-802991). 17 abstracts.   (51)

_____. 1977-March, 1983 (citations from the Selected water resources abstracts
data base). 1983. 389 p. (PB83-861757). Prepared in cooperation with Office of
Water Research and Technology, Washington, D. C. 288 abstracts fully indexed and
with a list of titles.   (52)

Snow studies. v. 1, 1964-1974 (a bibliography with abstracts). Robena J.
Brown. 1976. 216 p. (NTIS/PS-76/0808). 211 abstracts.   (53)

_____. 1975-November, 1980 (citations from the NTIS data base). 1981.
289 p. (PB81-802209). 283 abstracts on snow cover, snowbelt, snowdrifts, snow
removal, trafficability, snow rescue and survival, physical and mechanical
properties, and also detection by remote sensing.   (54)

_____. December, 1980-March, 1982. 1982. 39 p. (PB82-807967). 32
abstracts.   (55)

(4) Meteorology and Climatology

Paleoclimatology. 1964-March, 1982 (citations from the NTIS data base).
1982. 187 p. (PB82-807348). 180 abstracts involving interpretation of glacial
deposits, fossils, and paleogeographical data.   (56)

Precipitation washout. 1964-November, 1982 (a bibliography with abstracts).
1983. 221 p. (PB83-801811). 213 abstracts on the removal of pollutants, radioactive isotopes, and dust by rain and snow.   (57)

Fog prediction. 1964-November, 1981 (citations from the NTIS data base).
1981. 193 p. (PB82-802588). 185 abstracts.   (58)

Ice fog. 1964-February, 1982 (citations from the NTIS data base). 1982.
77 p. (PB82-806548). 67 abstracts.   (59)

Ice and fog: detection and warning systems. 1964-May, 1982 (citations from
the NTIS data base). 1982. 229 p. (PB82-809492). 222 abstracts.   (60)

Hail: meteorology, damage, prevention, and forecasting (a bibliography with
abstracts). v. 1. 1964-1975. Robena J. Brown. 1979. 246 p. (NTIS/PS-
79/0309/9GA). 238 abstracts on hail storms, formation, damage, warning systems;
atmospheric and cloud physics associated with hail, storm tracking, forecasts,
erosion, meteorological instruments, meteorological fronts and storms which
accompany hail and methods to modify these systems.   (61)

_____. 1976-September, 1982 (citations from the NTIS data base). 1982.
110 p. (PB82-811456). 104 abstracts.   (62)

Hurricanes forecasting, modification and research. 1964-January, 1981
(citations from NTIS data base). 1981. 297 p. (PB81-805160). 265 abstracts
on hurricane modeling, cloud seeding; remote sensing, air water interaction, heat
transfer, and wind motions.   (63)

(5) Coastal Zone

Coastal zone management and planning. v. 1. 1964-1976 (a bibliography with
abstracts). Robena J. Brown. 1978. 260 p. (NTIS/PS-78/0326). 255 abstracts.   (64)

_____. v. 2. 1977-June, 1981 (citations from the NTIS data base). 1981.
258 p. (PB81-807240). 251 abstracts   (65)

_____. July, 1981?-August, 1982. 1982. 39 p. (PB82-811407). 30 abstracts. (66)

Beach erosion. 1972-November, 1982 (citations from the Engineering Index
data base). 1982. 163 p. (P383-853549). 171 abstracts.   (67)

Beach erosion and protection. 1974-April, 1983 (citations from Oceanic abstracts). 1983. 204 p. (PB83-863126). Prepared in cooperation with Cambridge Scientific Abstracts, Washington, D. C. 224 abstracts. (68)

Shoreline erosion. 1974-November, 1982 (citation from Oceanic abstracts). 1982. 230 p. (PB83-853556). Prepared in cooperation with Cambridge Scientific Abstracts, Washington, D. C. 255 abstracts. (69)

Coastal regions: geomorphology. 1975-March, 1982 (citations from the International Information Service for the Physics and Engineering Communities data base) 1982. 164 p. (PB82-864869). 129 abstracts fully indexed and with a title list. (70)

(6) Ecosystems

Ecosystem models. Elizabeth A. Harrison. v. 1. 1964-October 1975 (a bibliography with abstracts). 1976. 219 p. (NTIS/PS-76/0903). 214 abstracts. (71)

_____. _____. v. 2. November, 1975-November, 1977 (a bibliography with abstracts). 1978. 187 p. (NTIS/PS78/1145). 181 abstracts. (72)

_____. _____. November, 1977-February, 1982 (citations from the NTIS data base). 1982. 314 p. (PB82-805037). 307 abstracts on ecosystem models in U. S. government funded research for marine biology, wildlife, plants, water pollution, microorganisms, food chains, radioactive substances, limnology, and diseases. (73)

Land reclamation, revegetation. 1977-April, 1983 (citations from Selected water resources abstracts data base). 1983. 154 p. In cooperation with Office of Water Research and Technology, Washington, D. C. (PB83-862797). 99 abstracts. (74)

(7) Energy

State-of-the-art reviews and bibliographies on energy. Audrey S. Hundemann. 1964-1978 (citations from the NTIS data base). 1980. 290 p. (PB80-812886). 280 abstracts on fossil fuels, wind, solar energy, hydrogen, geothermal energy, nuclear energy, and batteries. (75)

_____. 1979-January, 1983. 1983. 258 p. (PB83-803536). 249 abstracts. (76)

Energy supply and demand modelling. 1964-November, 1981 (citations from the NTIS data base). 1983. 304 p. (PB83-804450). 296 abstracts on models to estimate supply of and demand for electricity, oil, natural gas, coal and petroleum products on national, regional, and state levels. (77)

_____. December, 1981-February, 1983. 1983. 114 p. (PB83-804468). 106 abstracts. (78)

Strip mining. v. 1. 1964-1975 (citations from the NTIS data base). Audrey S. Hundemann. 1977. 161 p. (NTIS/PS-77/0950). 156 abstracts. (79)

_____. 1976-1979. 1982. 278 p. (PB82-807439). 273 abstracts pertaining primarily to environmental impacts, land reclamation, and satellite remote sensing of mines. (80)

_____. 1980-June, 1983. 187 p. (PB83-807560). 179 abstracts. (81)

Strip mining: impact on water resources. 1977-June, 1983 (citations from the Selected water resources abstracts data base). 1983. 160 p. (PB83-867200). Prepared in cooperation with Office of Water Research and Technology, Washington, D. C. 103 abstracts fully indexed and with a title list. (82)

Argonne National Laboratory. Selective bibliography of surface coal mining and reclamation literature. v. 2. Interior coal province. M. L. Patricoski, L. K. Daniels, and A. A. Sobek, 1979. 161 p. (ANL/LRP-1 [vol. 2]). 1300 references. (83)

Reports distributed by NTIS

Offshore drilling. Guy E. Habercom, Jr. v. 1. 1964-1975 (a bibliography with abstracts). 1978. 139 p. (NTIS/PS-78/0748). 132 abstracts. (84)

____. ____. 1976-September, 1981 (citations from the NTIS data base). 1981. 275 p. (PB82-801176). 268 abstracts on drilling procedures, equipment, environmental aspects, and legal implications involved in oceanic minerals resources recovery. (85)

____. October, 1981-December, 1982 (citations from the NTIS data base). 1983. 139 p. (PB83-803072). 131 abstracts. (86)

Offshore drilling: environmental effects. June, 1976-March, 1982 (citations from the Engineering index data base). 1982. 233 p. (PB82-863853). 209 abstracts fully indexed with a title list. (87)

Offshore drilling: environmental effect. 1976-January, 1983 (citations from the Energy data base). 1983. 309 p. (PB83-859595). 285 abstracts. (88)

Natural gas: supply, demand and utilization. 1978-January, 1983 (citations from the NTIS data base). 1983. 363 p. (PB83-803965). 354 abstracts. (89)

Nuclear electric power generation: economic analysis 1970-May, 1982 (citations from the NTIS data base). 1982. 196 p. (PB82-861030). 145 abstracts. (90)

____. 1976-January, 1982 (citations from the Energy data base). 1982. 193 p. (PB82-861048). 175 abstracts. (91)

Power plant siting. v. 1. 1964-1977 (a bibliography with abstracts). Audrey S. Hundemann. 1979. 275 p. (NTIS/PS-79/1071). 268 abstracts, with emphasis on nuclear power plant siting. (92)

____. 1978-January, 1982 (citations from the NTIS data base). 1982. 175 p. (PB82-804816). 134 abstracts. (93)

____. February, 1982-April, 1983. 1983. (PB83-805671). 134 abstracts. (94)

(8) Oceanography

Law of the sea: maritime boundaries and jurisdictions. 1974-July, 1982 (citations from Oceanic abstracts). 1982. 190 p. (PB82-870569) Prepared in cooperation with Cambridge Scientific Abstracts, Washington, D. C. 250 abstracts fully indexed and with a list of titles. (95)

Remote sensing of the ocean. Robena J. Brown. Part 1. Physical, chemical, and geological properties. v. 1. 1970-1975 (a bibliography with abstracts). 1978. 179 p. (NTIS/PS-78/0562). 173 abstracts. (96)

____. Physical, chemical, and geological properties. 1976-January, 1983 (citations from the NTIS data base). 1983. 217 p. (PB83-802330). 209 abstracts. (97)

Remote sensing of the ocean dynamics. 1970-January, 1983 (citations from the NTIS data base). 1983. 251 p. (PB83-803908). 243 abstracts. (98)

Ocean wave sensing. 1964-December, 1982 (citations from the NTIS data base). 1983. 315 p. (PB83-802256). 307 abstracts. (99)

Tsunamis. 1964-February, 1982 (citations from the NTIS data base). 1982. 250 p. (PB82-806654). 242 abstracts. (100)

Sea ice. 1975-November, 1982 (citations from the International Information Service for the Physics and Engineering Communities data base). 1982. 265 p. (PB83-854059). 237 citations on observations and measurements of the properties, movement, and distribution or location of sea ice and sea ice meltwater, worldwide. (101)

Icebreakers and icebreaking. 1964-January, 1982 (citations from the NTIS data base). 1982. 281 p. (PB82-806225). 271 abstracts. (102)

_____. 1970-February, 1982 (citations from the Engineering Index data base) 1982. 91 p. (PB82-8062333). 84 abstracts of worldwide literature. (103)

_____. 1974- December, 1982 (citations from Oceanic abstracts). 1982. 158 p. (PB83-856971). Prepared in cooperation with Cambridge Scientific Abstracts, Washington, D. C. 175 abstracts. (104)

(9) Air, Water, and Noise Pollution and Waste Disposal

Remote sensing applied to environmental pollution detection and management. 1964- January, 1983 (citations from the NTIS data base). 1983. 286 p. (PB83-803882). 277 abstracts. (105)

Remote sensing applied to pollution monitoring. 1976-June, 1980 (citations from the International Aerospace abstracts data base). Gerald F. Zollars. Alburquerque, New Mexico: University of New Mexico. Technology Application Center. 1980. 61 p. (PB80-815632). 53 entries. (106)

Air quality monitoring. v. 1. 1970-1974 (a bibliography with abstracts). Edward J. Lehmann and Diane M. Cavagnaro. 1976. 156 p. (NTIS/PS-76/0638). 151 abstracts. (107)

_____. v. 2, 1975-1976 (a bibliography with abstracts). Diane M. Cavagnaro. 1978. 291 p. (NTIS/PS-78/0757). 284 abstracts. (108)

_____. 1977-1978 (citations from the NTIS data base). Diane M. Cavagnaro. 1980. 221 p. (PB80-813462). 215 abstracts. (109)

_____. 1979-February, 1982. 1983. 326 p. (PB83-807149). 318 abstracts. (110)

_____. March, 1982-May, 1983. 1983. 89 p. (PB83-807156). 81 abstracts. (111)

Air pollution economics. v. 1. 1964-1974 (a bibliography with abstracts). Edward J. Lehmann. 1976. 211 p. (NTIS/PS-76/0663). 206 abstracts. (112)

_____. v. 2. 1975-1976 (a bibliography with abstracts. Diane M. Cavagnaro 1978. 136 p. (NTIS/PS-78/0797). 129 abstracts. (113)

_____. v. 3. 1977 (a bibliography with abstracts). Diane M. Cavagnaro. 1979. 136 p. (NTIS/PS-79/0939). 130 abstracts. (114)

_____. 1978 (citations from the NTIS data base). Diane M. Cavagnaro. 1980. 156 p. (PB80-813835). 151 abstracts. (115)

_____. 1979-July, 1980 (citations from the NTIS data base). Diane M. Cavagnaro. 1980. 211 p. (PB80-813827). 206 abstracts. (116)

_____. August, 1980-January, 1983. 1983. 227 p. (PB83-803288). 220 abstracts. (117)

Atmospheric modeling of air pollution. v. 1. 1964-1973 (a bibliography with abstracts). Edward J. Lehmann. 1976. 124 p. (NTIS/PS-76/0508). 119 abstracts. (118)

_____. v. 2. 1974-1976. Diane M. Cavagnaro. 1978. 168 p. (NTIS/PS-78/0630). 163 abstracts. (119)

_____. 1977-1978 (a bibliography with abstracts). Brian Carrigan. 1980. 225 p. (PB80-811623). 216 abstracts. (120)

_____. 1979-October, 1981 (citations from the NTIS data base). 1981. 254 p. (PB82-801499). 248 abstracts. (121)

_____. November, 1981-January, 1983 (citations from the NTIS data base). 1983. 70 p. (PB83-803015). 63 abstracts. (122)

Reports distributed by NTIS

Air pollution emission factors. 1964-November, 1982 (citations from the NTIS data base). 1982. 315 p. (PB83-801456). 307 abstracts on emission factors for various industry, stationary, and mobile sources of air pollution. (123)

Automobile air pollution: abatement through management and planning. v. 1. 1970-1978 (citations from the NTIS data base). Edward J. Lehman. 1980. 252 p. (PB80-806375). 245 abstracts. (124)

_____. 1979-June, 1982. 1982. 140 p. (PB82-810649). 131 abstracts. (125)

Acid precipitation. 1970-July, 1983 (citations from Pollution abstracts) 1983. 297 p. (PB83-869495). Prepared in cooperation with Cambridge Scientific Abstracts, Washington, D. C. 324 abstracts. (126)

_____. June, 1970-July, 1983 (citations from the Engineering Index data base). 1983. 248 p. (PB83-869487). 249 abstracts. (127)

_____. June, 1974-September, 1983 (citations from the International aerospace abstracts data base). 1983. 128 p. (PB83-872408). Prepared in cooperation with the National Aeronautics and Space Administration, Washington, D.C. 149 abstracts. (128)

_____. 1977-1982 (citations from the Selected water resources abstracts data base). 1982. 233 p. (PB83-857714). 169 abstracts fully indexed and with a list of titles. (129)

Acid precipitation: a bibliography. P. S. Blackburn. Department of Energy, Oak Ridge, Tennessee. Technical Information Center. 1983. 734 p. (DE83008750). 3,197 references to information in the Department of Energy's Energy data base through February 1983. (130)

_____: effects on terrestrial ecosystems. 1976-September, 1983 (citations from the Energy data base). 1983. 269 p. (PB83-782424). Prepared in cooperation with the U. S. Department of Energy. 274 abstracts with index and title list. (131)

_____: effects on the aquatic ecosystem. 1977-September, 1983 (citations from the Energy data base). 1983. 230 p. (PB83-872242). Prepared in cooperation with the U. S. Department of Energy. 242 abstracts. (132)

Acid precipitation: legal, political, and health aspects. 1976-September, 1983 (citations from the Energy data base). 1983. 185 p. Prepared in cooperation with the U. S. Department of Energy. 184 abstracts. (133)

Urban air pollution. v. 1. 1970-1975 (a bibliography with abstracts). Edward J. Lehmann. 1977. 202 p. (NTIS/PS-77/0650). 197 abstracts. (134)

_____. v. 2. 1976-1977 (a bibliography with abstracts). Diane M. Cavagnaro. 1979. 176 p. (NTIS/PS-79/0767). 170 abstracts. (135)

_____. _____. 1978-July, 1979 (citations from the NTIS data base). 1980. 227 p. (PB80-814411). 221 abstracts. (136)

_____. August, 1979-November, 1981. 135 p. (PB82-802463). 129 abstracts. (137)

Water pollution economics. v. 1. 1964-1974 (a bibliography with abstracts). Edward J. Lehmann. 1976. 213 p. (NTIS/PS-76/0665). 208 abstracts. (138)

_____. v. 2. 1975-August, 1977 (a bibliography with abstracts). Diane M. Cavagnaro. 1978. 190 p. (NTIS/PS-78/0926). 183 abstracts. (139)

_____. September, 1977-September, 1980 (citations from the NTIS data base). (PB81-800054). 1980. 310 p. 304 abstracts. (140)

_____. October, 1980-January, 1982. 72 p. (PB82-804881). 65 abstracts. (141)

Water pollution in estuaries and coastal zones. v. 1. 1964-1974 (a bibliography with abstracts). Robena J. Brown. 1976. 170 p. (NTIS/PS-76/0851). 165 abstracts. (142)

_____. v. 2. 1975-October, 1978. Robena J. Brown. 1979. 258 p. (PB80-801319). 252 abstracts. (143)

_____. 1978-February, 1982 (citations from the NTIS data base). 1982. 139 p. (PB82-807603). 132 abstracts. (144)

Oil pollution detection and sensing. v. 1. 1964-1975 (a bibliography with abstracts). Mona F. Smith. 1977. 214 p. (NTIS/PS-77/0933). 209 abstracts. (145)

_____. 1976-April, 1983 (citations from the NTIS data base). 1983. 278 p. (PB83-806380). 267 abstracts. (146)

Oil spills: environmental effects. 1977-March, 1983 (citations from the Selected water resources abstracts data base). 1983. 117 p. (PB83-862649). Prepared in cooperation with Office of Water Research and Technology, Washington, D. C. 83 abstracts fully indexed and with list of titles. (147)

Oil shale waste disposal: environmental impacts. 1976-March, 1983 (citations from the Energy data base). 1983. 160 p. (PB83-862060). 136 abstracts. (148)

Coal mine refuse disposal. June, 1976-February, 1983 (citations from the Energy data base). 1983. 236 p. (PB83-860965). 215 abstracts. (149)

Coal mine wastes, 1977-January, 1983 (citations from the Selected water resources abstracts data base). 1983. 191 p. Prepared in cooperation with Office of Water Research and Technology, Washington, D. C. 126 abstracts. (150)

Acid mine drainage. 1977-December, 1982 (citations from the Selected water resources abstracts data base). 1982. 272 p. (PB83-858548). Prepared in cooperation with Office of Water Research and Technology, Washington, D. C. 184 abstracts. (151)

Acid mine drainage. October, 1978-May, 1983 (citations from the NTIS data base). 1983. 115 p. (PB83-807297). 108 abstracts. (152)

Ground water pollution. Part 1. General studies. v. 1. 1964-1976 (citations from the NTIS data base). Robena J. Brown. 1978. 280 p. (NTIS/PS-78/0138). 275 abstracts. (153)

_____. v. 2. 1977-January, 1980. Robena J. Brown. 1980. 260 p. (PB80-806391). 253 abstracts. (154)

_____. February, 1980-December, 1982. 1983. 198 p. (PB83-802207). 190 abstracts. (155)

Ground water pollution. Part 2. Pollution from irrigation and fertilization. v. 1. 1964-1976 (citations from the NTIS data base). Robena J. Brown. 1978. 245 p. (NTIS/PS-78/0140). 240 abstracts. (156)

_____. v. 2. 1977-January, 1980. Robena J. Brown. 1980. 125 p. (PB80-806409). 118 abstracts. (157)

Ground water pollution: saline ground water. 1964-May, 1981 (citations from the NTIS data base). 1982. 269 p. (PB83-800813). 261 abstracts on irrigation return flow, soil studies, hydrology, aquifers, water quality, salt water intrusion, and effects on water supplies. (158)

_____. June, 1981-September, 1982. 1982. 47 p. (PB83-800821). 39 abstracts. (159)

Ground water pollution (citations from the American Petroleum Institute data base). Report for 1964-January, 1981. 1981. 186 p. (PB82-800129). 177 abstracts on contamination of ground water, especially from petroleum and petrochemical sources. (160)

Ground water pollution monitoring. 1976-May, 1983 (citations from the Energy data base). 1983. 137 p. (PB83-864470). Prepared in cooperation with the U. S. Department of Energy. 98 abstracts fully indexed and with a title list. (161)

Urban noise pollution. 1970-October, 1981 (citations from the NTIS data base). 1983. 271 p. (PB83-804575). 264 abstracts. (162)

Reports distributed by NTIS   48

_____. November, 1981-March, 1983. 89 p. (PB83-804583). 81 abstracts. (163)

Noise pollution economics. 1964-November, 1981 (citations from the NTIS data base). 1981. 155 p. (PB82-802646). 149 abstracts. (164)

Highway traffic noise. 1964-February, 1983 (citations from the NTIS data base). 1983. (PB83-804781). (165)

Airport noise. 1964-January, 1983 (citations from the NTIS data base). 1983. 375 p. (PB83-803387). 366 abstracts. (166)

Noise control for motor vehicles. 1964-March, 1983 (citations from the NTIS data base). 1983. 204 p. (PB83-805424). 195 abstracts of U. S. government sponsored research on control of noise by trucks, automobiles, buses, and motorcycles. (167)

_____. 1970-January, 1982 (citations from the Engineering Index data base). 1982. 249 p. (PB82-805078). 244 abstracts on worldwide literature. (168)

Sewage treatment costs and economics. 1970-1978 (citations from the NTIS data base). 1980. 192 p. (PB81-801979). 185 abstracts. (169)

_____. 1979-May, 1983. 1983. 226 p. (PB83-806919). 217 abstracts. (170)

Solid waste disposal economics. v. 1. 1964-1976 (a bibliography with abstracts). Diane M. Cavagnaro. 1978. 185 p. (NTIS/PS-78/0894). 179 abstracts. (171)

_____. 1977-1981 (citations from the NTIS data base). 1983. 299 p. (PB83-805903). 292 abstracts. (172)

_____. 1982-April, 1983. 1983. 184 p. (PB83-805911). 177 abstracts. (173)

Regional and urban solid waste disposal: Management planning (citations from the NTIS data base). 1964-November, 1982. 1983. 314 p. (PB83-802447). 306 abstracts. (174)

_____. Part 2. Local case studies. 1964-November, 1982. 1983. 342 p. (PB83-802454). 334 abstracts). (175)

_____. Part 3. Handling and disposal technology. 1964-November, 1982. 1983. 348 p. (PB83-802371). 340 abstracts. (176)

Sanitary landfills. v. 1. 1964-1977 (citations from the NTIS data base). Audrey S. Hundemann. 1979. 279 p. (PB80-802812). 272 abstracts. (177)

_____. _____. 1978-May, 1983. 1983. 214 p. (PB83-806992). 206 abstracts. (178)

_____. _____. v. 1. 1970-1977 (citations from the Engineering index data base). 1979. 279 p. (PB80-802838). 272 abstracts. (179)

_____. _____. 1978-May, 1983 (citations from the Engineering index data base). 1983. 271 p. (PB83-807529). 229 abstracts. (180)

Hazardous materials waste disposal. v. 1. 1964-1976 (a bibliography with abstracts). Diane M. Cavagnaro. 1979. 234 p. (NTIS/PS-79/0672). 255 abstracts on pesticides, explosives, chemical warfare agents, and other types of hazardous chemicals; management planning, spills, toxicity, water pollution abatement, and National Disposal Sites; landfills, incineration, and deep wells. Radioactive wastes are excluded. (181)

_____. _____. 1977-1979 (citations from the NTIS data base). 1981. 208 p. (PB82-801234). 201 abstracts. (182)

_____. 1980-January, 1983. 1983. 266 p. (PB83-802660). 260 abstracts. (183)

Hazardous materials transportation: general studies. 1964-1976. (citations from the NTIS data base). 1982. 237 p. (PB82-803685). 230 abstracts. (184)

_____. 1977-February, 1983. 1983. (PB83-804260). 253 abstracts. (185)

_____. 1970-August, 1982 (citations from the Engineering index data base). 1982. 335 p. (PB83-800201). 328 abstracts. (186)

(10) Regional Economics

Regional and local economic development. 1975-March, 1981 (citations from the NTIS data base). 1982. 243 p. (PB82-810045). 236 abstracts. (187)

_____. April, 1981-May, 1982. 1982. 147 p. (PB82-810052). 139 abstracts. (188)

(11) Population

Population projections for area planning. Mary E. Young. v. 1. 1964-1976 (a bibliography with abstracts). 1978. 172 p. (NTIS/PS-78/0989). 166 abstracts. (189)

_____. 1977-1979 (citations from the NTIS data base). 1982. 237 p. (PB82-804220). 230 abstracts on predictions of population growth or change in state, regional, country, or municipal areas, on projections for area economic analysis, employment, land and resource use, energy, and transportation needs. (190)

_____. 1980-March, 1983. 1983. 162 p. (PB83-804856). 153 abstracts. (191)

Population mobility. 1964-1978 (citations from the NTIS data base). Mary E. Young. 1980. 250 p. (PB80-809619). 243 abstracts of research reports on population migrations; census statistics on populations; effects of housing, employment, and services availability on population movements; and population mobility between urban and rural areas. (192)

_____. 1979-October, 1982. 1982. 207 p. (PB83-800581). 198 abstracts. (193)

(12) Ethnic Groups

Economic development of ethnic minorities. 1964-1979 (citations from the NTIS data base). 1982. 253 p. (PB82-808494). 248 abstracts on the economic conditions of non-European ethnic minorities in the United States: American Indians, Negroes, Chinese Americans, Japanese Americans, other Orientals, Mexican American, Puerto Ricans, Filipinos, and Eskimos. (194)

_____. 1980-March, 1982. 1982. 63 p. (PB82-808502). 56 abstracts. (195)

American Indians. v. 1. 1964-1975 (a bibliography with abstracts). Gerald H. Adams. 1977. 170 p. (NTIS/PS-77/0894). 164 abstracts. (196)

_____. 1976-1980 (citations from the NTIS data base). 1982. 317 p. (PB82-808783). 310 abstracts on tribal organizations, Indian reservation affairs, agricultural and industrial development, forest management, land use, natural resources, etc. (197)

_____. 1981-March, 1982. 1982. 79 p. (PB82-808791). 72 abstracts. (198)

Negroes in the U. S.--social, industrial, and behavioral interactions. v. 1. 1965-1972 (a bibliography with abstracts). Gerald H. Adams. 1975. 127 p. (NTIS/PS-75/842). 122 abstracts. (199)

_____. 1973-March, 1982 (citations from the NTIS data base). 1982. 325 p. (PB82-807140). 318 abstracts on rural and urban affairs, racial-labor market conditions, employment and unemployment, family relations, and the armed forces. References are made to migration, education, and racism. (200)

Ghetto sociodynamics. 1964-March, 1982 (citations from the NTIS data base). 1982. 87 p. (PB82-807306). 80 abstracts. (201)

Migrant workers. 1964-October, 1981 (citations from the NTIS data base). 1981. 110 p. (PB82-801283). 104 abstracts on housing, employment, medical and health care, and interaction of the migrant and the community. (202)

(13) Urban Areas

Land use in urban areas. v. 1. 1964-August, 1975 (a bibliography with abstracts). Carolyn Shonyo. 1976. 188 p. (NTIS/PS-76/0764). 183 abstracts. (203)

_____. September, 1975-December, 1980 (citations from the NTIS data base). Edith Kenton. 1980. 312 p. (PB81-801342). 295 abstracts on urban land use including transportation planning, water resource management, air pollution, and land use studies. Excludes local studies. (204)

Reports distributed by NTIS

____. 1980-May, 1982. 1982. 68 p. (PB82-811019). 60 abstracts. (205)

Effects of land use and urbanization on water resources and water quality (a bibliography with abstracts). v. 1. 1971-1976. Edward J. Lehmann. 1978. 190 p. (NTIS/PS-78/08487). 184 abstracts. (206)

____. 1977-August, 1981 (citations from the NTIS data base). 1981. 200 p. (PS82-800350). 193 abstracts. (207)

____. September, 1981-November, 1982. 1983. 72 p. (PB83-802520). 64 abstracts. (208)

Quality of life in the urban environment. Mary E. Young. v. 1. 1964-July, 1976 (a bibliography with abstracts). 1977. 216 p. (NTIS/PS-77/0696). 214 abstracts on attitude of people toward cities, urban quality of life, transtion, housing, and social services. (209)

____. v. 2. August, 1976-1977. 1979. 255 p. (NTIS/PS-79/880). 247 abstracts. (210)

____. 1978-February, 1983 (citations from the NTIS data base). 1983. 190 p. (PB83-803510). 183 abstracts. (211)

Remote sensing applied to urban and regional planning. 1964-January, 1983 (citations from the NTIS data base). 1983. 88 p. (PB83-803874). 79 abstracts on land use mapping, traffic surveys, urban transportation planning, and taking inventories of natural resources for urban planning. (212)

Urban information systems. Mary E. Young. Part 1. General. v. 1. 1964-1976 (a bibliography with abstracts). 1978. 174 p. (NTIS/PS-78/1027). 170 abstracts of reports not sponsored by USAC (Urban Information Systems Interagency Committee). (213)

____. v. 2. 1977-September, 1978. 1978. 121 p. (NTIS/PS-78/1028). 118 abstracts. (214)

____. part 2. USAC reports (a bibliography with abstracts). Report for 1964-September, 1978. 1978. 367 p. (NTIS/PS-78/1029). 363 abstracts. (21)

Urban parking. 1964-June, 1982 (citations from the NTIS data base). 1982. 249 p. (PB82-810102). 241 abstracts. (21)

Urban storm sewers and water runoff. v. 1. 1964-1973 (a bibliography with abstracts). Robena J. Brown and Edward J. Lehmann. 1975. 182 p. (NTIS/PS-75/603). 177 abstracts. (21)

____. v. 2. 1974-1976. Robena J. Brown. 1978. 210 p. (NTIS/PS-78/1216). 205 abstracts. (21)

____. 1977-October, 1979 (citations from the NTIS data base). 1981. 244 p. (PS81-805244). 236 abstracts. (21)

____. November, 1979-May, 1982. 1982. 148 p. (PB82-810458). 140 abstracts. (22)

____. 1977-June, 1982 (citations from the Selected water resources abstracts data base). 1982. 247 p. (PB82-868639). Prepared in cooperation with Office of Water Research and Technology, Washington, D. C. 204 abstracts fully indexed and with a list of titles. (22)

City redevelopment. 1964-April, 1980 (citations from the NTIS data base). Edith Kenton. 1980. 207 p. (PB80-808017). 200 abstracts on renewal of cities in the United States. (22)

New towns and new communities--planning and development. 1964-October, 1981 (citations from the NTIS data base). 1981. 180 p. (PB82-801168). 173 abstracts of new towns and communities in the United States: land use, service, environmental aspects, transportation, housing, employment, commerce, and other topics. (22)

(14) Housing

Housing. Gerald H. Adams. v. 1. 1970/August, 1975 (a bibliography with abstracts). 1976. 209 p. (NTIS/PS-76/0706). 204 abstracts. (22)

____. v. 2. September, 1975-August, 1976. 1976. 252 p. (NTIS/PS-76/0707). 247 abstracts. (22)

Housing: general studies. 1976-April, 1981 (citations from the NTIS data base). 1982. 278 p. (PB82-811126). 270 abstracts on a wide range of research on housing in the United States. (226)

_____. May, 1981-May, 1982. 1982. (PB82-811134). (227)

Housing: public housing. 1976-May, 1982 (citations from the NTIS data base). 1982. 196 p. (PB82-811118). 188 abstracts. (228)

Housing: Federal housing assistance programs. 1976-1981 (citations from the NTIS data base). 1982. 315 p. (PB82-811142). 307 abstracts. (229)

_____. January, 1982-May, 1982. 1982. 68 p. (PB82-811159). 60 abstracts. (230)

(15) Transportation

Air transportation: demands and needs. 1968-September, 1981 (citations from the NTIS data base). 1983. 341 p. (PB83-805077). 334 abstracts on needs and demand for air transportation including air traffic control, airports, cargo aircraft, short takeoff aircraft, and air transportation in general. (231)

_____. October, 1981-March, 1983. 1983. 26 p. (PB83-805085). 19 abstracts. (232)

Surface transportation: demands and needs. 1964-1979. 1983. 457 p. (PB83-805200). 453 abstracts divided into four sections: urban, rail, marine, and general. (233)

_____. 1980-March, 1983. 1983. 213 p. (PB83-805218). 203 abstracts. (234)

Dual mode transportation (a bibliography with abstracts). Final report for 1964-May, 1978. Edith Kenton. 1978. 169 p. (NTIS/PS-78/0538). 163 abstracts on inter-city networks, rapid transit railways, buses, automobile travel, automated guideways, personal rapid-transit systems, airport access, and modal split. (235)

Airport development: social and economic effects. 1968-February, 1983. 1983. 175 p. (PB83-804880). 166 abstracts. (236)

Multimodal transportation planning. 1972 February, 1983 (citations from the NTIS data base). 1983. 126 p. (PB83-804294). 117 abstracts on multimodal passenger and freight transportation planning for urban areas and intercity corridors including work travel patterns, trip generation, urban transportation demand, modal choice, and travel forecasting models. (237)

Transportation users: demands and need. 1964-September, 1982 (citations from the NTIS data base). 1982. 244 p. (PB83-800862). 236 abstracts, mainly on urban mass transit systems and needs of users, including the elderly, the poor, commuters, and students. (238)

Travel habits and patterns. v. 1. 1964-1973 (a bibliography with abstracts). Gerald H. Adams. 1976. 88 p. (NTIS/PS-76/0025). 83 abstracts. (239)

_____. v. 2. 1974-June, 1982 (citations from the NTIS data base). 1982. 326 p. (PB82-810037). 318 abstracts. (240)

METRO-rapid transit for the Washington, D. C. area. 1964-September, 1982 citations from the NTIS data base). 1982. 159 p. (PB83-801001). 149 abstracts. (241)

BART-Rapid transit for the San Francisco Bay area. 1964-September, 1982 citations from the NTIS data base). 1982. 290 p. (PB83-800995). 270 references. (242)

Bus transportation: local studies. 1964-1979 (citations from the NTIS data base). 1982. 308 p. (PB82-808767). 301 abstracts on bus systems in communities of the United States, arranged by states or other areas, on topics such as community relations, environmental issues, benefits and costs, alternatives, travel patterns and modes, demand, and social aspects. (243)

_____. 1980-August, 1983. 1983. 60 p. (PB83-808154). 52 abstracts. (244)

Bus transportation: national and general studies. 1964-1979 (citations from the NTIS data base). 1982. 314 p. (PB82-808866). 307 abstracts on variety of topics, such as scheduling, travel demand, costs, stations, subsidies, fuel, user groups, and highway aspects. (245)

Reports distributed by NTIS

_____. 1980-August, 1983. 1983. 154 p. (PB83-808147). 146 abstracts. (246)

Highway and freeway planning: social and economic effects. 1964-March, 1980 (citations from the NTIS data base). Edith Kenton. 1983. (PB83 804757). (247)

Highway beautification. 1964-March, 1980 (citations from the NTIS data base). Edith Kenton. 1980. 107 p. (PB80-805781). 100 abstracts. (248)

Railroad freight transportation. 1975-1980 (citations from the NTIS data base). 1982. 356 p. (PB82-811209). 348 abstracts. (249)

_____. 1981-September, 1983. 1983. 162 p. (PB83-872531). 161 abstracts. (250)

Waterway transportation. 1970-December, 1982 (citations from the NTIS data base). 1982. 198 p. (PB83-858191). 171 abstracts. (251)

_____. 1970-December, 1982 (citations from the Engineering index data base). 1982. 310 p. (PB83-856534). 342 abstracts. (252)

Supertankers and superports. 1964-December, 1982 (citations from the NTIS data base). 1983. 236 p. (PB83-802538). 228 abstracts. (253)

_____. 1970-December, 1982 (citations from the Engineering index data base). 1983. 139 p. (PB83-802637). 132 abstracts. (254)

_____. 1974-May, 1983 (citations from Oceanic abstracts). 1983. 103 p. (PB83-864405). Prepared in cooperation with Cambridge Scientific Abstracts, Washington, D. C. 132 abstracts fully indexed and with a title list. (255)

(16) Agricultural Resources

Remote sensing of agricultural resources. October, 1973-January, 1983 (citations from the NTIS data base). 1983. 320 p. (PB83-803890). 311 abstracts. on crop identification, acreage measurement, land mapping, and forest density studies. (256)

Remote sensing applied to agricultural resources. 1979-June, 1980 (citations from the International Aerospace Abstracts data base). Gerald F. Zollars. Alburquerque, New Mexico: University of New Mexico. Technology Applications Center. 1980. 57 p. (PB80-815624). 223 entries. (257)

(17) Tourism and Recreation

Tourism and vacation travel: state and local government planning. 1964-March, 1983 (citations from the NTIS data base). 1983. 233 p. (PB83-804369). 214 abstracts on use of tourism for economic development of local communities, especially in wilderness, coastal zone, lake, waterway, and Indian Reservation areas. (258)

Outdoor recreation. Mary E. Young. v. 1. 1964-1977 (a bibliography with abstracts). 1979. 275 p. (NTIS/PS-79/0111). 270 abstracts on swimming, camping, skiing, hunting, and outdoor sport and athletics together with area planning studies, demand projections, and safety measures. (259)

_____. v. 2. 1978-April, 1982 (citations from the NTIS data base). 1982. 293 p. (PB82-808650). 200 abstracts on swimming, camping, skiing, hunting, and outdoor sports and athletics. (260)

Recreation demand: water resources. 1977-August, 1982 (citations from Selected water resources abstracts data base). 1982. 137 p. (PB82-874033). Prepared in cooperation with Office of Water Research and Technology, Washington, D. C. 84 abstracts fully indexed and including a title list. (261)

Recreation facilities: water resources. 1977-August, 1982 (citations from the Selected water resources abstracts data base). 1982. 234 p. (PB82-874041). Prepared in cooperation with Office of Water Research and Technology, Washington, D. C. 161 abstracts fully indexed and including a title list. (262)

e. Publications of State and Municipal Governments

PARISH, David W. State government reference publications: an annotated bibliography. 2nd ed. Littleton, Colorado: Libraries Unlimited, 1981. 355 p. (1st ed. 1974. 237 p.). Indexes. 196

    Annotated guide to 1756 documents of state departments, agencies, and bureaus.

U. S. LIBRARY OF CONGRESS. Exchange and Gift Division. Monthly checklist of state publications, Washington, D. C.: Government Printing Office, 1910- . Monthly. 197

    A checklist of publications as issued by state governments and as received by the Library of Congress.

MUNICIPAL government reference sources: publications and collections. Edited for the American Library Association Government Documents Round Table by Peter Hernon and others. New York: Bowker, 1978. 341 p. 198

    Concentrates on large urban areas. Arranged by state and within state by municipality. Subject index.

8. MAPS, ATLASES, and REMOTE SENSING

a. Guides to Maps and Atlases

There is no comprehensive up-to-date inventory of maps produced by all of the various agencies of the United States government. For recent and authoritative information one can turn to:

NATIONAL Cartographic Information Center, U. S. Geological Survey, 507 National Center, Reston, Virginia 22092. Telephone: (703) 860-6045. 199

THOMPSON, Morris. M. Maps for America: cartographic products of the U. S. Geological Survey and others. Reston, Virginia: U. S. Geological Survey; distributed Washington, D. C.: Superintendent of Documents, Government Printing Office, 1979. 265 p. (A centennial volume, 1879-1979). Index. 200

    Account of mapping agencies of the United States government, especially but not solely the U. S. Geological Survey.

U. S. LIBRARY OF CONGRESS. Map Division. United States atlases: a catalog of national, state, county, city, and regional atlases in the Library of Congress and cooperating libraries. Compiled by Clara Egli LeGear. Washington, D. C.: Government Printing Office, 1950-1953. 2 v. Title of v. 1 varies slightly. 201

    Lists 7,064 atlases found in the Library of Congress and 132 cooperating libraries.

U. S. NATIONAL ARCHIVES. Guide to cartographic records in the National Archives. Washington, D. C.: Government Printing Office, 1971. 444 p. (National Archives publication no. 71-16). Index. 202

    560 annotated descriptive entries covering more than 1.6 million maps and about 2.25 million aerial photographs in the holdings of the National Archives Cartographic Branch [now the Center for Cartographic and Architectural Archives], as of 1966, arranged by administrative agencies of the Federal Government.

Maps, Atlases, and Remote Sensing   54

FIRE insurance maps in the Library of Congress: plans of North American cities
and towns produced by the Sanborn Map Company. A checklist compiled by the
Reference and Bibliography Section, Geography and Map Division. Washington,
D. C.: Library of Congress: for sale by the Superintendent of Documents, U. S.
Government Printing Office, 1981. 773 p. County index. Index to cities and
towns.   203

    9,805 entries (all but 15 in the United States) arranged by states in
alphabetical order and within states by cities and towns in alphabetical order,
with notation of date and number of sheets in each edition. The Sanborn Map
Company compiled detailed large-scale maps for commercial, industrial, and
residential districts of more than 12,000 cities and towns in the United States,
in about 50,000 editions, with about 700,000 sheets. Brief historical introduction by Walter W. Ristow. A major source of information on land-use and its
evolution in American cities.

HOEHN, R. Philip, and others. Union list of Sanborn fire insurance maps held in
institutions in the United States and Canada. Santa Cruz, California: Western
Association of Map Libraries, 1976-1977. 2 v.   20

    Covers 25,000 fire insurance maps held by libraries in the United States
and Canada (excluding the Library of Congress), arranged alphabetically by state
and city.

MILLER, E. Willard. State atlases: major sources of spatial information.
Journal of geography, v. 81, no. 1 (1982), p. 34-36.   20

    51 selected state atlases with review of seven outstanding recent examples.

McGAUGH, Maurice E. Geographies, atlases, and special references on the states
and provinces of Anglo-America. Mount Pleasant, Michigan: Central Michigan
University. Geography Department, October, 1970. 36 p. mimeographed.   20

    About 325 entries on geographies, atlases, references, and bibliographies
of individual states of the United States, arranged by state.

    Also published as Geographies, atlases, and special references on the
states and provinces of Anglo-America: a bibliography. Special Libraries
Association. Geography and Map Division. Bulletin, nos. 83-86 (1971). Part 1.
Bibliography of state and regional geographies of the United States, no. 83
(March, 1971), p. 40-47. 114 references. Part 2. Atlases for the states and
regions of the United States no. 84 (June, 1971) p. 31-36. 122 references.
Part 3. Selected references for the geographical study of states and regions
of the United States, no. 84, p. 37-39. 50 references. Part 7. Bibliographies
and special references for study of United States and Canadian geography. Part
8. Titles of special interest for bibliography of states and provinces, and
supplement, no. 86 (December, 1971), p. 44-50. 42 entries. [Parts 4, 5, and 6
in no. 85 (September 1971), p. 13-18 are devoted to Canada].

STEPHENSON, Richard W., and GALNEDER, Mary. Anglo-American state and provincial
thematic atlases: a survey and bibliography. The Canadian cartographer, v. 6,
no. 1 (June 1969), p. 15-45.

    55 atlases with commentary and list of reviews.

COBB, David A., and IVES, Peter B. State atlases: an annotated bibliography.
Chicago, Illinois: Council of Planning Librarians, CPL bibliography no. 108,
1983. 21 p.

    138 annotated entries on atlases of individual states of the United States,
arranged by states. Most of the listed atlases fall into two periods: 1850-1910
or 1950-1982.

Maps, Atlases, and Remote Sensing

STEPHENSON, Richard W., comp. Land ownership maps: a checklist of nineteenth century United States county maps in the Library of Congress. Washington, D.C., U. S. Library of Congress, Geography and Map Division, 1967. 86 p. 209

1,449 county land ownership maps in the United States. An introductory essay discusses the evolution of these maps.

b. Atlases and Maps

U. S. GEOLOGICAL SURVEY. The National atlas of the United States of America. Washington, D. C.: U. S. Geological Survey, 1970. 417 p. Index of places. 210

General reference maps. Special subject maps: physical, history, economic, socio-cultural, administrative, mapping and charting, and the world. Maps of landforms, geophysical forces, geology, marine features, soils, climate, water; fishing, and forestry, agriculture, mineral and energy resources, manufacturing, and business. Index contains 41,000 entries with latitude, longitude, and map location.

RAND McNALLY and Co. Rand McNally commercial atlas and marketing guide. Chicago: Rand McNally, 1876- . Annual. 211

Large double-page maps of states are individually indexed to record counties, townships, and 110,000 cities, towns, villages, and cross-road settlements. Special tables of population, businesses, manufactures, agriculture, transportation, and other information of commercial value.

Best source of up-to-date detailed information on smaller settlements of the United States.

ABLER, Ronald F., and ADAMS, John S., eds. A comparative atlas of America's great cities: twenty metropolitan regions. Minneapolis, Minnesota: University of Minnesota Press, for the Association of American Geographers, 1976. 503 p. 212

Comparable maps of relief, generalized land use, housing, population, and socioeconomic characteristics of the population for 20 cities of the United States: Boston, New York-Northern New Jersey, Philadelphia, Hartford-Connecticut Valley, Baltimore, New Orleans, San Francisco-Oakland, Pittsburgh, St. Louis, Cleveland, Chicago, Detroit, Minneapolis-St. Paul, Seattle, Dallas-Fort Worth, Houston, Los Angeles, Miami, Atlanta, and Washington, D. C. Comparable maps for metropolitan physical environments, open space, housing, transportation and communication, metropolitan growth, socioeconomic segregation, employment and poverty, and urban renewal and redevelopment.

PAULLIN, Charles O. Atlas of the historical geography of the United States. Ed. by John K. Wright. Washington, D. C.: Carnegie Institution of Washington, and New York: American Geographical Society, 1932. 162 p. 688 maps on 166 places. (Carnegie Institution of Washington. Publication no. 401). Index. 213

Maps cover a wide range of physical, historical, social, political, and economic topics: natural environment; reproduction of early maps; Indians; explorers' routes; lands; population; colleges, universities, and churches; boundaries; political parties and opinion; political and social reforms; industries and transportation; foreign commerce; distribution of wealth; city plans; military history; and external relations. Original compilations. Notes on sources.

RONEY, John F., Jr., ZELINSKY, Wilbur, and LOUDER, Dean R., eds. This remarkable continent: an atlas of United States and Canadian society and culture. College Station, Texas: Texas A and M University Press, 1982. 316 p. Bibliography, p. 306-309. Index. 214

cont.

Maps, Atlases, and Remote Sensing

Wide-ranging coverage of cultural and popular regions, settlement, divisions of the land, structures, social organization and behavior, language and place names, ethnicity, religion, politics, foodways, music and dance, sports and games, and place perception.

OXFORD regional economic atlas: the United States and Canada. Prepared by the Cartographic Department of the Oxford University Press. John D. Chapman and John C. Sherman, advisory editors. 2nd ed. Prepared with the assistance of Quentin H. Stanford. London: Oxford University Press, 1975. 128 p., plus index (gazetteer). Bibliography, p. vi-ix. (1st ed. 1967). 215

Includes urban plans (of larger cities), regional relief maps, and many aspects of physical geography, demography, agriculture, forestry, fishing, fuels and energy, mining and industry, and transport. Gazetteer index gives map location and latitude and longitude of about 10,000 places.

RAND McNALLY road atlas: United States/Canada/Mexico. 1924- . Annual. Chicago: Rand McNally. 216

In the land of the automobile a good road atlas is often the most convient and accessible collection of state and metropolitan maps. The 1982 edition of this atlas, 128 p., carries the subtitle: "Completely revised and up to date. Latest population figures for 23,000 cities and towns. More than 250 large-scale city maps." The basic maps are of individual states of the United States and provinces of Canada. At end of volume extensive lists of cities and counties by states with population figures and map locations.

ANDRIOT, John L. Township atlas of the United States. 2nd ed. McLean, Virginia: Andriot Associated, 1979. 1,184 p. Index. 21

Maps for each state of (1) state and county boundaries with a table of counties and their location on the map; (2) census county divisions; (3) minor civil divisions, regardless of name; (4) public land survey townships; (5) urbanized areas. Maps are reproduced from a variety of publications of the U. S. Bureau of the Census and the U. S. Geological Survey but are conviently assembled here. Three indexes, specially compiled for this volume, aid in locating (1) 3,067 counties and 43,294 named minor civil divisions in a single alphabetical index for the entire United States; (2) about 25,000 populated places in alphabetical order separately for each state; and (3) 3,850 populated places located on 275 maps of urbanized areas.

U. S. BUREAU OF THE CENSUS. Boundaries of counties and county equivalents as of January 1, 1970. Washington, D. C.: Government Printing Office, 1971 (Stock no. 0301-1896). 2

Large single sheet invaluable for plotting county data to study or depict distributions for the whole United States. Similar maps were produced for each decade 1840-1960, and also for 1915, 1935, and 1937, partly by the U. S. Department of Agriculture.

KNOWLES, Richard, and STOWE, Peter W. E. North America in maps: topographical map studies of Canada and the USA. London: Longman, 1976. 95 p. Bibliographies. 2

c. Aerial Photographs and Remote Sensing

AERIAL photography status maps, January 1981. Salt Lake City, Utah: U. S. Department of Agriculture. Agricultural Stabilization and Conservation Service. Aerial Photography Field Office, 1981. Unpaged. 220

79 maps of states or parts of states showing last aerial photography covering individual counties with date, scale, and number of index sheets to cover the county. Coverage is generally at the scale of 1:20,000 secured through 8 1/4 inch lens but scales vary from 1:10,000 to 1:40,000. Information may be obtained from Aerial Photography Field Office, USDA-ASCS, 2222 West 2300 South, P. O. Box 30010, Salt Lake City, Utah 84130.

U. S. GEOLOGICAL SURVEY. Geographic research in the U. S. Geological Survey: Bibliography--1966-1980. By Mary E. Graziani. Washington, D. C.: U. S. Geological Survey, 1982. 59 p. (U. S. Geological Survey, Circular 865). Author index. Subject index. 221

About 450 studies in remote sensing sponsored by the Office of Geographic Research, Geography Program, or Geographic Applications Program of the United States Geological Survey, 1966-1980, arranged by author. The subject index provides an entry by topic or region.

PHOTO-GEOGRAPHIC international (firm). Photo-atlas of the United States: a complete photographic atlas of the U.S.A. using satellite photography. Pasadena, California: Ward Ritchie Press, 1975. 127 p. Scale of most maps about 1:1,140,000 or 1 inch to 18 miles. 222

d. Map Collections

CARRINGTON, David K., and STEPHENSON, Richard W. Map collections in the United States and Canada: a directory. 3rd ed. New York: Special libraries Association. A project of the Geography and Map Division, 1978. 230 p. Index. (1st ed. 1954). 223

684 map collections in the United States with information on address, telephone number, map curator, staff, size and nature of collections, classification and cataloging, hours, and reproduction facilities, arranged by states and within states by cities, in alphabetical order.

9. ENCYCLOPEDIA

WORLDMARK encyclopedia of the states. Moshe Y. Sachs, ed. New York: Worldmark Press; distributed by New York: Harper and Row, 1981. 690 p. 224

Data and textual information for each of the 50 states. Fifty subject headings, such as location, size, extent; topography; climate; flora and fauna, environmental protection; population; ethnic groups; languages, religions, transportation, history; economy; labor; agriculture; animal husbandry, fishing; forestry; mining; energy and power, industry; housing; and education. Bibliographies.

10. GAZETTEERS

THE NATIONAL gazetteer of the United States of America. Prepared by the U. S. Geological Survey in cooperation with the U. S. Board on Geographic Names. 1982- . For sale Alexandria, Virginia: U. S. Geological Survey. Distribution Branch. Washington, D.C.: Government Printing Office. Separate volume for each state. 225

cont.

Reviews; Dissertations and Theses 58

Based on the Geographic Names Data Base, which in 1982 contained about two million names used throughout the United States and its territories. The first published volume, New Jersey (1982, 220 p.), contained about 10,000 names. Microfiche or printout copies of interim materials used in preparation of printed volumes are available from the U. S. Geological Survey, NCIC, 507 National Center, Reston, Virginia 22092. Based on names found on topographic maps, charts, and other published documents, excluding names of streets and roads. Information provided includes name, feature class, county, coordinate, and name of map on which located.

GEO-DATA: the world almanac gazetteer. 1st ed. ed. by George Thomas Kurian. Detroit, Michigan: Gale Research Co., 1983. 623 p. Published in cooperation with the World Almanac Publications. 226

The United States, p. 5-358 consists of three sections: 1. U. S. cities and towns with 20 items of information for each city and town in the United States with a population of 10,000 or more in 1975, arranged by states, then by cities and towns within each state; 2. U. S. counties with 10 items of information for each of the 3,142 counties in the United States, arranged by states; and 3. U. S. states with about 50 items of information for each state. In general the County and city data book [151] or the State and metropolitan area book [152] of the U. S. Bureau of the Census provide better sets of statistics but Geo-Data contains some additional information.

11. REVIEWS

VAN BALEN, John. Geography and earth science publications, 1968-1972: an author, title, and subject guide to books reviewed, and an index to the reviews. Ann Arbor, Michigan: Pierian Press, 1978. 313 p. Subject, regional, and title indexes. 227

_____. _____. 1973-1975. 1978. 232 p. 228

Bibliographic listing of books in geography and related earth sciences reviewed in geographical periodicals and a record of the reviews published in 21 periodicals in the first volume and 38 in the second. Extensive coverage of books published in or on the United States.

12. DISSERTATIONS AND THESES

BROWNING, Clyde E. A bibliography of dissertations in geography: 1901 to 1969: American and Canadian universities. Chapel Hill, North Carolina: University of North Carolina. Department of Geography, 1970. 96 p. Studies in geography, no. 1, 1970. 96 p. 229

1,582 doctoral dissertations arranged by 23 subject categories. A regional classification records the entry numbers by large regions.

BROWNING, Clyde E. A bibliography of dissertations in geography: 1969 to 1982. American and Canadian universities. Chapel Hill, North Carolina: University of North Carolina. Department of Geography. Studies in geography, no. 18, 1983. 145 p. Author index. 230

2,270 entries for doctoral dissertations in geography accepted by universities in the United States and Canada 1969-1982, based on annual listings in the Professional geographer or, after 1979 in Guide to graduate departments of geography in the United States and Canada, arranged by subject categories (number of dissertations in parentheses): agricultural (140), cartography (42), climatology (104), cultural (85), economic (53), environmental perception (73), environmental studies (156), geographic thought (26), geomorphology (188), historical (102), housing and residential (62), industrial (67), land use and landscapes (47), medical (30), other physical (68), planning and national development (27), political (69), population (111), recreation (59), regional (34), resources (29), retail and rural markets (54), settlement (56), social and ethnic (56), spatial diffusion (24), techniques (48), transportation and trade (101), urban (201), water resources (68), and not elsewhere classified (90).

HODSON, Dean R. A bibliography of dissertations in geography on Anglo-America, 1960-1972. Monticello, Illinois: Council of Planning Librarians, Exchange bibliography, no. 583-584, 1974. 202 p. 231

About 2,900 entries arranged by regions.

STUART, Merrill M. A bibliography of master's theses in geography: American and Canadian universities. Tualatin, Oregon: Geographic and Area Studies Publications, 1973. 274 p. 232

5,054 master's theses arranged by 27 fields and alphabetically by author in each field. Regional classification index.

COMPREHENSIVE dissertation index, 1861-1972. Ann Arbor, Michigan: Xerox University Microfilms, 1973. 37 v. 233

v. 16. Geography and geology. Geography. p. 1-166. A computer-generated index based on keywords in dissertation titles. Single word headings in alphabetical order, i.e. United States is under United or States and land use is under Land or Use or Los Angeles is under Los. See other such headings as agricultural, economic, industries, patterns, recreation (or tourism or tourist), transportation, urban (or city, cities, or towns), climates, conservation, geomorphology, resources, vegetation, or water. For regional works look under names of regions, such as South, Southeast, Southeastern, Southern, Southwestern, West, Western, North, Northeastern; under names of states such as California, Michigan, or Wisconsin, under names of cities such as Chicago or Los Angeles, or under other place names such as Appalachians. Alphabetical author listing, v. 33-37.

____. Annual supplements. 1973- . Annual. Each year has 5 volumes, 2 for science, 2 for social sciences and humanities, and 1 author index. Geography and regional planning are located in v. 4: social sciences and humanities, part 2. Arrangement is as in the basic index above. 234

13. DIRECTORIES

ASSOCIATION of American Geographers. Directory, 1982. Washington, D. C.: Association of American Geographers, 1982. 186 p. 235

Name, mailing address, birth date, birth place, education, employment, specialty, and geographic area of interest of 5,402 members. Earlier editions 1949, 1952, 1956, 1961, 1967, 1970, 1974, and 1978.

ASSOCIATION of American Geographers. Guide to graduate departments of geography in the United States and Canada. 1968/1969- . Annual. Washington, D. C.: Association of American Geographers. 236

Annual listing of departments of geography in the United States and Canada that offer graduate degrees. Programs and research facilities. Staff with specializations. Address and telephone number. Alphabetical directory of staff. Geographical index of institutions. The 1983-1984 volume provided information on 52 graduate departments of geography in the United States offering the doctorate in geography and on 125 departments in the United States that offer the master's degree [plus in Canada 16 departments offering a doctor's degree and 22 offering a master's].

14. TEXTUAL TREATISES OF THE GEOGRAPHY OF THE UNITED STATES

WHITE, C. Langdon, FOSCUE, Edwin J., and McKNIGHT, Tom L. Regional geography of Anglo-America. 5th ed. Englewood Cliffs, New Jersey: Prentice-Hall, 1979. 585 p. Index. 237

Selected bibliographies at the end of each chapter: general bibliography on Canada and the United States, p. 8-10; the physical environment, p. 32; population, p. 53-54; cities, p. 86-87; regions and regionalism in general, p. 99; Northeastern Anglo-America, p. 125-126; French Canada, p. 146-147; Megalopolis, p. 179-180; the Appalachians and the Ozarks, p. 205; the Inland South, p. 233-235; the Southeastern Coast, p. 269-270; the Anglo-American Heartland, p. 313-315; the Great Plains, p. 349-351; the Rocky Mountains, p. 379-380; the Intermontane Basins and plateaus. p. 419-420; the California region, p. 459-460; the Hawaiian Island, p. 480; the North Pacific Coast, p. 512-513; the Boreal Forest, p. 543-545; the Tundra, p. 567-568. About 700 references.

PATERSON, John H. North America: a geography of Canada and the United States. 6th ed. New York: Oxford University Press, 1979. 463 p. Bibliography, p. 436-455. 238 [7th ed., 1984. ca 480 p.].

About 800 references arranged by chapters both systematic and regional.

THOMAN, Richard S. The United States and Canada: present and future. Columbus, Ohio: Merrill, 1978. 471 p. Index. Bibliographies. 239

DURY, George H., and MATHIESON, Raymond S. The United States and Canada. 2nd ed. London: Heinemann Educational, 1976, 1980. 327 p. Bibliography, p. 299-304. (1st ed. 1970). 240

STARKEY, Otis P., ROBINSON, J. Lewis, and MILLER, Crane S. The Anglo-American realm. 2nd ed. New York: McGraw-Hill, 1975. 369 p. Bibliographies. (1st ed. 1969. 533 p.). 241

ESTALL, Robert C. A modern geography of the United States: aspects of life and economy. Harmondsworth, Middlesex, England; Baltimore, Maryland: Penguin Books, 1972. 401 p. Index. Bibliography, p. 388-393. About 90 references arranged by chapters. Revised edition, 1976. Bibliography, p. 452-459. 242

GRIFFIN, Paul F., CHATHAM, Ronald L., and YOUNG, Robert N. Anglo-America: a systematic and regional geography. Palo Alto, California: Fearon Publishers, 1968. 456 p. 243

Bibliographies at ends of both systematic and regional chapters include about 435 references.

WATSON, J(ames) Wreford. North America: its countries and regions. London: Longmans, 1963. 854 p. rev. ed. New York: F. A. Praeger, 1967. 881 p. General index and index of authors cited. Bibliography, p. 819-840 in both editions. (Geographies for advanced study). 244

876 references, arranged by systematic and regional chapters: 116 on North America as a whole; 310 on Canada; 402 on the United States; and 48 on Mexico.

MEAD, William R., and BROWN, Eric H. The United States and Canada: a regional geography. London: Hutchinson, 1962. 368 p. Index. 245

Brief bibliographies at ends of chapters.

BLUME, Helmut. USA. Eine geographische Landeskunde. Darmstadt: Wissenschaftliche Buchgesellschaft. Band 1. Der Grossraum in strukturellem Wandel. 1975, reprinted, 1978. 346 p. Bibliography, p. 305-321. Band 2. Die Regionen der USA. 1979. 499 p. Bibliography, p. 443-472. (Wissenschaftliche Länderkunden 9). Subject and place indexes. 246

Textual Treatises of the Geography of the United States

Good selection of about 1,000 references on the geography of the United States. The bibliography in volume 1 has about 400 references arranged by topical chapters: general studies of the land and its people; physical geography; natural hazards; resource exploitation and conservation; historical foundations of the cultural landscape; population problems; cities and urban dynamics; the economy (agriculture and the primary sector; industry and trade); atlases and maps.

The bibliography in volume 2 has about 600 references arranged by regional chapters: regionalization; of the United States; the Atlantic Megalopolis and its hinterland; the Middle West; the Florida peninsula; California; the Pacific Northwest; New England; the Deep South; the Southern Mountains; the Wheat Belt; Grazing and Irrigated Regions of the Great Plains and the Cordillera; island-like areas of dense population in the West; urban agglomerations; Alaska; Hawaii; Caribbean possessions; Pacific possessions.

BIRDSALL, Stephen S., and FLORIN, John W. Regional landscapes of the United States and Canada. 2nd ed. New York: John Wiley, 1981. Index. (1st ed. 1978. 416 p.). 247

Striking photos and maps. Few bibliographic references.

REGIONS of the United States. John Fraser Hart, ed. New York: Harper and Row, 1972. 155-374 p. Bibliographic references. (Reprint from Annals of the Association of American Geographers, v. 62, no. 2 [June 1972], p. 155-374). 248

JAMES, Preston E., and JONES, Clarence F., eds. American geography: inventory and prospect. Syracuse, New York: Syracuse University Press for the Association of American Geographers, 1954. 590 p. Index. 249

26 systematic chapters by specialists on each of the principal fields of geography. Extensive references to work by American geographers predominantly on the United States.

II. PHYSICAL GEOGRAPHY, RELATED EARTH SCIENCES, THE ENVIRONMENT, AND RESOURCES

1. GENERAL INFORMATION SOURCES

SOURCEBOOK on the environment: a guide to the literature. Edited by Kenneth A. Hammond, George Macinko, and Wilma B. Fairchild. Chicago, Illinois: University of Chicago Press, 1978. 613 p. Author and subject indexes. Sponsored by the Association of American Geographers. 250

A good introduction to geographical approaches to the study of the environment with careful selection of about 3,800 references, arranged at end of 24 topical chapters and by 26 specialists. Section 1, Environmental perspectives and prospects. Section 2, Environmental modification: case studies. Section 3, Major elements of the environment (air and air quality; water and water quality; landforms and soils; vegetation; animals in the biosphere the coastal zone; human population and the environment; and energy and environment. Section 4, Research Aids consists of three appendixes: A. Selected periodicals of environmental interest; B. Review of United States Federal environmental legislation; and C. Selected list of environmental organizations in the United States; Federal environmental agencies, departments, and offices; and U. S. Congressional committees and environmentally related subcommittees.

A DIRECTORY of information resources in the United States: geosciences and oceanography. National Referral Center. Washington, D. C.: Library of Congress: for sale by Superintendent of Documents, Government Printing Office, 1981. 375 p. Subject index. Organization locator. 251

1,000 entries. Detailed subject index.

ENVIRONMENT: a bibliography of social science and related literature. Compiled by Denton E. Morrison, Kenneth E. Hornback, W. Keith Warner. Washington. D. C.: Environmental Protection Agency. Office of Research and Monitoring. For sale by Superintendent of Documents, U. S. Government Printing Office, 1973. 860 p. (Socioeconomic Environment Studies Series). (EPA-600/5-74-011). Subject-title index. 252

4,892 entries arranged alphabetically by author. Subject index arranged the titles by 42 categories, such as air, climate, energy, forests, natural resources, and water. or fields such as geography and regional studies, anthropology, conservation, economics, ecology, government, history, politics, recreation, and sociology, or problems such as conflicts, natural hazards, pollution, or waste. An assemblage of diverse types of material on the environment very broadly defined. Includes many titles in geography.

EARTH resources: a continuing bibliography with indexes (National Aeronautics and Space Administration. Scientific and Technical Information Branch). Washington, D. C. 1- (Jn 1974-). Quarterly. (NASA SP-7041). Subject, personal author, corporate source, contract number, report/accession number, and accession number indexes. 253

A selection of annotated references to reports and journal articles introduced into the NASA scientific and technical information system in Scientific and Technical Aerospace Reports (STAR) and International Aerospace Abstracts (IAA) arranged by fields: agriculture and forestry; environmental changes and cultural resources; geodesy and cartography; geology and mineral resources; oceanography and marine resources; hydrology and water management; data processing and distribution systems; instrumentation and sensors; and general (including economic analysis). About 600 abstracts in each quarterly issue.

UNITED STATES DEPARTMENT OF THE INTERIOR. Office of Library and Information Services. Information sources and services directory. Washington, D. C.: U. S. Department of the Interior. Office of Library and Information Services, 1979. 300 p. plus organizational index, subject index, geographical index, and field office locations. 254

1,075 entries extensively annotated, arranged by bureaus and comparable units of the Department of the Interior: Office of the Secretary; U. S. Geological Survey; Heritage Conservation and Recreation Service; Bureau of Indian Affairs; Bureau of Land Management; Bureau of Mines; National Park Service; Bureau of Reclamation; U. S. Fish and Wildlife Service.

The Department of the Interior has major responsibility in management of natural resources of the United States and thus this welcome and detailed directory of its subdivisions and programs is an important tool for any study of the lands, waters, and animal and plant life of the country.

A GUIDE to obtaining information from the USGS 1981. Compiled by Paul F. Clarke, Helen E. Hodgson, and Gary W. North. Alexandria, Virginia: U. S. Geological Survey, Text Products Section. Distribution Branch, 1981. 42 p. (Circular 777). 255

Handy, brief guide to sources of information (general information; specialized subjects; publications; specialized reports; libraries; list of USGS products and sources and where they may be obtained (abstracts, bibliographies, catalogs, and lists; book reports; indexes; maps, charts, and diagrams, etc.) and list of sources of USGS information products, addresses, and telephone numbers.

U. S. GEOLOGICAL Survey. Office of the Data Base Administrator. Scientific and technical, spatial, and bibliographic data bases of the U. S. Geological Survey, 1979. Reston, Virginia: U. S. Geological Survey. Circular no. 817, 1980. 181 p. Indexes for acronyms, contact persons, geographic coverage, keywords, and names of data bases. 256

223 data bases listed by Computer Center, Conservation Geologic, Topographic and Water Resources divisions and the office of Land Information and Analysis.

EISTER, Margaret F. Selected bibliography and index of earth science reports and maps relating to land-resource planning and management published by the U. S. Geological Survey through October 1976. Washington, D. C.: U. S. Geological Survey. 1978. 76 p. (Bulletin, no. 1442). Subject index. Area index (by state and county). 257

About 600 references. Among major topics covered are climatic factors, economic factors, engineering factors, geological hazards (earthquakes, floods, landslides, subsidence, tsunamis, volcanoes), geology, ground water, land use man-made features, soils, surface water, waste disposal, and water.

CARBERRY, Michael. A bibliography of land and natural resources information systems. Monticello, Illinois: Council of Planning Librarians. Exchange bibliography, no. 1139, 1976. 24 p. Index. 241 references. 258

2. GEOMORPHOLOGY AND GEOLOGY

(See also Publications of the Geological Survey, 1879-1961, 1962-1970, 1971-[186], other guides, data bases, and bibliographies of the United States Geological Survey [255-257], and Geology under Government reports. Announcements and index [195 (4-11)].

THORNBURY, William D. Regional geomorphology of the United States. New York: Wiley, 1965. 609 p. 259

About 1,300 references, arranged regionally at the end of each of 28 chapters.

CORBIN, John Boyd. An index of state geological survey publications issued in series. New York, Scarecrow Press, 1965. 667 p. Author index. Subject index. 260

About 7,000 publications of state geological surveys arranged by states in alphabetical order and within each state by reports in numerical order.

_____. _____. Supplement, 1963-1980. Metuchen, New Jersey, and London: Scarecrow Press, 1982. 449 p. Author index. Subject index. 261

About 5,000 additional publications, 1963-1980.

KEIFFER, F. V. An annotated bibliography of geology and land use planning. Monticello, Illinois: Council of Planning Librarians. Exchange bibliography, no. 1230, 1977. 63 p. 301 references. 262

3. ENERGY AND MINERALS

See also Energy under Government reports. Announcements and index [195 (75-94)].

WEBER, R. David. Energy information guide. v. 1. General and alternative energy sources. Oxford, England: Clio; Santa Barbara, California: ABC-Clio, 1982. 334 p. Author, title, subject, and document number indexes. 263

861 annotated entries arranged by chapters: environmental impact; general sources of energy; conservation; general alternative sources; solar energy; wood power; wind power; geothermal energy; other alternatives. Entries in each chapter are arranged by type of publication: dictionaries; encyclopedias; handbooks and manuals; documentary sources; directories; statistical sources; indexes, abstracts, and bibliographies; and data bases. Limited to works in English dealing primarily with the United States.

v. 2 is to cover nuclear and electric power. v. 3 is to cover fossil fuels. The three volumes are to include more than 2,000 entries.

1980 EIA publications directory: a user's guide (U. S. Department of Energy. Energy Information Administration. National Energy Information System), Washington, D. C.: Government Printing Office, June, 1981. 191 p. 264

505 publications which provide detailed data and analysis of energy production in the United States. Subject index includes headings both for topics and for areal units such as individual states. Semiannual supplements, 1981- .

EIA data index: an abstract journal (U. S. Department of Energy. Energy Information Administration. Office of Energy Information Services), Washington, D. C.: Government Printing Office, December, 1980. 773 p. Subject, report number, and federal energy data indexes. 265

2,501 abstracts of tables, graphs, and other formatted data reported in publications of the EIA arranged by subject categories: coal and coal products; petroleum, natural gas; oil shales and tar sands; nuclear fuels; hydro energy; solar energy; geothermal energy: wind energy; electric power, nuclear power plants; energy analysis and modeling; energy conservation, consumption, and utilization; engineering; atmospheric environmental sciences; environmental-social aspects of energy technologies; and general and miscellaneous. Very full subject index. Semiannual supplements, 1981- .

ENERGY research abstracts (United States Department of Energy. Technical Information Center), Oak Ridge, Tennessee. 1- (1976-). Semimonthly. Corporate author, personal author, subject, contract number, report number, and order number correlation indexes in each issue, with semiannual and annual cumulations. 266

Massive abstracting (nearly 40,000 abstracts a year) of technical literature on energy, arranged by a detailed classification with extensive indexing.

Energy and Minerals

ENERGY abstracts for policy analysis (United States Department of Energy. Technical Information Center), Oak Ridge, Tennessee. v. 1- (1975-). Monthly. Each issue has corporate, author, subject, and report number indexes. Annual index volume. 267

Abstracts arranged subjects: energy analysis and modeling; economics and sociology; environment, health, and safeth; natural resources; research, development, demonstration, and commercialization; nuclear energy; transport and storage; waste heat utilization; conservation; supply, demand, and forecasting; policy, legislation, and regulation; fossil fuels; hydrogen and synthetic fuels; electric power; consumption and utilization; and unconventional sources and power generation.

ENERGY and environment information resource guide. M. Lynne Neufeld and Martha Cornog, compilers. Philadelphia, Pennsylvania: National Federation of Abstracting and Indexing Services, 1982. 53 p. 268

Only the most basic sources, arranged by 10 subject headings: general; environment--general; air pollution and air quality; water pollution and water quality; earth and land topics; energy--general; fossil fuels; renewable energy sources; nuclear energy; and electricity.

CUFF, David J., and YOUNG, William J. The United States energy atlas. New York: Free Press, a division of Macmillan; London: Collier-Macmillan, 1980. 416 p. Index. Bibliography. 269

Maps, bar graphs, pie charts, diagrams, black-and-white photos, text, and sources on coal, petroleum and natural gas, oil shale and tar sands, nuclear fuels, geothermal heat, solar radiation, wind power, hydroelectric generation, ocean thermal energy, and biomass. More than 100 tables.

BALACHANDRAN, Sarojini. Energy statistics: a guide to information sources. Detroit, Michigan: Gale Research Co., 1980. 272 p. (Natural world information guide series, v. 1). Directory of publishers. Personal and corporate author index. Subject index. 270

Inventory of energy-related statistics, in alphabetical arrangement by topic or place, found in 40 widely used serials. Sources analyzed. Additional sources of statistical data arranged by coal, electric power, natural gas, nuclear energy, petroleum, solar, and other emerging sources, composite sources, and energy and transportation.

MILLER, E. Willard, and MILLER, Ruby M. The American coal industry: economic, political, and environmental aspects. Monticello, Illinois: Vance bibliographies. Public administration series: Bibliography, no. P-572, 1980. 72 p. 271

About 1,000 references organized by topics: general, economic, political, and environmental aspects of the coal industry, each subdivided into numerous subtopics.

AVERITT, Paul, and LOPEZ, Lorreda. Bibliography and index of U. S. Geological Survey publications relating to coal, 1882-1970. Washington, D. C.: Government Printing Office, 1972. Reprinted 1977. 173 p. (U. S. Geological Survey. Bulletin, no. 1377). Index. 272

1,312 geological reports, maps, and statistical summaries.

WALKER, Flora K. Bibliography and index of U. S. Geological Survey publications relating to coal, January 1971-June 1974. Washington, D. C.: U. S. Geological Survey. Circular no. 709, 1975. 14 p. Index. 27

About 130 additional references.

Water Resources, Hydrology, Water Management, and Floods

ROWE, James E. Coal surface mining reclamation. Monticello, Illinois: Vance Bibliographies. Public Administration Series: Bibliography, no. P-252. 1979. 28 p. 274

About 400 references.

WEIS, Ina J. Strip mining--environmental aspects: a bibliography. Monticello, Illinois: Vance bibliographies. Public administration series: Bibliography, no. P-1038, 1982. 46 p. About 300 annotated references arranged by states. 275

COOK, Joseph L., and COOK, Earleen H. Oil shale as a possible fossil fuel resource. Monticello, Illinois: Vance bibliographies. Public administration series: Bibliography, no. P-580, 1980. 33 p. 276

About 450 references.

HAMILTON, Michael S. Power plant siting (with special emphasis on western United States). Monticello, Illinois: Council of Planning Librarians. Exchange bibliography, no. 1359-1360, 1977. 100 p. 277

More than 300 annotated references arranged by sections: state statute compilation; broadview materials on siting; western state material (Arizona, California, Colorado, Idaho, Montana, Nevada, New Mexico, Oregon, Utah, Washington, Wyoming); federal materials; electric utility industry; siting criteria and methodologies; and energy-environment overview and problems.

COPPA, Frank J. Energy policy: a bibliographical overview. Monticello, Illinois: Vance Bibliographies. Public Administration Series: Bibliography, no. P-275. 1979. 12 p. 278

About 160 references organized by: introduction to energy policy; the state-local context; the national-international context; conservation; energy and the environment; and development and regulation of energy.

U. S. Bureau of Mines. Mineral facts and problems. Washington, D. C.: Government Printing Office, 1970. 1,291 p. (Bulletin 650). Lists of references. 279

4. WATER RESOURCES, HYDROLOGY, WATER MANAGEMENT, AND FLOODS

See also Water resources, hydrology, floods, and snow under Government reports. Announcements and index [195 (12-55)].

SELECTED water resources abstracts (U. S. Department of the Interior. Office of Water Research and Technology). 1- (1968-). Semimonthly 1968-1981 (except v. 1, no. 1-9, monthly, published by the Bureau of Reclamation, Denver, Colorado); monthly 1982- . Subject, author, and organization indexes, cumulate annually. 280

6,000-13,000 abstracts annually in a classed arrangement with 10 major classes and many subdivisions: nature of water; water cycle; water supply augmentation and conservation; water quantity management and control; water quality management and protection; water resources planning; resources data; engineering works; manpower, grants, and facilities; and scientific and technical information. Subject index includes both topical and place headings, such as names of individual states, cities, lakes, rivers and river basins, and aquifers, in the United States. The annual cumulated subject index is particulary useful.

WATER Resources Scientific Information Center, Office of Water Research and Technology, U. S. Department of the Interior, Room 1308, Washington, D. C. 20240. 281

Maintains computerized data bases containing about 150,000 references (as of 1983) and full-text abstracts of published literature related to water resources, with on-line access at retrieval network centers. Publishes Selected water resource abstracts.

cont.

Has published a large number of bibliographies utilizing the data bases, partly in its extensive Bibliography series. Some bibliographies refer specifically to parts of the United States, e.g. bibliographies of Lake Superior, Lake Michigan, Lake Huron, Lake Erie, and Lake Ontario (all published in 1972). These quickly become dated but can be updated through the annual and monthly subject indexes to Selected water resource abstracts or through on-line access to the data base, which include geographical headings for individual lakes, states, cities, rivers and river basins, and aquifers.

GIEFER, Gerald J. Sources of information in water resources: an annotated guide to printed materials. Port Washington, N. Y.: Water Information Center, 1976. 290 p. Index of authors, subjects, and most titles. 282

1,584 numbered annotated entries arranged by a general section and a subject section. Subject section arranged by: nature of water; water cycle; water supply; water quality; water resources planning; and engineering works, each subdivided. Includes bibliographies, guides and manuals, indexes and abstract journals, handbooks, directories, and data compilations. A comprehensive survey of sources of information on many aspects of water resources and their management in the United States.

GIEFER, Gerald J. and TODD, David K., eds. Water publications of state agencies: a bibliography of publications on water resources and their management published by the states of the United States. Port Washington, N. Y.: Water Information Center, 1972. 319 p. 283

Water resources publications issued by 335 state agencies in the 50 states of the United States, arranged by state and agency.

_____. _____. First supplement, 1971-1974. Huntington, N. Y.: Water Information Center, 1976. 189 p. 284

ANNOTATED bibliography on hydrology, United States and Canada. A series with diverse forms of bibliographic entry and publication. 285

a. Annotated bibliography on hydrology 1941-1950 (United States and Canada). Prepared by the American Geophysical Union...in cooperation with the Subcommittee on Hydrology, Federal Inter-Agency River Basin Committee... Prepared for publication by the Bureau of Reclamation, Department of the Interior. Washington, D. C.: Government Printing Office, 1952. 408 p. (U. S. Federal Inter-Agency River Basin Committee. Subcommittee on hydrology. Notes on activities. Bulletin, no. 5). Index for subjects and places.

About 4,500 entries.

b. Annotated bibliography on hydrology 1951-54 and sedimentation 1950-54 (United States and Canada). Prepared under the auspices of Subcommittee on Hydrology and Sedimentation--Inter-Agency Committee on Water Resources. Compiled and edited for Subcommittees by American Geophysical Union. Washington, D. C.: Government Printing Office, 1956. 207 p. (U. S. Inter-Agency Committee on Water Resources. Joint Hydrology-Sedimentation Bulletin, no. 7).

More than 2,000 entries.

c. Annotated bibliography on hydrology and sedimentation United States and Canada 1955-58. Compiled by H. C. Riggs. Prepared in cooperation with the Subcommittees on Hydrology and Sedimentation, Inter-Agency Committee on Water Resources. Washington, D. C.: Government Printing Office, 1962. 236 p. (U. S. Geological Survey. Water-supply paper, no. 1546). Combined subject and geographic location or river-basin index.

About 2,000 entries.

d. Annotated bibliography on hydrology and sedimentation 1959-1962 (United States and Canada). Compiled and edited under the auspices of the Subcommittees on Hydrology and Sedimentation, Inter-Agency Committee on Water Resources by Carroll E. Bradberry and Associates. Washington, D. C.: Government Printing Office, 1964. 323 p. (U. S. Interagency Committee on Water Resources. Joint Hydrology-Sedimentation Bulletin, no. 8). Index for subjects and places.

About 3,000 entries.

e. Annotated bibliography on hydrology and sedimentation 1963-1965. United States and Canada. Compiled and edited under the auspices of the Hydrology and Sedimentation Committees, Water Resources Council, by Engineering Science, Inc. Washington, D. C.: Government Printing Office, 1969. 527 p. (Water Resources Council. Joint Hydrology-Sedimentation Bulletin, no. 9). Index for subjects and places.

About 5,000 entries.

f. Annotated bibliography on hydrology and sedimentation 1966-1968. United States and Canada. Compiled and edited under the auspices of the Hydrology and Sedimentation Committees, Water Resources Council, by Engineering Science, Inc. Washington, D. C.: Government Printing Office, 1970. 613 p. (Water Resources Council. Joint Hydrology-Sedimentation Bulletin, no. 10).

About 5,500 entries.

For references on water 1968- see Selected water resources abstracts (U. S. Department of the Interior. Office of Water Research and Technology [280].

WATER atlas of the United States. By James J. Geraghty, David W. Miller, Frits Van der Leeden, and Fred L. Troise. Cartographers, Miklos Pinther and Robert S. Collins. Port Washington, New York: Water Information Center, 1973. 122 plates with text on facing pages. 24x36 cm.   286

86 maps on conterminous United States, 20 on Alaska, and 16 on Hawaii, on physiography, precipitation, temperatures, evaporation and potential evapotranspiration, water transfers, rivers and drainage basins, reservoirs, runoff, river flows, flood losses, ground-water areas, thermal springs, water use, water laws, dissolved solids, salinity, hardness, water pollution, fishable fresh-water areas, natural wetlands, withdrawal of water, per capita water use, and similar topics.

PLANNING and Management Consultants, Ltd., Carbondale, Illinois. An annotated bibliography on water conservation: a report submitted to U. S. Army Engineer Institute for Water Resources, by Duane D. Baumann, et al. Fort Belvoir, Virginia: U. S. Army Engineer Institute for Water Resources; for sale Springfield, Virginia: National Technical Information Service, 1979. 181 p. Author index. (AD-A070 870).   287

About 200 annotated entries. The annotations provide extensive abstracts or summaries of findings.

SHARMA, Prakash C. Water resource development: a selected research bibliography. Monticello, Illinois: Council of Planning Librarians. Exchange bibliography, no. 764, 1975. 14 p.   288

About 160 selected references, mainly for the period 1950-1972 divided into books and articles.

CUDRNA, Frank L., Jr. Watershed planning: a selected research bibliography. Monticello, Illinois: Council of Planning Librarians. Exchange bibliography, no. 1014, 1976. 57 p.   289

cont.

569 references arranged by river basin planning and regional wastewater treatment and by watershed planning, mostly to publications in the United States, 1967-1975.

DEAN, Robert D., and WILSON, Carolyn. Development planning for water resources. Monticello, Illinois: Council of Planning Librarians. Exchange bibliography, no. 162, 1970. 22 p. 290

About 250 references arranged by general works; economics of water resources development; uses and benefits; and planning.

LANDMAN, Georgina B., and THILOFF, T. W. The legal aspects of flood plain zoning and management: an annotated bibliography. Monticello, Illinois: Council of Planning Librarians. Exchange bibliography, no. 1093, 1976, 26 p. 291

About 180 references, arranged by sections: legal aspects; economic aspects and flood insurance; planning, engineering, geologic, and geographic aspects; miscellaneous sources on flood control; government documents and government publications: land use abstracts publications.

FERGUSON, Bruce K. Bibliography on regulation of development for stormwater management. Monticello, Illinois: Vance bibliographies. Public Administration Series: Bibliography P-54, 1978. 13 p. 292

160 references.

ILLINOIS. University. Water Resources Center. Annotated bibliography on Great Lakes hydrology. By Larry B. Buetikofer and Dale D. Meredith. Urban, Illinois: University of Illinois. Water Resources Center, 1972. 68 p. 293

233 references, arranged under the following headings: precipitation; evaporation; runoff; groundwater; lake levels and flows; hydrologic budget; currents, winds, and water temperatures; and general.

ROGOFF, Marc Jay. Water resource development in the Great Lakes Basin: a selected bibliography. Monticello, Illinois: Council of Planning Librarians. Exchange bibliography, no. 1309, 1977. 9 p. 294

About 100 references, with emphasis on institutional structures and issues in water resource management.

MOE, Christine E. Rio Grande flood control and drainage. Monticello, Illinois: Vance Bibliographies. Public administration series: Bibliography no. P-769, 1981. 295

About 300 references.

WEATHERS, John W. Flood damage prevention: an indexed bibliography. 8th ed. Knoxville, Tennessee: Tennessee Valley Authority and Water Resources Research Center, The University of Tennessee, 1976. 61 p. Subject index. 296

800 entries, arranged by years. Emphasis on nonstructural measures for flood damage abatement, flood insurance, and floodproofing with only selected items on structural measures for flood control. Subject categories in index: building codes, channel encroachment, developmental policies, encroachment statutes, flood control, flood damage prevention, flood information reports, flood insurance, flood plain mapping, flood plain regulation, flood proofing, floods, forecasting and warning, inter-governmental relations, legal aspects, open space recreation, subdivision regulations, tax adjustments, urban renewal, use of flood plains, water resources development, and zoning.

U. S. Water Resources Council. Bibliography of water conservation. Washington, D. C.: Water Resources Council, 1981. 46 p. 297

BAUMANN, Duane D., and DWORKIN, Daniel. Water resources for our cities. Washington, D. C.: Association of American Geographers, 1978. 35 p. Bibliography, p. 33-35. (Resource papers for college geography, no. 78-2). 298

BAUMANN, Duane D., and others. An annotated bibliography on water conservation. Fort Belvoir, Virginia: U. S. Army Engineer Institute for Water Resources, for sale by National Technical Information Service, U. S. Department of Commerce, 1979. 181 p. (Planning and Management Consulants, Ltd., Carbondale, Illinois. IWR contract report 79-3. Contract no. DACW 72-78-M-0752). Author index. 299

Each entry is extensively annotated.

BURTON, Ian. Types of agricultural occupance of flood plains in the United States. Chicago, Illinois: University of Chicago. Department of Geography, Research paper no. 75, 1962. Bibliography, p. 163-167. 300

BURTON, Ian, KATES, Robert, and SNEAD, Rodman. The human ecology of coastal flood hazard in Megalopolis. Chicago, Illinois: University of Chicago. Department of Geography. Research paper no. 115, 1969. 196 p. Bibliography, p. 191-196. 88 references. 301

DZIEGIELEWSKI, Benedyki, BOLAND, John J., and BAUMANN, Duane D. An annotated bibliography on techniques of forecasting demand for water. Carbondale, Illinois: Planning and Management Consultants Ltd., 1981. 76 p. (IWR-CR-81-C03. Contract DACW72-80-C-0028). 302

U. S. Water Resources Council. The nation's water resources: the first national assessment. Washington, D. C.: Government Printing Office, 1968. 7 parts. 303

_____. _____, 1975-2000: second national water assessment. Washington, D. C.: Water Resources Council. For sale by the Superintendent of Documents. U. S. Government Printing Office, 1978-1980. 4 v. v. 1. Summary, 86 p. v. 2. Water quantity, quality, and related land consideration. 5 parts. v. 3. Analytical data summary, 89 p. plus 5 appendices. v. 4. Regional reports. 21 regions. 304

WHITE, Gilbert F. Strategies of American water management. Ann Arbor, Michigan: University of Michigan Press, 1969. 155 p. Bibliographical references. 305

WHITE, Gilbert F. Human adjustment to floods. Chicago, Illinois: University of Chicago. Department of Geography. Research paper 29, 1953 (reprint of 1945 edition). 225 p. Bibliography, p. 213-225. 306

247 references arranged by topics: floods and flood plains (31); flood-plain occupance (27); factors affecting flood-plain occupance (50); flood protection (70); other adjustments to floods (55); public policy (14). A broad survey of the literature up to 1942.

WOLLMAN, Nathaniel, and BONEM, Gilbert W. The outlook for water: quality, quantity, and national growth. Baltimore, Maryland: Johns Hopkins Press for Resources for the Future, 1971. 286 p. Bibliographical references. 307

5. COASTAL RESOURCES AND MANAGEMENT

See also Coastal zone under Government reports. Announcements and Index. [195 (64-70)].

CENTER for Natural Areas. An annotated bibliography of coastal zone management work products: a compilation of State, Territory, and Federal work products produced via funding from the Coastal zone management act of 1972, as amended. Washington, D. C.: National Oceanic and Atmospheric Administration. Office of Coastal Zone Management, 1980. 391 p. Index with descriptors (subjects) and reports by states. Cover title: Coastal zone management: an annotated bibliography. 308

About 1,500 entries arranged by states, territories, federal office.

SEA Grant publications index 1968-72. Parmula K. Weedman, compiler. Washington, D. C.: U. S. Department of Commerce. National Oceanic and Atmospheric Administration. Environmental Data Service. Environmental Science Information Center, May, 1973. 2 v. v. 1. Document listing, 289 p. v. 2. Key-Word-in Context (KWIC), Author, Corporate, Grant Number, National Technical Information Service Number, and Additional Report Number Indexes. 341 p. 309

SEA grant publications index (University of Rhode Island. Pell Marine Science Library. National Sea Grant Depository). Narragansett, Rhode Island, 1973- Annual. 310

Lists all materials received by the National Sea Grant Depository with the exception of newsletters. Listing by documents. Separate indexes by subject (KWIC), author, corporate body, grant number, NTIS number, and additional report number.

BIBLIOGRAPHY of publications of the Coastal Engineering Research Center and the Beach Erosion Board, December 1981. By Andre Szuwalski and Linda Clark, Fort Belvoir, Virginia: U. S. Army, Corps of Engineers. Coastal Engineering Research Center, 1981. 243 p. 311

Annotated listing of reports in 12 series with author index, subject (keyword) index, and list of keywords. Subject index includes both topical and place entries. Covers material in geology, oceanography, ecology, and coastal engineering.

COASTAL Engineering Research Center (CERC) and Beach Erosion Board (BEB) Publication List, January 1982. Fort Belvoir, Virginia: U. S. Army, Corpos of Engineers. Coastal Engineering Research Center, 1982. 33 p. 312

Reports listed by 17 different series.

HEIKOFF, Joseph M. Shorelines and beaches in coastal management: a bibliography. Monticello, Illinois: Council of Planning Librarians. Exchange bibliography, no. 876, 1975. 63 p. 313

About 650 entries arranged by subjects: coastal zone management; physiography, hydrography, and oceanography; shorelines and beaches; wetlands and estuaries; storms and the shoreline; sedimentation, dredging and mining; recreation; power plants and energy; ports; legislation and legal aspects; and U. S. Army Corps of Engineers projects.

MITCHELL, James K. A selected bibliography of coastal erosion protection and related human activity in North America and the British Isles. Natural hazard research. Working paper, no. 4. 1968. 66 p. 314

About 700 references arranged by three main sections with sub-divisions: physical background to coastal erosion, nature and control of coastal erosion, and human dimensions of coastal erosion.

COOK, Joseph Lee, and COOK, Earleen H. Shore erosion: a survey of the literature since 1969. Monticello, Illinois: Vance bibliographies. Public administration series: Bibliography, no. P-439, 1980. 23 p. 315

    About 275 references.

MOE, Christine. Effects of offshore oil and gas development on coastal communities. Monticello, Illinois: Vance bibliographies. Public administration series: Bibliography, no. P-380, 1979. 15 p. 316

    About 170 references with emphasis on environmental impacts.

GULF South Research Institute. Barrier islands of the Atlantic and Gulf coasts of the United States: an annotated bibliography. Jacques D. Bagur, Project Leader. Washington, D. C.: U. S. Department of the Interior. Fish and Wildlife Service. 1978. 215 p. Author and subject indexes. 317

    953 annotated entries on the physical features and the fish and wildlife resources, arranged areally by state and island from Maine to Texas.

MITCHELL, James K. Community response to coastal erosion: individual and collective adjustments to hazard on the Atlantic Shore. Chicago, Illinois: University of Chicago. Department of Geography. Research paper no. 156, 1974. 209 p. Bibliography, p. 190-206. 318

    258 references arranged by topics: coastal erosion, 52; coastal management, 22; natural hazard research, 10; environmental perception, 11; coastal perception, 35; adjustments to erosion, 40; and collective decision making, with subdivisions: theory, 36; conflict as a decision theme, 21; resource management decisions and citizen participation, 31.

6. CLIMATE

See also Meteorology and climatology under Government reports. Announcements and index [195 (56-63)].

SELECTIVE guide to climatic data sources. By Keith D. Butson and Warren L. Hatch, National Climatic Center, Asheville, N. C. Washington, D. C.: U. S. Department of Commerce. National Oceanic and Atmospheric Administration. Environmental Data and Information Service, December, 1979. 142 p. Index of published climatological data by element. (Key to meteorological records documentation no. 4.11 319

    Detailed analysis of 61 different publications of climatological information on the United States, arranged in five parts: current serial publications issued frequently; marine publications including atlases; decennial and intermittent publications; special publications (including atlases); and data catalogs and indexes.

COURT, Arnold. The climate of the conterminous United States, chapter 3 in The climates of North America, ed. by R. A. Bryson and F. Kenneth Hare, v. 11 of World survey of climatology, ed. by H. E. Landsberg. Amsterdam; London; New York: Elsevier Scientific Publishing Co., 1974, p. 193-343. Reference index. Geographical index. Subject index. 320

    159 references on the climate of the conterminous United States, p. 261-266. See also references on Alaska and Canada, p. 188-192. Text, maps, and extensive tables.

AMERICAN Meteorological Society. Bibliography on hurricanes and severe storms of the Coastal Plains Region. Washington, D. C.: Coastal Plains Center for Marine Development Services. Publication 70-2, 1970. 71 p. Subject index. Author index. 321

cont.

Climate   74

More than 250 annotated references on hurricanes and severe storms that have affected the Carolinas and Georgia, 1946-1970. Also three selected bibliographies: literature on hurricanes and storms for non-technical readers (16 references); general and historical material of interest to scientists and engineers (17 references); literature on economic effects of hurricanes and storms (25 references).

HACIA, Henry. A selected annotated bibliography of the climate of The Great Lakes. Silver Spring, Maryland: U. S. Department of Commerce. National Oceanic and Atmospheric Administration. Environmental Data Service. Technical memo, EDS BS-7, 1972. 70 p. Author index. Subject heading index. 322

201 annotated references 1903-1971 arranged chronologically. The subject heading index, p. 68-70, provides the most useful entry into this bibliography.

U. S. ENVIRONMENTAL SCIENCE SERVICES ADMINISTRATION. Climatic atlas of the United States. Washington, D. C.: U. S. Government Printing Office, 1968. 80 p. Large atlas format. Reprinted 1983. 323

217 climatic maps and 15 tables, prepared primarily by John L. Baldwin. (Republished Detroit, Michigan: Gale Research, 1975. 262 p., in smaller format under the title Weather atlas of the United States).

BALDWIN, John L. Climates of the United States. Washington, D. C.: U. S. Department of Commerce. National Oceanic and Atmospheric Administration. Environmental Data Service; for sale by Superintendent of Documents, U. S. Government Printing Office, 1973. 113 p. 324

Textual discussion of climates and climatic elements of the United States, plus 63 maps.

VISHER, Stephen S. Climatic atlas of the United States. Cambridge, Massachusetts: Harvard University Press, 1954. 403 p. Index. 325

Small-scale maps on aspects of climate of the United States for which usable data are available.

RUFFNER, James A., and BAIR, Frank E. Weather almanac: a reference guide to weather and climate of the United States and its key cities, including reference data on storms and weather extremes. 3rd ed. Detroit, Michigan: Gale Research Co., 1981. 326

Includes sections on U. S. weather in atlas format; storms and severe weather information; air pollution; and weather of 108 selected U. S. cities.

THE CLIMATES of the states. National Oceanic and Atmospheric Administration narrative summaries, tables, and maps for each state. 2nd ed. with new material by James A. Ruffner. Detroit, Michigan: Gale Research Co., 1980. 2 v. 1,182 p. 32?

State climatological reports for each of the 50 states based on first-order weather reporting stations with extensive tables. Materials on the individual states were originally issued in parts by the National Oceanic and Atmospheric Administration in the series, Climates of the states, climatology [climatography] of the United States, no. 60, parts 1-52 [no part 50], 1976-1978. v. 1. Alabama-North Carolina. v. 2. Ohio-Wyoming. Appendices.

7. VEGETATION

See also A. W. Küchler and Jack McCormick. Vegetation maps of North America [60].

EGLER, Frank E., ed. A cartographic guide to selected regional vegetation literature, where plant communities have been described. Part I. Northeastern United States. Montréal, 1959. 50 l. (Montréal. Université. Institut Botanique. Sarracenia, no. 1). 328

Annotated references on "vegetation" as distinct from "flora," arranged by states and localities from Maine to New Jersey with maps of each state showing location of described plant communities. Part II. Southeastern United States. Montréal, 1961. 87 l. Maps. (Sarracenia, no. 6).

VANKAT, John L. The natural vegetation of North America: an introduction. New York and Chichester: John Wiley, 1979. 261 p. Index. Bibliographies at end of part 1, p. 66-68, and at end of each chapter of part 2. The major vegetation formations of North America: tundra, p. 94-95; coniferous forest, 130-131; deciduous forest, p. 156-157; grassland, p. 178-179; desert, 203-204; temperate shrubland, woodland, and savanna, 223-224; and tropical, 248-249. 329

DAUBENMIRE, Rexford F. Plant geography: with special reference to North America. New York and London: Academic Press, 1978. 338 p. Index. Bibliography, p. 293-309. 442 references. 330

Two parts: floristic plant geography and ecologic plant geography.

ROSENKRANTZ, Barbart Gutmann, and KOELSCH, William A. American habitat: a historical perspective. New York: Free Press, 1973. 372 p. Bibliographical references. 331

WEAVER, John E. North American prairie. Lincoln, Nebraska: Johnson Publishing Co., 1954. 348 p. Index. Bibliography, p. 332-339. 332

WEAVER, John E., and ALBERTSON, F. W. Grasslands of the Great Plains: their nature and use. Lincoln, Nebraska: Johnson Publishing Co., 1956. 395 p. Index. Bibliography, p. 379-387. 333

8. SOILS

U. S. Soil Conservation Service. List of published soil surveys: January 1982. Washington, D. C.: U. S. Department of Agriculture, Soil Conservation Service, 1982. 18 p. 334

List of soil surveys, mostly for individual counties of the United States, listed by state (in alphabetical order), and within each state by counties in alphabetical order, with year of publication. Lists about 3,400 published soil surveys. Most of the soil surveys published since 1957 contain soil maps printed on a photomosaic base, usually at a scale of 1:24,000, 1:20,000, or 1:15,840. For many counties in the United States the soil survey is the best published source of information on the physical geography and the areal distribution of agricultural potential.

McAVIN, Margaret J., FERGUSON, Bruce K., and BOCKHEIM, James G. Soil surveys and their applications to land use planning. Monticello, Illinois: Vance Bibliographies. Public administration series: Bibliography, no. P-507. 1980. 31 p. 335

About 350 references organized by topics: soil surveys (classification; mapping) and land-use applications, especially development (building-pavement construction; waste disposal; stormwater runoff-flooding-erosion-sedimentation); farming; and forestry.

GAINES, Stanley H. Bibliography on soil erosion and soil and water conservation. With abstracts by Francesca Vincent, Marion Bloom, and James F. Carter. Washington, D. C.: Government Printing Office, 1938. 651 p. (U. S. Department of Agriculture, Miscellaneous publication no. 312). Author index. List of citations by geographic regions. 336

    4,388 numbered annotated entries, arranged by broad subject. Nearly all references are on the United States.

FOTH, Henry D., and SCHAFER, John W. Soil geography and land use. New York and Chichester: John Wiley, 1980. 484 p. Index. Bibliographies at end of chapters. 337

9. LAND USE

AUSTIN, Morris E. Land resource regions and major land resource areas of the United States (exclusive of Alaska and Hawaii). Washington, D. C.: Government Printing Office, 1965. 82 p. Reissued slightly revised, 1972. (U. S. Department of Agriculture. Soil Conservation Service. Agriculture handbook, no. 296). 338

    Textual description of land use, elevation and terrain, climate, water, and soils of 156 major land resource areas (numbered 1-156) and 20 land resource regions (labelled A-U, omitting Q) on accompanying color map at scale of 1:10,000,000.

BAKER, Simon, and DILL, Henry W., Jr. The look of our land: an airphoto atlas of the rural United States. Washington, D. C.: Government Printing Office, 1970-1971. 5 v. (U. S. Department of Agriculture. Economic Research Service. Agriculture Handbook, nos. 373, 384, 406, 409, and 419.) 339

    The Far West. 1970. 48 p. (no. 372). Includes regions A-C.
    North Central. 1970. 64 p. (no. 384). Includes regions K-M.
    The East and the South. 1971. 99 p. (no. 406). Includes regions N-U.
    The Mountains and the Desert. 1971. 68 p. (no. 409). Includes regions D and E.
    The Plains and Prairies. 1971. 84 p. (no. 419). Includes regions F-J.

    Airphotos illustrate land use patterns and terrain in land resource regions. Portions of small-scale airphoto index sheets and a stereopair of airphotos accompany the textual description of each area.

MARSCHNER, Francis J. Land use and its patterns in the United States. Washington, D. C.: Government Printing Office, 1949. 277 p. 168 plates. Colored map. Bibliography, p. 273-277. 167 references. (U. S. Department of Agriculture. Agriculture Handbook, no. 153). 340

    Discussion of settlement, division, and use of land; physical conditions and land use; and type-of-farming areas of the United States. 168 aerial photographs showing land use patterns of the 48 conterminous states, together with interpretative text, and a color map at a scale of 1:5,000,000 "Major Land Uses of the United States."

JACKSON, Richard H. Land use in America. New York: John Wiley, London: Edward Arnold, 1981. 226 p. Index. Bibliographical notes at the end of each chapter. 341

CLAWSON, Marion. America's land and its use. Baltimore, Maryland: Johns Hopkins Press for Resources for the Future, 1972. 166 p. Bibliography, p. 161-162. 342

CLAWSON, Marion. Man and land use in the United States. Lincoln, Nebraska: University of Nebraska Press, 1964. 178 p. 343

CLAWSON, Marion. The Federal lands revisted. Baltimore, Maryland: The Johns Hopkins University Press for Resources for the Future, 1983. 288 p. Index. Bibliography. 344

CLAWSON, Marion. Suburban land conversion in the United States: an economic and governmental process. Baltimore, Maryland: Johns Hopkins Press for Resources for the Future, 1971. 406 p. Index. Bibliographical footnotes. Additional references at the end of some chapters.   344

Devoted particularly to the Northeastern urban complex of the United States.

ROBBINS, Roy M. Our landed heritage: the public domain, 1776-1970. 2nd ed. Lincoln, Nebraska: University of Nebraska Press, 1976. 503 p. Index. Bibliography, p. 475-485. (1st ed., 1970).   345

PLATT, Rutherford H. Land use control: interface of law and geography. Washington, D. C.: Association of American Geographers, 1975. 39 p. Bibliography, p. 37-39. (Resource papers for college geography, no. 75-1).   346

PLATT, Rutherford H. and Macinko, George, eds. Beyond the urban fringe: land use issues of nonmetropolitan America. Minneapolis, Minnesota: University of Minnesota Press, 1983. 416 p. Index. Bibliographies.   347

10. CONSERVATION

SMITH, Guy-Harold, ed. Conservation of natural resources. 4th ed. New York: John Wiley, 1971. 685 p. Bibliography, p. 655-660. (1st ed., 1950).   348

PARSON, Ruben L. Conserving American resources. 3rd ed. Englewood Cliffs, New Jersey: Prentice-Hall, 1972. 608 p. Bibliographical notes arranged by chapters, p. 565-593. (1st ed., 1956. 550 p.).   349

BURTON, Ian and KATES, Robert W., eds. Readings in resource management and conservation. Chicago, Illinois: University of Chicago Press, 1965. 609 p. Bibliographical footnotes and references at ends of papers.   350.

BRUNN, Stanley D. Key word identifiers of theses and dissertations from departments of geography in Canada and the United States on land use, water use, resource conflict, resource policy, and facility location. Monticello, Illinois: Council of Planning Librarians. Exchange bibliography, no. 1512, 1978. 71 p. Topical index. Regional index.   351

Lists 236 doctoral dissertations and 546 masters theses, 1926-1976.

11. NATURAL LANDSCAPES AND OPEN SPACE

OWINGS, Loren C. Environmental values, 1860-1972: a guide to information sources. Detroit, Michigan: Gale Research Co., 1976. 324 p. Index. (Man and the environment information guide series, v. 4).   352

Annotated references arranged by chapters with textual introductions: Man and nature in America--general works; travel reports on scenery and the search for the picturesque; American landscape painting; conservation and the preservation of natural beauty--the national parks; conservation and the idea of wilderness; conservation and the ecological ethic; American nature writing; nature study in America; camping and outdoor life; "back to nature"--reports on country life in America; and general reference works, all with subdivisions.

HENDEE, John C., STANKEY, George H., and LUCAS, Robert C. Wilderness management. Washington, D. C.: U. S. Department of Agriculture, Forest Service; for sale by the Superintendent of Documents, Government Printing Office, 1978. 381 p. (U. S. Department of Agriculture. Forest Service. Miscellaneous publication no. 1365). Index. Bibliography at the end of each chapter.   353

Covers a wide range of topics, with well-selected bibliographies on each.

CONRAD, Adam Halicki. Wilderness preservation, planning and management: an annotated bibliography. Monticello, Illinois: Council of Planning Librarians. Exchange bibliography no. 1516, 1978. 54 p.   354

    References divided into monographs, periodical and newspaper articles, and U. S. Government documents. Focus is on publications in the 1970s.

RICKERT, John E., and PICKARD, Jerome P. Open space land, planning and taxation: a selected bibliography. Washington, D. C.: Housing and Home Finance Agency. Urban Renewal Administration. For sale by Superintendent of Documents, U. S. Government Printing Office. 1965. 58 p. Prepared by the Urban Land Institute. Author index.   355

    297 annotated entries arranged by fields.

HUNT, Charles B. Natural regions of the United States and Canada. San Francisco, California: Freeman, 1974. 725 p. Bibliographies at the end of each chapter.   356

    314 references.

GRABER, Linda H. Wilderness as sacred space. Washington, D. C.: Association of American Geographers, 1976. 124 p. (Monograph series, no. 8). Bibliography, p. 117-124.   357

RUNTE, Alfred. National Parks: the American experience. Lincoln, Nebraska: University of Nebraska Press, 1979. 240 p. Index. Bibliography, p. 227-230.   358

12. ENVIRONMENT AND ENVIRONMENTAL PROTECTION

(See also Sourcebook of the environment: a guide to the literature [250], p. 63 and Environment: a bibliography of social science and related literature [252], p. 63).

MESHENBERG, Michael J. Environmental planning: a guide to information sources. Detroit, Michigan: Gale Research Co., 1976. 492 p. (Man and the environment information guide series, v. 3). Author index. Title index. Subject index.   359

    1739 annotated entries arranged by subject chapters: the environment and environmental issues, environmental planning, environmental impact analysis, environmental plans, soil, geology, natural hazards, water in the planning process, climatology, vegetation, wildlife, population and urban growth, environmental design, historic preservation, environmental health, noise, environmental law, energy, and the "new" land-use planning. Appendix listing of serials, newsletters, and abstracting and information services, almost all from the United States.

FIELD, Barry C., and WILLIS, Cleve E. Environmental economics: a guide to information sources. Detroit, Michigan: Gale Research Co., 1979. 243 p. (Man and the environment information guide series, v. 8). Author index. Title index. Subject index. Appendices.   360

    About 1,000 annotated entries on conceptual foundations of environmental economics and studies of water, air, solid wastes, urban environment, noise and congestion, wildlife, recreation, pesticides, land use, and energy studies, particularly but not solely in the United States.

EPA cumulative bibliography 1970-1976. Springfield, Virginia: Published by National Technical Information Service for Library Systems Branch, Management and Organization Division, Office of Administration, Office of Planning and Management, United States Environmental Protection Agency, 1977. 2 v. 1,362 p. EPA reports bibliography. Separate pagination for a series of indexes: titles, subjects, corporate authors, personal authors, contract numbers, and accession/report numbers.   361

Subject index includes both topical headings and place headings for individual states, lakes, rivers, waterways, river basins, and cities in the United States.

EPA publications bibliography. Quarterly abstract bulletin. (U. S. Environmental Protection Agency. Office of Planning and Management. Library Systems Branch). Washington, D. C. January-March 1977- . Quarterly, with annual cumulative index. 362

Each issue consists of abstracts and bibliography with title, subject, sponsoring EPA office, corporate author, personal author, contract number, and accession/report number indexes. Indexes cumulate annually. Subject index includes names of states, rivers, lakes, and cities in the United States.

U. S. ENVIRONMENTAL PROTECTION AGENCY. Office of Research and Development. Indexed bibliography of Office of Research and Development reports. Washington, D. C.: U. S. Environmental Protection Agency. Office of Research and Development, 1974. 263 p. (EPA-600/9-74-001). 363

Bibliographic section arranged by report numbers. Index section includes indexes by title, programs, performing organizations, and personal authors. No subject entry but program area index provides one sort of organization. Reports listed are mostly technical.

WORSHAM, John P., Jr. The National Environmental Policy Act and related materials: a selected bibliography. Monticello, Illinois: Vance Bibliographies. Public Administration Series: Bibliography P-43. 1978. 24 p. 364

About 325 references under topics such as environmental impact statements, environmental law, energy considerations, housing, transportation planning, legislation, and general application in the United States.

WORSHAM, John P., Jr. Environmental impact statements: a selected bibliography of the report and periodical literature. Monticello, Illinois: Vance Bibliographies. Public Administration Series: Bibliography P-17, 1978. 10 p. 365

About 100 references by subject areas.

DARLING, F. Fraser, and MILTON, John P., eds. Future environments of North America. Garden City, New York: Natural History Press, 1966. 767 p. Bibliographies. 366

Reports at a conference convened by the Conservation Foundation, April 1965.

MANNERS, Ian R., and MIKESELL, Marvin W., eds. Perspectives on environment. Essays requested by the Panel on Environmental Education. Commission on College Geography. Washington, D. C.: Association of American Geographers. Commission on College Geography. Publication no. 13, 1974. 395 p. Bibliography at the end of each essay. 367

WATSON, J. Wreford, and O'RIORDAN, Timothy, eds. The American environment: perceptions and policies. London and New York: John Wiley, 1976. 340 p. Index. Bibliographies. 368

19 papers on perceptions of the environment, perceptions of the city, transportation, and perceptions and policies of land use, each with a bibliography.

GREENBERG, Michael, ANDERSON, Richard, and PAGE, G. William. Environmental impact statements. Washington, D. C.: Association of American Geographers, 1978. 35 p. Bibliography, p. 31-34. (Resource papers for college geography, no. 78-3). 369

Pollution

BUTTEL, Frederick H., and MORRISON, Denton E. The environmental movement: a research bibliography with some state-of-the-art comments. Monticello, Illinois: Council of Planning Librarians. Exchange bibliography, no. 1308, 1977. 27 p. About 250 references. 370

DUNLAP, Riley E. Studies in environmental politics and policy: a bibliography. Monticello, Illinois: Council of Planning Librarians. Exchange bibliography, no. 917, 1975. 26 p. About 300 entries. 371

DUNLAP, Riley E. Sociological and social-psychological perspectives on environmental issues: a bibliography. Monticello, Illinois: Council of Planning Librarians. Exchange bibliography, no. 916, 1975. 37 p. 372

    About 400 entries arranged under five sections: the environmental movement; environmental attitudes; social impact assessment; other sociological studies; and general sociological perspectives on environmental issues.

BOWMAN, James S. Politics of ecology: the environment and public policy: a bibliography. Monticello, Illinois: Council of Planning Librarians. Exchange bibliography, no. 696 (1974). 39 p. 397 references, 1970-1974. On the United States. 373

13. POLLUTION

    See also Air, water, and noise pollution and waste disposal under Government reports. Announcements and index [195 (105-186)].

POLLUTION abstracts with indexes. (Cambridge Scientific Abstracts), Bethesda, Maryland. v. 1- (1970-). Bimonthly. Annual cumulated subject index. 374

    5,000-9,000 abstracts a year arranged by categories: air pollution; marine pollution; freshwater pollution; sewage and wastewater treatment; waste management; land pollution; toxicology and health; noise; radiation; and environmental action. Author index and subject index in each issue. Each abstract or annotation is assigned up to 12 controlled terms which describe each work. Abstracts material in 34 languages. International in scope but includes much material on pollution in the United States.

KIRALDI, Louis, and BURK, Janet L. Pollution: a selected bibliography of U. S. government publications on air, water, and land pollution. Kalamazoo, Michigan: Western Michigan University. Institute of Public Affairs, 1971. 78 p. 375

    Entries arranged by land pollution, air pollution, and water pollution, each subdivided by reference books (abstracts, bibliographies, etc.) and general publications by government agencies. Limited to 1965-1970 and thus dated but useful in indicating relevant government agencies and the types of publications they issued as of 1970, at the time of the establishment of the Environmental Protection Agency.

GERRARD, Michael B. The economics of pollution: a bibliography. Monticello, Illinois: Vance bibliographies. Public administration series: Bibliographies nos. P-312 and P-313, 1979. 94 p., 90 p. 376

    About 2,600 references mainly for the period 1970-1978 arranged by subjects under four main headings: methods and issues; role of industries; effects of pollution; and the control of pollution. Detailed table of contents.

KNIGHT, Allen W., and SIMMONS, Mary Ann. Water pollution: a guide to information sources. Detroit, Michigan: Gale Research Co., 1980. 278 p. (Man and environment information guide series, v. 9). Indexes. 377

BRAGDON, Clifford R. Noise pollution: a guide to information sources. Detroit, Michigan: Gale Research Co., 1979. 524 p. (Man and environment information guide series, v. 5). Indexes. 378

RUDD, Robert L. Environmental toxicology: a guide to information sources. Detroit, Michigan: Gale Research Co., 1977. 266 p. (Man and environment information guide series, v. 7). Author index. Subject index.   379

1023 annotated entries arranged by subjects: sources, consequences of intentional environmental pollution, consequences of unintended environmental pollution, and special aspects.

MOE, Christine. Environmental impacts of offshore oil spills on the Gulf Coast. Monticello, Illinois: Vance bibliographies. Public administration series. Bibliography, no. P-379. 1979. 16 p.   380

About 175 references.

MELOSI, Martin V. A bibliography on urban pollution problems in American cities from the mid-nineteenth through the mid-twentieth centuries. Monticello, Illinois: Vance bibliographies. Public administration series. Bibliography, no. P-694. 1981. 16 p.   381

About 160 references arranged by: bibliographies; general; air pollution; noise pollution; public health and sanitation; public works and engineering; refuse and street cleaning; and water pollution, water purification, and waste treatment.

VAN NEST, William J., and HAGEVIK, George H. Air pollution and urban planning: a selective annotated bibliography. Monticello, Illinois: Council of Planning Librarians. Exchange bibliography, no. 257, 1972. 64 p.   382

About 200 entries annotated in detail.

GEHR, Marilyn. Solid waste management: a selected and annotated bibliography. Monticello, Illinois: Council of Planning Librarians. Exchange bibliography, no. 1295. 1977. 68 p.   383

About 300 references arranged by the basics; technical information (automobiles, beverage containers, energy production, hazardous wastes, organics, paper and plastics, and recycling and resource recovery); and project plans and operating programs (states, localities, industry).

14. HAZARDS

See also Bibliography on hurricanes and severe storms of the Coastal Plains Region [321], Flood damage prevention [296].

COCHRAN, Anita. A selected, annotated bibliography on natural hazards. Natural hazard research. Working paper, no. 22, 1972. 86 p. Author index. Subject index.   384

317 numbered annotated references, primarily in the United States, arranged by subject: general, agricultural frost, avalanche, drought, earthquake, flood, hail, landslides, snow, tornado, tropical cyclone (hurricane and typhoon), tsunami, and volcanic eruption.

WHITE, Gilbert F., and HAAS, J. Eugene. Assessment of research on natural hazards. Cambridge, Massachusetts: MIT Press, 1975. 487 p. Index. Bibliography, p. 441-470.   385

About 300 references to research on natural hazards in the United States.

COLORADO. University. Institute of Behavioral Science. Program of Technology, Environment, and Man. Monograph series. 1- (1975-). Irregular.   386

cont.

Monographs on natural hazards, particularly in the United States, their assessment, distribution, frequency, and effects, including studies of drought (no. 4), earthquakes and tsunamis (5), floods (6), hurricanes (7), frost and freezing (15), landslide (16), snow avalanches (17), urban snow (18), local windstorm (19), and hail (24).

HILDING, Sabine C. Subsidence in the Houston-Galveston area: a bibliography. Monticello, Illinois: Vance bibliographies. Public administration series: Bibliography, no. P-691, 1981. 24 p.   387

About 240 references.

TYCKOSON, David A., and HARNLY, Caroline D. Mount St. Helens, the 1980 eruptions: a bibliography. Monticello, Illinois: Vance bibliographies. Public Administration series: Bibliography, no. P-786, 1981. 42 p.   388

About 250 references arranged subjects: general; agricultural; atmospheric studies; biological and environmental effects; business and commerce; chemical studies; geologic studies; industrial and engineering; medical and health effects; social and cultural effects; books; government documents.

BURTON, Ian, KATES, Robert W., and WHITE, Gilbert F. The environment as hazard. New York: Oxford University Press, 1978. 240 p. Bibliography, p. 226-235.   389

III. HUMAN GEOGRAPHY AND RELATED SOCIAL SCIENCES

1. URBAN GEOGRAPHY AND RELATED STUDIES

a. General

ASSOCIATION of American Geographers. Comparative metropolitan analysis project. John S. Adams, editor.

    v. 1. Contemporary metropolitan America: twenty geographical vignettes. Cambridge, Massachusetts: Ballinger, 1976. 4 v. Extensive bibliographies at the end of the text on each city. 390

        v. 1. Cities of the nation's historic metropolitan core, 354 p. Index.
        v. 2. Nineteenth century ports, 314 p. Index.
        v. 3. Nineteenth century inland centers and ports, 507 p. Index.
        v. 4. Twentieth century cities, 350 p. Index.

Case studies of 20 major American cities by leading American urban geographers. Boston, New York-New Jersey, Philadelphia, Hartford-Central Connecticut, Baltimore, New Orleans, Chicago, St. Paul-Minneapolis, Seattle, Miami, Los Angeles, Atlanta, and Detroit also published as separate volumes. San Francisco-Oakland (v. 2); Pittsburgh, St. Louis, and Northeast Ohio (v. 3); Dallas-Fort Worth, Houston, and Washington (v. 4) published only in the combined 4-volume collection.

    v. 2. Urban policymaking and metropolitan dynamics: a comparative geographical analysis. Cambridge, Massachusetts: Ballinger, 1976. 576 p. Index. 391

13 chapters by specialists on urban policy, land speculation and urban morphology, abandoned housing, national housing and urban renewal goals, environmental goals, school goals, crime, health care, open space, urban elderly, metropolitan governance, urban spatial-political systems, and malapportionment and gerrymandering in the ghetto. References at the end of each chapter.

    v. 3. A comparative atlas of America's great cities: twenty metropolitan regions. See entry 212.

MUNICIPAL yearbook 1934- . Annual. Washington, D. C.: International City Management Association, 1934- . Annual. v. 50, 1983, 50th anniversary edition, 1983. 460 p. 392

An authoritative source with many tables of data. Profiles of individual cities (Table 1/18, p. 13-47 provides for cities of more than 10,000 population, 1980 population data, 1979 employment data, workforce classification, housing, and government finances. Other tables have similar data for counties. Extensive listing of personnel. Sources of information, p. 415-437 provides a good up-to-date selection of data sources on many topics relevant to the study and operation of cities.

YEATES, Maurice, and GARNER, Barry. The North American city. 3rd ed. New York: Harper and Row, 1980. 557 p. Index. Bibliography, 519-543. 393

About 550 references.

PALM, Risa. The geography of American cities. New York; Oxford: Oxford University Press, 1981. 365 p. Index. 394

Bibliographical notes at ends of chapters: introduction; the city and the countryside; ethnicity; political economy and urban structure; resources and urban growth; cities and their physical environment; political economy, attitudes, and the physical environment of cities; the system of cities in the United States;

cont.

the development of the city system; the changing city system; land values in the city; locational decisions in the private and public sectors of the economy; residential structure; mobility within the city; the changing metropolitan area.

HARTSHORN, Truman A. Interpreting the city: an urban geography. New York: John Wiley, 1980. 498 p. Author and subject indexes. Bibliographies at ends of chapters. 395

KING, Leslie., and GOLLEDGE, Reginald G. Cities, space, and behavior: the elements of urban geography. Englewood Cliffs, New Jersey: Prentice-Hall, 1978. 393 p. Index. Bibliographical notes at ends of chapters. 396

RUGG, Dean S. Spatial foundations of urbanism. 2nd ed. Dubuque, Iowa: William C. Brown, 1979. 375 p. (1st ed., 1972. 313 p.). Index. Bibliography, p. 357-366. 397

NORTHAM, Ray M. Urban geography. 2nd ed. New York: John Wiley, 1979. 512 p. Index. Bibliographical references. (1st ed., 1975. 410 p.). 398

HOLCOMB, H. Briavel, and BEAUREGARD, Robert A. Revitalizing cities. Washington, D. C.: Association of American Geographers, Resource publications in geography, 1981. 84 p. Bibliography p. 73-84. 399

About 300 references.

MURPHY, Raymond E. The American city: an urban geography. 2nd ed. New York: McGraw-Hill, 1974. 566 p. (1st ed., 1966). Index. 400

References at the end of each chapter.

GEOGRAPHICAL perspectives and urban problems. Washington, D. C.: National Academy of Sciences, 1973. 107 p. Bibliographies at ends of articles. 40

A symposium organized by the Committee on Geography of the Division of Earth Sciences, National Academy of Sciences, September 20 and 21, 1971, Washington, D.C.

HOFMEISTER, Burkhard. Stadt und Kulturraum Angloamerika. Braunschweig: Friedr. Vieweg und Sohn, 1971. 341 p. Subject, place name and personal name indexes. Bibliography p. 320-330. 40

522 references on the cities of Anglo-America arranged by sections and subsections of the book.

DUNCAN, Otis Dudley, SCOTT, W. Richard, LIEBERSON, Stanley, DUNCAN. Beverly, and WINSBOROUGH, Hal H. Metropolis and region. Baltimore, Maryland: The Johns Hopkins Press, for Resources for the Future Inc., 1960. 587 p. Index. Bibliography, p. 561-575, which is also an index of citations. 40

282 references.

GALE, Stephen, and MOORE, Eric G., eds. The manipulated city: perspectives on spatial structure and social issues in urban America. Chicago, Illinois: Maaroufa Press, 1975. 366 p. 4

References at ends of chapters.

HAUSER, Philip M., and SCHNORE, Leo F., eds. The study of urbanization. New York: John Wiley, 1965. 554 p. 4

Notes at end of each chapter with rich bibliographical citations not limited to the United States but especially full on American sources on this country.

KHARITONOV, V. M. Urbanizatsiia v S.Sh.A. (Urbanization in the USA). Moskva: Izdatel'stvo Moskovskogo Universiteta, 1983. 198 p. Bibliography, p. 193-(199). 245 references. 405a

MAYER, Harold M., and KOHN, Clyde F., eds. Readings in urban geography. Chicago, Illinois: The University of Chicago Press, 1959. 625 p. Index to authors. Index to subjects. 406

    Not limited to the United States but conveniently assembles many important papers on aspects of American cities, with bibliographical footnotes.

SWARTZ, Robert D., BALL, John M., DOHRS, Fred E., and RIDD, Merrill K., eds. Metropolitan America: geographic perspectives and teaching strategies. Oak Park, Illinois: National Council for Geographic Education, 1972. 420 p. Bibliographical footnotes. (The 1972 yearbook for National Council for Geographic Education). 407

    Studies of and in Detroit, Michigan, as a case study.

STRAND, Sverre. Urban geography 1950-70: a comprehensive bibliography of urbanism as reflected in the articles and book reviews of 72 American, Canadian, British, Dutch, and Scandinavian geographical periodicals. Monticello, Illinois: Council of Planning Librarians. Exchange bibliography, no. 358-360, 1973. 272 p. 408

    2,949 entries in classed arrangement. Two regional indexes. Author index. Not limited to the United States but extensive coverage of the literature on cities of the United States.

SOMMER, John W. Bibliography of urban geography, 1940-1964. Hanover, New Hampshire: Dartmouth College. Department of Geography, 1966. 94 p. (Geography publications, no. 5). Author index. Topical index. 409

    1,310 articles on urban geography in 71 geographical periodicals. Articles arranged by region.

AY, William W. Urban studies in geography: a bibliography of dissertations and theses in geography, 1960-1970. Monticello, Illinois: Council of Planning Librarians. Exchange bibliography, no. 189, 1971. 60 p. 410

    About 200 doctoral dissertations and about 700 masters' theses, presented in the United States and Canada, 1960-1970.

UNIVERSITY of Chicago. Center for Urban Studies. A directory of urban and urban related master theses and Ph.D. dissertations of the University of Chicago. n.d. 218 p. Index to studies by subject. (Master's theses, p. 6-23; Ph.D. dissertations, p. 24-40). Index to Chicago area studies (Master's theses, p. 42-45; Ph.D. dissertations, p. 45-48). 411

    List of Master's theses by departments, p. 50-144. List of Ph.D. dissertations by department, p. 145-218: Geography, master's theses, p. 85-94, 123 entries. Geography, Ph.D. dissertations, p. 176-182, 80 entries.

ELLAR, Barry S., and GRAFF, Thomas O. Bibliography on urban and regional information systems: focus on geographic perspectives. Monticello, Illinois: Council of Planning Librarians. Exchange bibliography, no. 316-317, 1972. 88 p. Author-agency index. 412

    About 800 entries arranged by general; specification; acquisition; processing; and applications.

SHEARER, Barbara Smith, and SHEARER, Benjamin F. Periodical literature on United States cities: a bibliography and subject guide. Westport, Connecticut; London, England: Greenwood Press, 1983. 574 p. Subject and author indexes. 41

   4,919 references to selected periodical articles published 1970-1981 on 170 United States cities with a population of 100,000 or more, arranged alphabetically by city subdivided by subject categories: architecture and the arts; education and the media; environment; government and politics; housing and urban development; social and economic conditions; transportation; and general works. List of included cities by states. p. xv-xvii.

   Articles are mainly from national circulation general periodicals.

WHITE, Anthony G. A source list for the beginner in urban research, Monticello, Illinois: Council of Planning Librarians. Exchange bibliography, no. 338, 1972, 36 p. 41

   Divided into sections: 120 books and articles on urban research; professional journals; governmental research organizations; private and semiprivate research organizations; about 200 university urban affairs research institutes.

ZEITLIN, Morris. Guide to the literature of cities: abstracts and bibliography, Monticello, Illinois: Council of Planning Librarians, Exchange bibliography, nos. 305-315 and 328, 1972. 11 parts. 4

   Extended abstracts on major works in urban history, land use, transportation, housing, renewal, sociology, government, the metropolitan region; design, planning; and socialist cities. Not limited to cities of the United States but contains many references primarily on these cities.

NILSEN, Kirsti. Bibliography of bibliographies prepared by U. S. Government agencies of interest to community planners. Monticello, Illinois: Council of Planning Librarians, Exchange bibliography, no. 527, 1974. 23 p. 153 references arranged by agency. 4

BOYER, Richard, and SAVAGEAU, David. Place rated almanac: your guide to finding the best place to live in America. Chicago, Illinois: Rand McNally, 1981. 385 p. 4

   277 standard metropolitan statistical areas rated on the basis of climate and terrain, housing, health care and environment, crime, transportation, education, recreation, culture and the arts, and economics. Large amount of data.

b. Urban Systems

JOHNSTON, Ronald J. The American urban system: a geographical perspective. New York: St. Martin's Press, 1982. 348 p. 4

   159 references grouped at the ends of sections: the study of urban geography, p. 49-50; the American urban system, p. 150-153; the internal structure of urban areas, p. 240-243; and urban patterns and processes and the urban crisis, p. 336-337.

BRUNN, Stanley D., and WHEELER, James O., eds. The American metropolitan system: present and future. New York: John Wiley, 1980. 216 p. Index. (V. H. Winston and Sons; A Halsted Press book). 4

   References at ends of chapters, each by different authors, which deal with many aspects of the evolving urban system of the United States.

YEATES, Maurice H. North American urban patterns. New York: John Wiley; London: Edward Arnold. 1980. 168 p. Index. Bibliography, p. 149-154. 100 references. 420

Chapters on defining the major urban regions; the major urban regions and patterns of growth; causes of the differential growth patterns; issues arising from macro-urban development; some responses to issues facing the major urban regions; and future growth. Bibliographical notes at end of chapters.

CHRISTIAN, Charles M., and HARPER, Robert A., eds. Modern metropolitan systems. Columbus, Ohio: Charles E. Merrill, 1982. 495 p. Index. Bibliography, p. 481-484. 421

BERRY, Brian J. L., and HORTON, Frank E. Geographic perspectives on urban systems with integrated readings. Englewood Cliffs, New Jersey: Prentice-Hall, 1970. 564 p. Index. 422

Extensive bibliographical footnotes at end of each chapter. Not limited to the United States but contains many references to the literature on cities in the United States.

BERRY, Brian J. L., and GILLARD, Quentin. The changing shape of metropolitan America: commuting patterns, urban fields, and decentralization processes, 1960-70. Cambridge, Massachusetts: Ballinger, 1977. 697 p. Index, p. 41-43. 423

An atlas of the commuting areas of the Standard Metropolitan Statistical Areas (SMSAs) of the United States in 1970 and of the changes that took place in these areas between 1960-1970. Where data are available, each of the 284 SMSAs has 6 maps: commuting to the central business district in 1960; commuting to the central city in 1970; change in commuting to the central city, 1960-1970; reverse commuting, 1960; reverse commuting, 1970; and change in reverse commuting, 1960-1970.

PHILLIPS, Phillip D. No growth and the evolution of the American metropolitan system, 1970-1976. Monticello, Illinois: Council of Planning Librarians. Exchange bibliography, no. 1289, 1977. 21 p. 143 references with discussion. 424

DUNN, Edgar S., Jr. The development of the U. S. urban system. Baltimore, Maryland: The Johns Hopkins University Press, for Resources for the Future, v. 1. Concepts, structures, regional shifts, 1980. 205 p. Index. Bibliography, p. 195-198. 125 references. 421 pages of appendix tables on microfiche in pocket. v. 2. Industrial shifts, implications, 1983. 266 p. Index. Bibliography, p. 259-260. 55 references. 120 pages of appendix tables on microfiche in pocket. 425

Detailed analysis with many tables of regional and structural shifts in the urban system of the United States 1940-1970 and the intervening decades.

"URBAN and regional systems," Progress in human geography, v. 4, no. 3 (1980), p. 399-405, by Larry S. Bourne; v. 5, no. 3 (1981), p. 420-431, and v. 6, no. 3 (1982), p. 431-440, by James W. Simmons and Larry S. Bourne; v. 7, no. 3 (1983), p. 414-419, by Jim Whitelaw. 173 references with commentary, many of which pertain to the United States. 426

PRED, Allan R. Major job-providing organizations and systems of cities. Washington, D. C.: Association of American Geographers, 1974. 69 p. Bibliography, p. 67-69. (Commission on college geography. Resource paper no. 27). 427

PRED, Allan R. City-systems in advanced economies: past growth, present processes, and future development options. London: Hutchinson; New York: John Wiley, 1977. 256 p. Index. Bibliography, p. 231-247. 428

GOTTMANN, Jean. Megalopolis: the urbanized northeastern seaboard of the United States. New York: Twentieth Century Fund, 1961. 810 p. Cambridge, Massachusetts: MIT Press, 1964. Index. Bibliographical footnotes. 429

c. Central Places and Capitals

BERRY, Brian J. L., and PRED, Allan R. Central place studies: a bibliography of theory and applications, including supplement through 1964 by H. G. Barnum et al. Philadelphia, Pennsylvania: Regional Science Research Institute, 1965. 203 p. (Bibliography series no. 1, with supplement). (1st ed., 1961. 153 p.). Author index. List of journals.

More than 1,000 annotated entries, organized topically.

ANDREWS, Howard F. Working notes and bibliography of central place studies, 1965-1969. Monticello, Illinois: Council of Planning Librarians. Exchange bibliography, no. 209, 1971. 41 p.

About 350 entries, partly annotated.

MAHNKE, Hans-Peter. Die Hauptstädte und die führenden Städte der USA. Stuttgart: Geographisches Institut der Universität. Stuttgarter geographische Studien, v. 78, 1970. 168 p. Bibliography, p. 147-167. About 400 references.

d. Growth

BERRY, Brian J. L. Growth centers in the American urban system. Cambridge, Massachusetts: Ballinger, 1973. 2 v. Index. Bibliography, v. 1, p. 189-191.

v. 1. Community development and regional growth in the sixties and seventies
v. 2. Working materials on the U. S. urban hierarchy and on growth center characteristics, organized by economic region. Tables for 171 economic areas and 193 socio-economic transects showing the topography of urban influences.

APPLEBAUM, Richard P. Size, growth, and U. S. cities. New York: Praeger, 1978. 140 p. Bibliography, p. 129-140.

CLAY, Phillip L. Metropolitan growth and change: a bibliography in metropolitan differentiation. Monticello, Illinois: Council of Planning Librarians. Exchange bibliography, no. 1062, 1976. 24 p. 206 references.

BURG, Nan C. Economic development in nonmetropolitan areas: special socioeconomic problems of rapid-growth communities. Monticello, Illinois: Council of Planning Librarians. Exchange bibliography, no. 1497, 1978. 24 p. About 300 references.

e. City Classifications

BERRY, Brian J. L., ed. City classification handbook: methods and applications. New York, Wiley-Interscience, 1972. 394 p. Index. Bibliographical footnotes.

BRICKFORD, Deborah. City classification and urban need. Monticello, Illinois: Vance bibliographies. Public administration series: Bibliography, no. P-752, 1981. 16 p. 131 references.

f. Internal Structure

PALM, Risa. "Urban geography: city structures," Progress in human geography, v. 5, no. 1 (1981), p. 79-86; v. 6, no. 1 (1982), p. 89-95; v. 7, no. 1 (1983), p. 109-115 (1983).

126 references with commentary.

g. Urban Ecology and Neighborhoods

BRODEN, Thomas F., and others. Identifying urban neighborhoods: an annotated bibliography. Chicago, Illinois: Council of Planning Librarians. CPL bibliography. No. 28. April 1980. 37 p.   440

BERRY, Brian J. L., and KASARDA, John D. Contemporary urban ecology. New York: Macmillan, 1977. 497 p. Indexes. Bibliography, p. 430-475.   441

h. Land Use and Zoning

CHAPIN, F. Stuart, Jr., and KAISER, Edward J. Urban land use planning. 3rd ed. Urbana, Illinois: University of Illinois Press, 1979. 656 p. Index. References at ends of chapters. (1st ed., 1957. 397 p.).   442

MAYER, Harold M., and HAYES, Charles R. Land uses in American cities. Champaign, Illinois: Park Press, 1983. 176 p. Index. Bibliography.   443

    Focus on residential, commercial, industrial, public and institutional, and especially transportation land use within cities of the United States.

LISTOKIN, David, GERLACH, Linda, and CYVINER, Barbara. Zoning--exclusionary zoning: a selected bibliography. Monticello, Illinois: Council of Planning Librarians. Exchange bibliography, no. 684, 1974. 304 references with discussion.   444

DAVIS, Elizabeth Gould, JOHNSON, Hugh A., and HAREN, Claude C., Urbanization and changing land uses; a bibliography of selected references, 1950-58. Washington, D. C.: U. S. Department of Agriculture. Miscellaneous publication, no. 825 1960. 212 p. Index.   445

    1319 annotated entries arranged by bibliographies; general; planning; cities and their fringes (general; government; taxation and services; annexation; and the rural-urban fringe); and rural areas.

i. Commerce

MURPHY, Raymond E. The central business district. Chicago, Illinois: Aldine-Atherton; London: Longman, 1972. 193 p. Index. Bibliography p. 187-189. 51 references.   446

VANCE, Mary. Central business districts. Monticello. Illinois: Council of Planning Librarians. Exchange bibliography no. 23, 1963. 116 p. Index.   447

    1346 entries organized by general, topical, and case studies.

BERRY, Brian J. L. Geography of market centers and retail distribution. Englewood Cliffs, New Jersey: Prentice-Hall, 1967. 146 p. Index.   448

    Bibliographical footnotes.

VANCE, James E. The merchant's world: the geography of wholesaling. Englewood Cliffs, New Jersey: Prentice-Hall, 1970. 167 p.   449

    Bibliographical footnotes.

COHEN, Yehoshua S. Diffusion of an innovation in an urban system: the spread of planned regional shopping centers in the United States 1949-1968. Chicago, Illinois: University of Chicago. Department of Geography. Research paper no. 140, 1972. 136 p. Bibliography, p. 131-136. 98 references.   450

VANCE, Mary. A bibliography on shopping centers. Monticello, Illinois: Vance
bibliographies. Architecture series: Bibliography no. A-820, 1982. 31 p. Index.   451

    413 numbered references.

KESSLER, Mary Z. Shopping centers. Monticello, Illinois: Council of Planning
Librarians. Exchange bibliography no. 208, 1971. 34 p.   452

    About 550 references, 1960-1970.

HOLMES, Jack D. L. Selected and annotated bibliography of the planned suburban
shopping center. Austin Texas: Texas. University. Bureau of Business Research.
Bibliography series. 13, 1957. 55 p. rev. ed. 1960.   453

    274 annotated entries. Now dated.

j. Urban Transportation

WHEELER, James O. The urban circulation noose. North Scituate, Massachusetts:
Duxbury Press, 1974. 137 p. Index. Bibliography, p. 131-133.   454

k. Housing

U. S. Department of Housing and Urban Development (early issues by U. S. Housing
and Home Finance Agency. Library). Library. Housing and planning references.
n.s. no. 1-127 (1948-May-June 1965); 1-109 (July-Ag. 1965-July-Ag 1983). Closed
August 1983.   455

    References arranged by subjects, such as city growth and planning, downtown
revitalization, economic conditions, economic development, energy, environmental
policy, ethnicity, harbors and ports, highways and streets, housing with many
subcategories, immigrants, industrial development, industrial location, land use,
metropolitan areas, minority groups, natural resources, new towns, office buildings,
planning, politics and government, population, public housing, real estate, schools,
sewage disposal and storm sewers, small business, social indicators, urban sociology, transportation, urban economics, urban renewal, urbanization, water resources,
zoning, and others. Also lists of Department publications and Department-sponsored
research, and new periodicals. Geographic index. Author index.

ROUSE, John E., Jr. Urban housing: public and private: a guide to information
sources. Detroit, Michigan: Gale Research, 1978. 319 p. (Urban studies information guide series, v. 5). Author, title, and subject indexes.   456

    Annotated entries on urban housing issues in the United States, mainly 1972-
1976, under headings: housing policies and priorities; housing finance; housing
markets; housing industry and construction; multi-family housing; public housing;
low-income housing; housing subsidies; open housing; housing for the elderly; and
housing and decentralization. Appendix lists housing periodicals, housing bibliographies, and housing associations. About 1200 annotated references.

WELLAR, Barry S., and GRAFF, Thomas O. Introduction and selected bibliography on
the quality of housing and its environment. Monticello, Illinois: Council of
Planning Librarians. Exchange bibliography, no. 270, 1972. 35 p. About 200
entries.   457

REES, Philip H. Residential patterns in American cities: 1960. Chicago, Illinois: University of Chicago. Department of Geography. Research paper no. 189, 1979. 405 p. Bibliography, p. 391-405. 203 references. 459

HARVEY, David W. Society, the city, and the space economy of urbanism. Washington, D. C.: Association of American Geographers, 1972. 56 p. Bibliographical notes, p. 53-54. Bibliography, p. 55-56. (Commission on College Geography. Resource paper no. 18). 460

    Part II focuses on American cities. The discussion of the housing market in Baltimore, Maryland, serves as an example.

    1. Social Processes, Ethnic Neighborhoods, and Ghettos

ROSE, Harold M. Social processes in the city: race and urban residential choice. Washington, D. C.: Association of American Geographers, 1969. 34 p. Bibliography, p. 31-34. (Commission on College Geography. Resource paper no. 6). 461

ARDEN, Joe T. The ghetto: a bibliography. Monticello, Illinois: Council of Planning Librarians. Exchange bibliography, no. 1310. 25 p. 462

    251 references organized around major themes: the concept and origin of the ghetto; changing population --ethnic ghetto vs. racial ghetto; spatial diffusion; economy; political system; health, education, and transportation; quality of life; civil disorders; other.

ROSE, Harold M. The Black ghetto: a spatial behavioral perspective. New York: McGraw-Hill, 1971. 147 p. 463

    Bibliographical footnotes.

MEYER, David R. Spatial variation of black urban households. Chicago, Illinois: University of Chicago. Department of Geography. Research paper no. 129, 1970. 127 p. Bibliography, p. 123-127. 464

    75 references arranged by topic: residential choice and intra-urban mobility (9); studies of Afro-Americans (13); housing and race (19); urban structure (16); miscellaneous (8); methodology (5); and sources of data (5).

LAKE, Robert W. The new suburbanites: race and housing in the suburbs. New Brunswick, New Jersey: Rutgers University. Center for Urban Policy Research, 1981. 303 p. Index. Bibliography, p. 289-298. 465

m. Urban Renewal

UHLIG, Klaus R. Die Stadterneuerung in den USA seit dem Housing Act 1949 bis 1969, insbesondere der innerstädtische Wohnungsbau sowie seine möglichen Einflüsse auf die stadtregionale Binnenmigration. Bonn: Uhlig, 1971. 264 p. Bibliography, p. 239-260. 466

    References on urban renewal 1949-1969.

n. Urban Preservation

FORD, Larry R. Urban preservation and the geography of the city in the USA, Progress in human geography, v. 3, no. 2 (1979), p. 211-238. 68 references with commentary. 467

Urban Geography 92

o. Governance and Services

GOVERNMENT Affairs Foundation. Metropolitan communities: a bibliography with special emphasis upon government and politics. Compiled by Victor Jones and others. Chicago, Illinois: Public Administration Service, 1957. 392 p. Index. 468

5120 briefly annotated entries on government and politics in metropolitan areas (functions and problems; governmental organization; and politics) and on the socio-economic background (social structure and process, population, and the metropolitan economy).

_____. _____. Supplement 1955-1957. Compiled by Victor Jones and Barbara Hudson. 1960. 229 p. Index. 469

2524 briefly annotated entries.

_____. _____. Supplement 1958-1964. Compiled by Barbara Hudson and Robert H. McDonald. 1967. 536 p. Index. 470

6282 briefly annotated entries.

_____. _____. Supplement 1965-1967. Compiled by Barbara Hudson and Robert H. McDonald. 1969. 272 p. Index. 47

2669 briefly annotated entries.

_____. _____. Supplement 1968-1970. Compiled by Barbara Hudson and Robert H. McDonald. 1972. 375 p. Index. 47

3979 briefly annotated entries.

REYNOLDS, David R. Metropolitan governance and service delivery in the United States: a review and synthesis of research findings, in György Enyedi, ed. Urban development in the USA and Hungary. Budapest: Akadémiai Kiadó, 1978. p. 169-186. Studies in geography in Hungary, 14. Bibliography, p. 183-186, with 90 references. 47

p. City Planning (See also 416)

ALEXANDER, Ernest R., CATANESE, Anthony J., and SAWICKI, David S. Urban planning: a guide to information sources. Detroit, Michigan: Gale Research, 1979. 165 p. Author, title, and subject indexes. (Urban studies information guide series, v. 2). 47

About 600 annotated references. Also related bibliographies and references and list of periodicals.

BESTOR, George C., and JONES, Holway R. City planning bibliography: a basic bibliography of sources and trends. 3rd ed. New York: American Society of Civil Engineers, 1972. 518 p. Author and subject indexes. 47

1837 entries, most annotated, arranged by subjects in an articulated organization. Separate listing of services and periodicals in planning and related fields.

HOLLEB, Doris B. Social and economic information for urban planning. Chicago, Illinois: University of Chicago. Center for Urban Studies. 1969. 2 v. 4

v. 1. Its selection and use. 187 p.
v. 2. A directory of data sources. 312 p. Listing of sources by types: population and vital statistics, housing, transportation, economic performance, education, social welfare, health, public safety, environmental quality, and leisure time. Appendices: bibliography of general statistical sources: social and economic data from the decennial censuses of housing and population; and the urban Negro American in the 20th century: a survey of resources.

REPS, John W. The making of urban America: a history of city planning in the United States. Princeton, New Jersey: Princeton University Press, 1965. 574 p. Index. Bibliography, p. 545-562.   477

GOEHLERT, Robert. City and regional planning: a bibliography of journal literature, 1945-1975. Monticello, Illinois: Vance Bibliographies. Public Administration Series: Bibliography P-124, 1978. 53 p.   478

 About 750 references.

RETEBENNER, Lyle. City planning and zoning in American legal periodicals. Monticello, Illinois: Council of Planning Librarians. Exchange bibliography, no. 28, 1965. 137 p. List of periodicals cited.   479

 About 2500 references arranged by topics and subtopics in alphabetical order.

ATTY, Paul. Planning publications: an annotated bibliography and reference guide. Chicago, Illinois: Council of Planning Librarians, CPL Bibliography, no. 68, 1981. 100 p.   480

 More than 450 planning reference works. Covers bibliographies and directories; community and economic developments, impact analysis; environment, land use, parks and recreation; real property, and urban design; lists periodicals, agencies, associations, organizations, and publishers.

q. Suburbs

MULLER, Peter O. Contemporary suburban America. Englewood Cliffs, New Jersey: Prentice-Hall, 1981. 218 p. Geographical index. Subject index. Bibliography, p. 183-209.   481

 About 400 references. Suggested readings at end of each chapter.

GOTTMANN, Jean, and HARPER, Robert A., eds. Metropolis on the move: geographers look at urban sprawl. New York: John Wiley, 1967. 203 p. Index. Bibliography, p. 193-195. 47 references.   482

ROSE, Harold M. Black suburbanization: access to improved quality of life or maintenance of the status quo? Cambridge, Massachusetts: Ballinger, 1976. 288 p. Index.   483

 Bibliographical notes, p. 265-279, arranged by chapters.

SKMUND, Joseph, II, and DENNIS, Deborah Ellis. Suburbia: a guide to information sources. Detroit, Michigan: Gale Research, 1979. 142 p. (Urban studies information guide series, v. 9). Author, title, and subject index.   484

 392 annotated entries, arranged by topics, such as demography, education, politics, economics, sociology, and minorities.

MASOTTI, Louis H., and DENNIS, Deborah Ellis. Suburbs, suburbia and suburbanization: a bibliography. Second edition. Monticello, Illinois: Council of Planning Librarians. Exchange bibliography, no. 524-525, 1974. 108 p. About 1300 entries. Relatively comprehensive coverage of publications in the United States up to 1973.   485

CLAWSON, Marion. Suburban land conversion in the United States: an economic and governmental process. Baltimore, Maryland: Johns Hopkins Press for Resources for the Future, Inc., 1971. 406 p. Index.   486

 Bibliographical footnotes and additional references at the end of some chapters.

CHRISTIAN, Charles M., and WILLIAMS, Connie L. The suburbanization of industrial firms and employment opportunities: a bibliography. Monticello, Illinois: Council of Planning Librarians. Exchange bibliography, no. 1324, 1977. 36 p. About 500 references. 487

BERLIN, G. Lennis, and LANCASTER, Joel R. Industrial suburbanization. Monticello, Illinois: Council of Planning Librarians. Exchange bibliography, no. 223, 1971. 22 p. About 300 entries. 488

DAVIDSON, Claud M. Rural and suburban towns: spatial characteristics of change in population and functional structure. Monticello, Illinois: Council of Planning Librarians. Exchange bibliography, no. 272, 1972. 18 p. About 200 entries. 489

r. Small Towns

JAKLE, John A. The American small town: twentieth-century place images. Hamden, Connecticut: Shoe String Press (Archon Books), 1982. 195 p. Index. Bibliography, p. 183-190. 490

s. New Towns

CLAPP, James A. New towns: an emphasis on the American experience. Monticello, Illinois: Council of Planning Librarians, Exchange bibliography, no. 982, 1976. 101 p. About 1000 partly annotated references. 491

MOE, Christine E. New towns and utopias. Monticello, Illinois: Vance bibliographies. Architecture series: Bibliography, no. A-253, 1980. 31 p. About 475 references, mostly on the United States. 492

U. S. Department of Housing and Urban Development. New communities: a bibliography. Washington, D. C.: Government Printing Office, 1970. 84 p. Indexes by countries and places. 493

Annotated bibliography with more than 600 entries in English. Not limited to the United States.

t. Single Enterprise Communities

PORTEOUS, J. Douglas. The single-enterprise community in North America. Monticello, Illinois: Council of Planning Librarians, Exchange bibliography, no. 207, 1971. 18 p. About 125 entries. 494

u. Problems

REGNELL, John B. United States urban revolution: cities in crisis. A selected and subject-classified bibliography of books relating to cities, 1960-1969. Reno, Nevada: University of Nevada. Bureau of Governmental Research, Miscellaneous paper no. 5, 1969. 105 p. Author index. 495

Books arranged by broad topics: the urbanization process; urban government and politics; urban renewal; urban architecture and environmental planning; urban sociology and social conditions; urban race relations; urban economics and poverty; urban community organization and development; urban church; and urban education. Within each category the main listing is by author but there is also a listing by title. Publishers addresses are provided in an appendix.

MEYER, Jon K. Bibliography on the urban crisis: the behavioral, psychological, and sociological aspects of the urban crisis. Chevy Chase, Maryland: U. S. National Institute of Mental Health. For sale by Washington, D. C.: Government Printing Office. 1969. 452 p. (Public Health Service publication no. 1948). Author index. Aubject index. 496

2779 numbered entries, arranged in 10 subject sections.

v. Urban Studies in Related Disciplines

SAGE urban studies abstracts. v. 1- (1973-). Beverly Hills, California: Sage
Publications, 1973- . Quarterly. Author and subject indexes. 497

250 abstracts in each issue on urbanism and urban research, land use and
urban development, industry and labor, and urban affairs.

MILLS, Barbara. An annotated interdisciplinary guide to sources of information in
the social sciences with special emphasis on urban studies. Monticello, Illinois:
Council of Planning Librarians. Exchange bibliography, no. 552, 1974. 76 p.
Index. 200 annotated entries. 498

WOOD, James L., NG, Wing-cheung, and WOOD, Patricia A. Urban sociology, bibliography.
Monticello, Illinois: Council of Planning Librarians. Exchange bibliography, no.
1336, 1977. 53 p. 499

About 700 references arranged by sections: the development of urban-industrial
and suburban society; urban methods; consequences of urban-industrial and suburban
society (family, community, ethnic, poverty, and personal consequences); urban
politics; strategies for change (community organizing, urban renewal, urban planning, urban social movements, protests and conflicts); additional urban resources.

HAWLEY, Amos H. Urban society: an ecological approach. 2nd ed. New York: John
Wiley, 1981. 383 p. Indexes. Bibliographies. (1st ed. New York: Ronald Press,
1971. 348 p.). 500

SCHNORE, Leo F. The urban scene: human ecology and demography. New York: The Free
Press; London: Collier-Macmillan, 1965. 374 p. Name index. Subject index. 501

Bibliographical footnotes at ends of chapters. Six parts: human ecology and
demography; metropolitan growth and decentralization; the functions and growth of
suburbs; the socioeconomic status of cities and suburbs; the changing color composition of metropolitan areas; and studies in urban circulation.

MURPHY, Thomas P. Urban indicators: a guide to information sources. Detroit,
Michigan: Gale Research, 1980. 234 p. (Urban studies information guide series,
v. 10). Author, title, and subject indexes. 502

Annotated entries on urban indicators in 6 chapters: urban indicators; types;
methodology; applications; program evaluation; future directions. List of journals,
abstracts and indexes, and associations.

SHACKELFORD, Jean A. Urban and regional economics: a guide to information sources.
Detroit, Michigan: Gale Research, 1980. 192 p. (Economics information guide
series, v. 14). Indexes. 503

About 600 annotated entries on topics such as growth and development, planning and policies, location theory, spatial analysis, and regional models and
techniques.

GOLDSTEIN, Gerald S., and MOSES, Leon N. A survey of urban economics, Journal of
economic literature, v. 11, no. 2 (June 1973), p. 471-515. 504

438 references arranged by:selected early literature on urban land use;
microeconomic approach to residential location; residential models; choice of
urban-suburban location; gravity models; institutions and the housing market;
residence and race;competition and factor substitution in the land market;
empirical studies of intra-metropolitan firm location; location theory of the
firm; growth; general references in urban economics; central place studies; and
additional references.

Discussion of the literature on urban growth; residential settlement, housing,
and land values; intra-urban location and competition among land uses; urban simulation (exposition and evaluation).

MURPHY, Thomas P. Urban politics: a guide to information sources. Detroit, Michigan: Gale Research, 1978. 248 p. (Urban studies information guide series, v. 1). Author, title, and subject indexes. 505

Annotated bibliography on American urban governmental structure; political leadership and political parties, community participation: socioethnic politics; urban public policy issues; metropolitan organization and suburbanization; and federal urban relations. Appendices list bibliographies, abstracts and indexes, reference books, textbooks, periodicals, and associations.

PALUMBO, Dennis J., and TAYLOR, George A. Urban policy: a guide to information sources. Detroit, Michigan: Gale Research, 1979. 198 p. (Urban studies information guide series, v. 6). Author, title, and subject indexes. 506

Annotated entries arranged by 5 chapters: models and analytical theories; community characteristics which determine policy; policy goals; policy formulation and implementation; and policy evaluation methods.

BUENKER, John D., GREENFIELD, Gerald Michael, and MURIN, William J. Urban history: a guide to information sources. Detroit, Michigan: Gale Research, 1981. 448 p. Author, title, and subject indexes. (American government and history information guide series, v. 9). 507

1911 annotated entries organized by broad subject categories: general studies; the urbanization process; the city in American thought and historiography; single city studies, regional studies; colonial cities and towns; urban institutions; planning, architecture, and urban renewal; class, ethnicity, and race; urban politics and government; and bosses, machines, and urban reform. Annotations provide a succinct summary of each entry.

HOOVER, Dwight W. Cities. New York: Bowker, 1976. 231 p. (Bibliographic guides for contemporary collections). Author and title indexes. 508

More than 1,000 annotated entries in classed arrangement.

ROSS, Bernard H., and FRITSCHLER, A. Lee. Urban affairs bibliography: an annotated guide to the literature of the field. 3rd ed. Washington, D. C.: American University. College of Public Affairs. School of Government and Public Administration, 1974. 85 p. (1st ed., 1969). 509

Annotated entries in classed arrangement. Limited to books.

FILIPOVITCH, Anthony J., and REEVES, Earl J. Urban community: a guide to information sources. Detroit, Michigan: Gale Research, 1978. 286 p. (Urban studies information guide series, v. 4). Author, title, and subject indexes. 510

Annotated entries grouped by subject, such as theories of community, physical aspects, social groups and classes, size and density, safety, quality of life. Primarily works in urban sociology in the United States and Britain. Lists of cited journals, bibliographies, abstracts and indexes.

BELL, Gwen, RANDALL, Edwina, and ROEDER, Judith E. R. Urban environments and human behavior: an annotated bibliography. Stroudsburg, Pennsylvania: Dowden, Hutchinson and Ross, 1973. 271 p. (Community development series, 2). Author and subject indexes. 511

References on behavior and urban forms from the design viewpoint, the social science viewpoint, the view of parts of the urban environment. Not limited to the United States but limited to works in English.

GOLDFIELD, David R., and BROWNELL, Blaine A. Urban America: from downtown to no town. Boston, Massachusetts: Houghton Mifflin, 1979. 435 p. Index. Bibliography, p. 407-417.   512

About 200 references arranged in five sections: Introduction: the city: people, space, and time; Part I, Genesis; Part II, The market place; Part III, Radial center; and Part IV, Vital fringe. Bibliographical notes also at ends of each of the 15 chapters.

CLAY, Grady. Close-up: how to read the American city. Chicago, Illinois: University of Chicago Press, 1980. 192 p. Index. Bibliographical references, p. 182-186. (Phoenix book P863) [originally published: New York: Praeger, 1974. 192 p.].   513

2. ECONOMIC GEOGRAPHY

a. General Economic Geography of the United States

MULLER, Peter O. Locational analysis and economic geography: a comprehensive bibliography of recent literature on theory, techniques, and the spatial organization of agriculture, manufacturing, and transportation. Philadelphia, Pennsylvania: Temple University. The Samuel Paley Library, 1972. 94 p.   514

Nearly 2,000 entries. Part 1 covers the scope, theory, and methods of economic geography. Part 2 covers location and other theory in agriculture, manufacturing, and transportarion geography.

_____. _____. Supplement, 1971-1977. 1977. 57 p.   515

About 900 entries. Includes both books and articles.

NATIONAL Planning Association. Basic maps of the U. S. economy, 1967-1990: population, employment, income. Washington, D. C.: National Planning Association, Center for Economic Projections, 1979. 292 p.   516

Part I presents data at the state level by 50 states. Part II presents data by 183 economic areas. Maps are grouped by four subjects: growth, population, employment, income. Data in tabular form presented on page facing each map. Plastic overlays provide boundaries and numbers for states and economic areas.

ALEXANDERSSON, Gunnar. The industrial structure of American cities. Stockholm, Sweden: Almquist and Wiksell; Lincoln, Nebraska: University of Nebraska Press, 1956. 133 p. Bibliographical footnotes.   517

b. Industrial Location

FSHER, James S., HANINK, Dean M., and WHEELER, James O. Industrial location analysis: a bibliography, 1966-1979. Athens, Georgia: University of Georgia. Department of Geography. Aids to geographic research, Bibliography no. 1, 1979. 76 p.   518

About 1,200 entries arranged by divisions and subdivisions: 1. Location analysis; 2. Systematic analyses; 3. Regional studies (Anglo-American, p. 41-47, about 100 entries; other regions); 4. Industrial development and planning.

WHEELER, James O. Industrial location: a bibliography, 1966-1972. Monticello, Illinois: Council of Planning Librarians. Exchange bibliography, no. 436. 1973. 68 p.   519

About 750 entries.

WE, James E. Industrial plant location. Monticello, Illinois: Vance bibliographies. Public administration series. Bibliography, no. P-575, 1980. 52 p.   520

About 750 references to empirical studies.

_____. The theory of industrial location. Monticello, Illinois: Vance bibliographies. Public administration series. Bibliography, no. P-576, 1980. 32 p.

About 450 references to theoretical studies, mainly in geography, economics, and sociology.

STEVENS, Benjamin H., and BRACKETT, Carolyn A. Industrial location: a review and annotated bibliography of theoretical, empirical and case studies. Philadelphia, Pennsylvania: Regional Science Research Institute. Bibliography series, no. 3. 1967. 199 p. Subject index by broad categories.

854 annotated entries listed alphabetically by author.

c. Manufacturing

MILLER, E. Willard. A geography of manufacturing. Englewood Cliffs, New Jersey: Prentice-Hall, 1962. 490 p. Index.

Anglo-America, p. 31-124. Bibliography, p. 120-124. 117 references.

MILLER, E. Willard. Manufacturing: a study of industrial location. University Park, Pennsylvania: Pennsylvania State University Press, 1977. 286 p. Index. Bibliographies, p. 78-79, 172-176, 279-280. 201 references.

LONSDALE, Richard E., and SEYLER, H. L., eds. Nonmetropolitan industrialization. New York: John Wiley, 1979. 196 p. Subject index. Bibliographical notes at ends of each chapter.

KALE, Steven. The impact of new or additional industry upon rurally oriented areas: a selectively annotated bibliography with emphasis on manufacturing. Monticello, Illinois: Council of Planning Librarians. Exchange bibliography, no. 1148, 1976. 28 p.

About 100 references.

COHEN, Yehoshua S., and BERRY, Brian J. L. Spatial components of manufacturing change, 1950-1960. Chicago, Illinois: University of Chicago. Department of Geography. Research paper no. 172, 1975. 262 p. Bibliography, p. 259-262. 52 references.

Statistical analysis of components of changes in location of manufacturing in the United States, 1950-1960.

WARREN, Kenneth. The American steel industry, 1850-1970: a geographical interpretation. Oxford: Clarendon Press, 1973. 337 p. Index. Bibliographical notes.

d. Mining

TOMPKINS, Dorothy Campbell. Strip mining for coal. Berkeley, California: University of California, Institute of Governmental Studies, 1973. 86 p. (Public policy bibliographies, 4). Index.

669 entries arranged by large subject categories: strip mining for coal (bibliographies and other sources; acid mine drainage, and legal aspects of strip mining); strip mining in the states (state-by-state references, Appalachian region, interstate activities); strip mining and the federal government (Tennessee Valley Authority); reclamation of strip mined land.

FRAWLEY, Margaret L. Surface mined areas: control and reclamation of environmental damage: a bibliography. Washington, D. C.: U. S. Department of the Interior, Office of Library Service, Information Service Division, 1971. 63 p. (Bibliography series no. 27). Name index. Subject index. (Available from the National Technical Information Service, Springfield, Virginia, as PB 203 448).

387 annotated entries, arranged by subjects under environmental effects, protective measures, and reclamation.

e. Agriculture

WORLD atlas of agriculture, under the aegis of the International Association of Agricultural Economists. Monographs edited by the Committee for the World Atlas. v. 3. Americas. Novara, Italy: Istituto Geografico de Agostini, 1969. 497 p. 531

United States, by James R. Anderson, p. 409-465. Bibliography, p. 464-465. 89 references.

HIGBEE, Edward C. American agriculture: geography, resources, conservation. New York: John Wiley, 1958. 399 p. Index. 532

References at ends of 27 chapters, 3 systematic and 24 regional.

HAYSTEAD, Ladd, and FITE, Gilbert C. The agricultural regions of the United States. Norman, Oklahoma: University of Oklahoma Press, 1955. 288 p. Index. Bibliography, p. 276-280. 533

ANDERSON, James R. A geography of agriculture in the United States: Southeast. Budapest, Hungary: Akadémiai Kiadó, 1973. 135 p. (Geography of world agriculture, v. 2). Bibliography, p. 132-[136]. 79 references. 534

GREGOR, Howard F. An agricultural typology of California, Budapest, Hungary: Akadémiai Kiadó, 1974. 106 p. (Geography of world agriculture, v. 4). Bibliography, p. 105-[107]. 51 references. 535

KUZINA, Irina Mikhailovna. Agrogeografiia kapitalisticheskikh stran (na primere S.Sh.A. i Kanady) (Agricultural geography of capitalist countries: case study of the United States and Canada). A. N. Rakitnikov, ed. Itogi nauki i tekhniki: Geografiia zarubezhnykh stran, v. 9. Moskva: VINITI, 1981. 155 p. Bibliography, p. 138-155. 536

307 references (174 in English, 128 in Russian, and 5 in French). Textual discussion in Russian of the development and the main features of contemporary agriculture in the United States, p. 19-68.

INDHORST, Hans-Wilhelm. Die Landwirtschaft der Vereinigten Staaten. Strukturelle und regionale Dynamik. Wiesbaden: Steiner, 1975. 54 p. (Wissenschaftliche Paperbacks Geographie). Bibliography, p. 52-54. 70 references on agriculture in the United States. 537

FURUSETH, Owen J., and PIERCE, John T. Agricultural land in an urban society. Washington, D. C.: Association of American Geographers, Resource publications in geography, 1982. 89 p. Bibliography, p. 81-89. About 200 references. 538

GREGOR, Howard F. Industrialization of U. S. agriculture: an interpretive atlas. Boulder, Colorado: Westview Press, 1982. 259 p. Index. Bibliographical notes at end of each chapter. 539

Discussion of the conceptualization, intensity, scale, structure, types, and performance of agricultural industrialization with 38 maps and 26 tables.

BIBLIOGRAPHY of agriculture. Date provided by National Agricultural Library, U. S. Department of Agriculture. Phoenix, Arizona:.Oryx Press, v. 1- . 1942- . Monthly with cumulated subject, personal, and organizational indexes. Publisher varies. 540

BIOLOGICAL and agricultural index: a cumulative subject index to periodicals in the fields of biology, agriculture, and related sciences, 1964- . New York: Wilson, v. 19- (S 1964-). Monthly (except August) with quarterly and annual cumulation. 541

Preceded by Agricultural index: subject index to a selected list of agricultural periodicals and bulletins, v. 1-18 (S 1916-Ag 1964).

BIOLOGICAL abstracts reporting worldwide research in life science. v. 1- ,
December 1926- . Philadelphia, Pennsylvania: Bio Sciences Information Service,
1926. Semimonthly (Subtitle, frequency and name of publisher have varied).
Author, biosystematic, generic, concept, and subject indexes in each issue,
cumulated semiannually. 542

U. S. Department of Agriculture. Yearbook of agriculture, 1894- . Washington,
D. C.: U. S. GovernmentPrinting Office, 1895- . Annual. Title varies. 543

    Some of the volumes are of particular interest in the study of factors
affecting agriculture in the United States. These are individually listed below.

SOILS and men: the yearbook of agriculture, 1938. (U. S. Department of Agriculture).
Washington, D. C.: Government Printing Office, 1938. 1,232 p. Index. Bibliography, p. 1181-1207. 544

    Major sections: the nation and the soil; the farmer and the soil; soil and
plant relationships; fundamentals of soil science; and soils of the United States.

CLIMATE and man: the yearbook of agriculture, 1941. (U. S. Department of Agriculture). Washington, D. C.: Government Printing Office, 1941. 1248 p. Index. 545

    Major parts: climate as a world influence; climate and agricultural settlement; climate and the farmer; the scientific approach to weather and climate; and
climatic data, with special reference to agriculture in the United States (including climatic summary for each state).

GRASS: the yearbook of agriculture, 1948. (U. S. Department of Agriculture).
Washington, D. C.: Government Printing Office, 1948. 892 p. Index. Bibliography, p. 855-878. 546

TREES: the yearbook of agriculture, 1949. (U. S. Department of Agriculture).
Washington, D. C.: Government Printing Office, 1949. 944 p. Index. Bibliography, p. 901-910. 547

WATER: the yearbook of agriculture, 1955. (U. S. Department of Agriculture).
Washington, D. C.: Government Printing Office, 1955. 751 p. Index. Bibliography,
p. 722-723. 548

    Sections: Our need for water; where we get our water; water and our soil;
caring for our watersheds; water and our forests; water for irrigation; water and
our crops; our ranges and pastures; gardens, turf, and orchards; drainage of
fields; water and our wildlife; pure water for farms and cities; and a look to
the future.

SOIL: the yearbook of agriculture, 1957. (U. S. Department of Agriculture).
Washington, D. C.: Government Printing Office, 1957. 784 p. Index. 549

    Sections: principles; fertility; practices; soil care; moisture; systems;
regions; special uses.

LAND: yearbook of agriculture, 1958. (U. S. Department of Agriculture). Washington,
D. C,: Government Printing Office, 1958. 605 p. Index. 550

AFTER a hundred years: the yearbook of agriculture, 1962. (U. S. Department of
Agriculture). Washington, D. C.: Government Printing Office, 1962. 688 p. Index. 551

    Sections: background (a retrospective look at the country since the establishment of the Department of Agriculture in 1862); plants; conservation; forests;
animals; insects; technologies; markets; economics; so people may know; homes.

f. Trade

REVZAN, David A. A geography of marketing: resource bibliography. Berkeley, California: University of California. Institute of Business and Economic Research. Research Program in Marketing, 1968. 259 p. Author index. 552

3,663 entries arranged by chapters: 1. Conceptual bases: multi-discipline literature, research methodology (economic location theory, regional economics and land economics, economic and business history, marketing, geography, sociology, other disciplines, and research methodology); 2. Locational and structural determinants and composition, geographical units, business activities, and clusters; 3. Human populations: locational characteristics; 4. Trading area patterns; 5. Spatial competition, commodity origins and flows, channel patterns; 6. Geographical variations; 7. The maximization of geographical alternatives in marketing; and 8. Uses of a geography of marketing.

BERRY, Brian J. L. Geography of market centers and retail distribution. Englewood Cliffs, New Jersey: Prentice-Hall, 1967. 146 p. Index. Bibliographical footnotes. 553

Includes illustrations from the United States.

VANCE, James E., Jr. The merchant's world: the geography of wholesaling. Englewood Cliffs, New Jersey: Prentice-Hall, 1970. 167 p. Bibliographical footnotes. 554

RISTOW, Walter W. Marketing maps of the United States: an annotated bibliography. 3rd ed. Washington, D. C.: Library of Congress. Map Division, 1958. 147 p. (1st ed. 1951). 554a

g. Transportation

ADAMS, Russell B., and GEYER, Mark C. Transportation: a geographical bibliography. Minneapolis, Minnesota: University of Minnesota. Department of Geography, 1970. 154 p. Author index. 555

Almost 2,000 references, including books, journals, and articles with emphasis on urban transportation and theoretical and quantitative studies, but with wide coverage of historical, economic, and regional studies and the principal modes. Not limited to the United States but includes many references that deal with transportation in this country.

SIDDALL, William R. Transportation geography: a bibliography. 3rd ed. Manhattan, Kansas: Kansas State University Library, 1969. 94 p. (Bibliography series no. 1). (1st ed., 1964. 46 p.). 556

About 1,700 articles or books, primarily from the period 1950-1969, mainly organized by type of transportation: ocean shipping, seaports, inland waterways, railroads, highways, pipelines, and air transportation, but including general and regional studies.

WHEELER, James O. Spatial studies in transportation: introduction and annotated bibliography. Monticello, Illinois: Council of Planning Librarians, Exchange bibliography, no. 324-325, 1972. 161 p. Subject index. 557

About 1,000 annotated entries.

WHEELER, James O. Research directions in urban transportation geography in the United States, in György Enyedi, ed. Urban development in the USA and Hungary. Budapest: Akadémiai Kiadó, 1978. p. 187-204. Studies in geography in Hungary, 14. Bibliography, p. 201-204, with 104 references. 558

TAAFFE, Edward J., and GAUTHIER, Howard L. Geography of transportation. Englewood Cliffs, New Jersey: Prentice-Hall, 1973. 226 p. Index. Bibliography, p. 211-222, arranged by chapters and topics. 559

ELIOT HURST, Michael E., ed. Transportation geography: comments and readings. New York: McGraw-Hill, 1974. 528 p. Bibliographic footnotes and bibliographies at end of parts, p. 50-52, 126-128, 187-188, 280-283, 377-380, 450-451, and 507-509. 560

DAVIS, Bob J. Information sources in transportation, material management, and physical distribution: an annotated bibliography and guide. Westport, Connecticut: Greenwood Press, 1976. 715 p. Index. 561

Arranged by 67 subjects and within each subject by type of material.

METCALF, Kenneth N. Transportation: information sources. An annotated guide to publications, agencies, and other data sources concerning air, rail, water, and pipeline transportation. Detroit, Michigan: Gale Research, 1965. 307 p. (Management information guide, no. 8). Author-title-source index. Subject index. 562

Entries arranged by sections: library facilities; government sources; statistical sources; fact source books; periodicals, indexes, abstracts, and services; research and university programs; literature and bibliography; professional and trade organizations and associations; and transportation industry literature.

RAKOWSKI, James P. Transportation economics: a guide to information sources. Detroit, Michigan: Gale Research, 1976. 215 p. (Economics information guide series, v. 5). Author, title, and subject indexes. 563

Annotated entries arranged by types of transportation: general, railroads, highways, air, water, and urban. Entries for books are annotated. Last chapter devoted to bibliographic sources, periodicals, associations, and government sources of information. Bibliography, p. 159-182.

CURRENT literature in traffic and transportation (Northwestern University. Transportation Library). v. 1- (1960-). Monthly. 564

Books and articles in classed arrangement: transportation, containerization, air transportation, rail transportation, water transportation, highway transportation, pipelines, freight commodities, physical distribution, travel, rural travel and transit, urban transportation, roads and traffic, and motor vehicles and drivers, with subdivisions.

HSU, Ann Yi-rong, and WHEELER, James O. A bibliography of highway impact studies, 1966-1976. Monticello, Illinois: Council of Planning Librarians. Exchange bibliography, no. 1401, 1977. 29 p. 565

About 400 references.

DYETT, Michael F. The Land use and urban development impacts of beltways: an annotated bibliography. Monticello, Illinois, Vance bibliographies. Public Administration series: Bibliography, no. P-809, 1981. 39 p. 566

About 200 references, some extensively annotated, arranged by subject: general; land use and location theory; beltway impact studies; other highway impact studies; foreign experience; methodologies; data for comparative statistical analysis; bibliographies.

ONIBOKUM, Adepoju G. Socio-economic impact of highways and commuter rail systems on land use and activity patterns: an annotated bibliography. Monticello, Illinois: Council of Planning Librarians. Exchange bibliography, no. 815, 1975. 35 p. 567

About 40 annotated references and 90 unannotated references.

GARRISON, William L., and others. Studies of highway development and geographic change. Seattle, Washington: University of Washington Press, 1959. 291 p. Index. Bibliography, p. 277-288. 568

WILLIS, Dawn E., comp. Urban mass transportation: a bibliography. Washington, D.C.:
U. S. Department of Transportation, Library Services Division, 1971. 140 p.
(Urban mass transportation. Bibliographic list no. 6). Author index. Subject
index.   569

    921 entries arranged by bibliographies, conferences, reports and books, and
periodical articles. The subject index must be used to locate works on a particular topic.

TRYGG, Lisa, and SGOURAKIS, Alice. Land use impacts of rapid transit. Monticello,
Illinois: Council of Planning Librarians. Exchange bibliography no. 1377. 1977.
32 p.   570

    About 300 references arranged by sections: bibliography; system-specific
studies and observations (Atlanta, Baltimore, Boston, Chicago, Montreal, Philadelphia, San Francisco, Toronto, Washington, D. C., and other cities); pre-World
War II; international; value capture; and bibliographies.

WHEELER, James O. A bibliography of recent studies of urban commodity flows.
Monticello, Illinois: Council of Planning Librarians. Exchange bibliography, no.
961, 1976. 10 p.   571

    About 140 entries on the urban distribution and transportation of goods,
mostly in the United States.

MODELSKI, Andrew W. Railroad maps of the United States: a selective annotated bibliography of original 19th-century maps in the Geography and Map Division of the
Library of Congress. Washington, D. C.: Library of Congress; for sale by Superintendent of Documents, Government Printing Office, 1975. 112 p.   572

    622 selected entries from among the 5,000 such maps held by the Library.

STARR, John T., Jr. The evolution of the unit train, 1960-1969. Chicago, Illinois:
Department of Geography. Research paper no. 158, 1976. 233 p. Bibliography,
p. 215-233. 324 references.   573

    Development of the unit train in freight transportation in the United States.

CHATFIELD, Mary. Inland waterways transportation: a bibliography and guide to information sources. Cambridge, Massachusetts: Harvard University, Graduate School of
Business Administration. Baker Library, 1966. 42 p.   574

    References arranged in two major sections: materials dealing with the industry
as a whole and materials dealing with particular waterways and areas of the United
States (21 in alphabetical order from Alabama to Wabash River and Valley).

SCHENKER, Eric, MAYER, Harold M., and BROCKEL, Harry C. The Great Lakes transportation system. Madison, Wisconsin: University of Wisconsin. Sea Grant College
Program, 1976. 292 p. Bibliographical footnotes and bibliographies at ends of   575
chapters, p. 29-33, 63-65, 92-96, 128-133, 173, 227-235, and 271-279.

HORSHAM, John P., Jr. A Survey of current literature on port development in the
United States. Monticello, Illinois: Vance Bibliographies. Architecture Series:
Bibliography, no. A-11. 1978. 23 p.   576

    About 225 references.

HORSHAM, John P., Jr. Water transportation and inland waterways information:
further considerations. (Supplement to Council of Planning Librarians. Exchange
bibliography no. 1168). Monticello, Illinois: Vance bibliographies. Public
administration series. Bibliography P-51, 1978. 26 p. About 270 references
arranged by topic or by state.   577

BARR, Charles W. <u>Waterfront development: a partial bibliography.</u> Monticello, Illinois: Council of Planning Librarians. <u>Exchange bibliography</u>, no. 1001, 1976. 31 p. 578

About 300 references arranged by bibliographies, general studies, and case studies by states in alphabetical order.

MAYER, Harold M. <u>The port of Chicago and the St. Lawrence Seaway.</u> Chicago, Illinois: The University of Chicago Press, 1957. 283 p. Bibliography, p. 273-283. 579

202 references.

STEVENSON, Arthur J. <u>The New York-Newark air freight system</u>. Chicago, Illinois: University of Chicago. Department of Geography. Research paper nos. 199-200, 1982. 440 p. Index. Bibliography, p. 407-430. 580

WOLFE, Harry P. <u>Domestic air freight: a selected bibliography.</u> Monticello, Illinois: Council of Planning Librarians. <u>Exchange bibliography</u>, no. 1020. 1976. 43 p. 581

About 400 references on domestic air freight in the United States, 1970-1975, divided into four sections: air cargo, air forwarding, air shipments, and air-truck transportation with subdivisions by subject.

h. Energy

BALACHANDRAN, Sarojini. <u>Energy statistics: a guide to sources.</u> Monticello, Illinois: Council of Planning Librarians. <u>Exchange bibliography</u>, no. 1065. 1976. 51 p. Index. 582

162 references, arranged by: composite sources; coal; electricity; natural gas; nuclear energy; petroleum; and solar and others. Directory of publishers. Predominantly but not solely devoted to sources in the United States.

BALACHANDRAN, Sarojini. <u>Energy statistics: an update to bibliography no. 1065,</u> Monticello, Illinois: Council of Planning Librarians. <u>Exchange bibliography</u>, no. 1247, 1977. 22 p. Subject index. 80 annotated references. 583

i. Land Resources and Land Use (See also entries 442-445)

JACKSON, Richard H. <u>Land use in America.</u> New York: John Wiley, 1981. 226 p. Index. (V. H. Winston and Sons. A Halsted press book). 584

Bibliographical footnotes for each chapter: land use in America; the public welfare; the Federal government and land use; the development of state land use controls; land use: a community dilemma; land use problems and metropolitan areas; changing methods of controlling land use; farmland preservation: necessity or misperception; implementing the control of land use; and land use in tomorrow's America: today's dilemma.

PLATT, Rutherford H., and MACINKO, George, eds. <u>Beyond the urban fringe: land use issues in nonmetropolitan America.</u> Minneapolis, Minnesota: University of Minnesota Press, 1983. 416 p. Index. Bibliographies at ends of papers. 585

NIEMANN, Bernard J., Jr., and MLADENOFF, David J. <u>Annotated bibliography of land planning and information systems.</u> Monticello, Illinois: <u>Vance bibliographies.</u> Public administration series: Bibliography, no. P. 308, 1979. 131 p. 586

416 annotated references: 242 on land planning and 174 on land information systems (land classification systems; remote sensing; cartographic techniques; land records or cadastre; and physical and demographic information systems).

WORSHAM, John P. Jr., with Edward E. May and John H. Brown. Land use planning information: basic considerations. Monticello, Illinois: Council of Planning Librarians. Exchange bibliography no. 633, 1974. 38 p. 588

About 450 references, under headings such as: agriculture, central business district, conservation, economic development, environmental planning, flood plains, forest and forestry, housing, information systems, land bank, land economics, land resource management, tenure, land use, location, models, national planning, open space, public lands, recreational areas, residential areas, soils, transportation, urban design, urban growth, and zoning.

HESS, David. Bibliography of state land resources planning, 1960-1974 (preliminary edition): indexed by topic, year, state, agency. Monticello, Illinois: Council of Planning Librarians. Exchange bibliography, no. 769-771, 1975. 512 p. 3 parts. 589

Includes documents produced or commissioned by State Governments in the areas of land-use management and planning of statewide signifance. About 4500 entries, arranged by 29 subjects. No. 772-774, 1975. 520 p. 3 parts. Arranged by states.

HESS, David. Bibliography of state land resources planning, 1970-1975 (supplemental edition): indexed by topic, year, state, agency. Monticello, Illinois: Council of Planning Librarians. Exchange bibliography, no. 845-847, 1975. 269 p. 590

About 2,500 references indexed under 40 main topic headings. No. 848-850, 1975. 264 p. Arranged by states.

BERCAW, Louise O., and HANNAY, Annie M., under the direction of Mary G. Lacy. Bibliography on land utilization, 1918-36. Washington, D. C. United States Department of Agriculture, Miscellaneous publication no. 284. For sale by the Superintendent of Documents, U. S. Government Printing Office, 1938. 1508 p. Index. 591

7,343 entries. Pages 14-757, entries 56-4328, are devoted to the United States with listings under subjects and under individual states, each in alphabetical order.

CULVER, Dorothy Campbell. Land utilization: a bibliography. Berkeley, California: University of California, Bureau of Public Administration, 1935, reissued 1937. 222 p. 592

2,887 entries arranged by broad subjects and subdivisions: public lands, land classification, land utilization (marginal lands; economic surveys; land-use planning; land uses by categories such as agricultural, forestry, recreation, wild-life conservation, water conservation and power development); land finance; and land protection.

_____. _____. Supplement, 1937. 139 p. 593

1,437 additional entries, similarly arranged.

U. S. Bureau of Land Management. Public lands bibliography. Washington: Government Printing Office, 1962. 106 p. 1288 references prior to 1954, arranged by articles and monographs, laws and legislation, and theses. 594

_____. _____. Supplement 1. Washington: Bureau of Land Management, 1965. 71 p. (Covers the years 1954-1962). 595

BERRY, Brian J. L., and others. Land use, urban form and environmental quality. Chicago, Illinois: University of Chicago. Department of Geography. Research paper no. 155, 1974. xxiii plus 440 p. Bibliography, p. 431-440. 596

144 references arranged by topics: air pollution, 26; water pollution, 43; solid wastes, 17; noise, 24; pesticides, 4; radiation, 4; and other, 26.

PLATT, Rutherford H. The open space decision process: spatial allocation of costs and benefits. Chicago, Illinois: University of Chicago. Department of Geography. Research paper no. 142, 1972. 189 p. Bibliography, p. 183-189. 597

117 references arranged by ideology, 47 references; land economics, 33; and law, 37. Materials used in case studies are noted in bibliographical footnotes. Focus is on the United States.

j. Housing

PAULUS, Virginia. Housing: a bibliography, 1960-1972. New York: AMS Press, 1974. 339 p. Author index and subject finding guide. 598

3,625 entries in classed arrangement on economic, legal, social and political, and demographic aspects of housing.

k. Regional Development and Economic Regions

THOMAN, Richard S. Selected bibliography on regional development in Canada and the United States with special reference to 1965-1971. Kingston, Ontario: The Author [now Department of Geography, California State University, Hayward, California 94542], 1971. 93 p. 599

About 1,100 entries arranged alphabetically by author under three headings: general method and policy; application to Canada; application to the United States.

BERRY, Brian J. L., and HANKINS, Thomas D. A bibliographic guide to the economic regions of the United States. Chicago, Illinois: University of Chicago. Department of Geography. Research paper no. 87, 1963. 101 p. List of articles by major journals. 600

378 entries arranged by concept or type of regions: regions in geography and other social sciences, economic regions, regions of uniformity, organizational regions, regional science, regional planning, and textbooks on North American regions. Introductory text and supplementary list of articles by journal.

CUMBERLAND, John H. Regional development: experiences and prospects in the United States of America. The Hague, The Netherlands: Mouton, 1971. 170 p. (United Nations Research Institute for Social Development, Geneva. Publication series: Regional Planning, v. 2). Bibliography, p. 165-170. 601

PERLOFF, Harvey S., and others. Regions, resources, and economic growth. Baltimore Maryland: Johns Hopkins Press for Resources for the Future, 1960. 716 p. Index. Bibliographical footnotes. 602

BOGUE, Donald J., and BEALE, Calvin L. Economic areas of the United States. New York: Free Press of Glencoe, 1961. xc. plus 1,162 p. plus Basic statistics for economic regions, subregions, and state economic areas, clxxxvi p. (Studies in population distribution, no. 15). Bibliographical note, p. 1162. 603

l. Related Studies in Economics and Business

ENCYCLOPEDIA of business information sources. 5th ed. Paul Wasserman, managing ed. Charlotte Georgi and James Way, associate editors. Detroit, Michigan: Gale Research, 1983. 728 p. (1st ed. 1970. 2 v.). 604

About 1,215 subjects. Under each subject are listed available encyclopedias, handbooks, bibliographies, abstract services and indexes, periodicals, directories, statistical sources, and commercially available on-line data bases.

MELNYK, Peter. Economics: bibliographic guide to reference books and information sources. Littleton, Colorado: Libraries Unlimited, 1971. 263 p. Index. 605

    1,464 annotated entries arranged in 10 subject chapters by type of material. Chapters are devoted to economic theory; economic conditions in various countries; finance; commerce and marketing; international economics; agricultural and land economics, economic geography; industry and transportation; labor; population and statistics; and periodicals. Not limited to the United States but contains many references on the United States.

JOURNAL of economic literature (The American Economic Association). Nashville, Tennessee. v. 1- (1963-). Quarterly. v. 1-6 (1961-1968) as Journal of economic abstracts. Index of authors of articles in the subject index. 606

    Includes book reviews, an annotated listing of new books, a listing of contents of current periodicals, a detailed subject index of articles in current periodicals (arranged according to a finely articulated classification system), and selected abstracts.

ECONOMICS selections: an international annotated bibliography, nos. 1-35 (1954-1963); 1963-1973, no. 4; v. 21- (1976-). New York: Gordon and Breach, 1954- . Quarterly. Title and sponsorship vary: nos. 1-35 (1954-1962) by the Department of Political Economy, The Johns Hopkins University; 1963-1973, no. 2-3, by the Department of Economics, University of Pittsburgh. 1973, no. 4 (including 1974 citations); v. 21- (1976-), edited by Maurice B. Ballabon. [v. 1-20 without volume designation covered 1954-1973]. 607

    Annotated entries arranged by subject. Author index in each issue.

ECONOMICS library selections: cumulative bibliography, series I and II, 1954-1962. Edited by the Department of Economics, University of Pittsburgh. New York: Gordon and Breach, 1965. 352 p. Index. 608

    7,695 entries in classed arrangement. Chapter 12, Land economics; economics of agriculture, mining, and housing; economic geography; natural resources; and regional economic planning, is of particular interest.

ECONOMICS selections: an international bibliography: cumulative bibliography, series I and II, 1963-1970. New York: Gordon and Breach, 1974. 393 p. 609

    Books classified during the year 1963 through 1970 in classed arrangement. This convenient cumulation omits the annotations of included items, for which one must turn to the journal itself.

____, volume III, 1971-1977. New York: Gordon and Breach, 1979. 316 p. Author index. 610

    6,300 English-language monographs. For annotations one must go to the original entries in Economic selections: an international bibliography.

____. Volume 4. 1978-1981. New York: Gordon and Breach, 1982. 256 p. 611

ECONOMIC books: current selections. A quarterly publication. Department of Economics and University Libraries. University of Pittsburgh. 1- (1974-). Quarterly. Clifton, New Jersey: Augustus M. Kelley, Publisher, 1974- . 612

    Arranged by subjects. Author index.

INDEX of economic articles in journals and collective volumes. v. 1- (1886/1924-). Homewood, Illinois: R. D. Irwin, 1961- . Annual. Title varies: v. 1-7 as Index of economic journals. (Prepared under the auspices of the Journal of economic literature of the American Economic Association). 613

cont.

Social Geography 108

v. 1. 1886-1924; v. 2, 1925-1939; v. 3, 1940-1949; v. 4, 1950-1954; v. 5, 1954-1959; v. 6, 1960-1963; v. 7, 1964-1965; v. 6A, 1960-1963; Collective volumes; v. 6A, Collective volumes 1960-1963; v. 7A, 1964-1965, Collective volumes. v. 8- , 1966- , annual.

Consists of 2 parts: a subject index arranged by 4-digit categories and an author index. These annual volumes have a more detailed classification than the quarterly Journal of economic literature and are thus more convenient to use. They also include articles in collective works, but have about a 4-year delay (the volume covering publications in 1978 was published in 1983).

HUTCHINSON, William K., ed. American economic history: a guide to information sources. Detroit, Michigan: Gale Research, 1980. 296 p. (Economics information guide series, v. 16). Author, title, and subject indexes. 614

More than 1,500 entries, mostly annotated, in topical arrangement.

BUSINESS statistics: the biennial supplement to the Survey of current business (U.S. Department of Commerce. Bureau of Economic Analysis). 1931- . Washington, D.C.: Government Printing Office, 1931- . Biennial. Title varies: 1932-1942 as Annual Supplement. Not published 1934, 1942-1947. 615

Annual data (monthly for recent years) for 2,600 statistical series. For latest data see Survey of current business, v. 1- (1921-). Monthly.

3. SOCIAL GEOGRAPHY

a. General

WATSON, J. Wreford. Social geography of the United States. London and New York: Longman, 1979. 209 p. Bibliographies at the ends of chapters. 616

JAKLE, John A., BRUNN, Stanley, and ROSEMAN, Curtis C. Human spatial behavior: a social geography. North Scituate, Massachusetts. Duxbury Press, 1976. 315 p. Index. Bibliographies. 617

SMITH, David M. The geography of social well-being in the United States: an introduction to territorial social indicators. New York: McGraw-Hill, 1973. 144 p. References at the end of each chapter. 618

ALBAUM, Melvin, with DAVIES, Shane, eds. Geography and contemporary issues: studies of relevant problems. New York: Wiley, 1973. 590 p. Index. 619

39 readings on poverty and the poor in America; Black America and the Black ghetto; urban life and housing; environmental deterioration, hazards, and stress; population growth and pressure; conflict and conflict resolution. Bibliographical references at the end of each article.

PEET, Richard, ed. Radical geography: alternative viewpoints on contemporary social issues. Chicago: Maaroufa Press, 1977; London: Methuen, 1978. 387 p. Bibliographical references. 620

HARVEY, David W. Social justice and the city. London: Edward Arnold; Baltimore, Maryland: Johns Hopkins University Press, 1973. 336 p. Indexes of authors and subjects. Bibliography, p. 315-325. 621

Discusses liberal and socialist formulations of social processes, social justice, spatial results, and similar problems.

JAKLE, John A. The spatial dimensions of social organization: a selected bibliography for urban social geography. Monticello, Illinois: Council of Planning Librarians, Exchange bibliography, no. 118, 1970. 50 p. About 750 references. 622

b. Elderly

WARNES, Anthony M., ed. Geographical perspectives on the elderly. Chichester, England; New York: John Wiley, 1982. 478 p. Indexes. Bibliography, p. 449-465. 623

Chapter 6. County patterns of elderly migration in the United States, by James R. Bohland and Lexa Treps, p. 139-158. Bibliography, p. 157-158. 22 references. Chapter 8. Housing for the elderly in the United States, by Wiley P. Mangum, p. 191-221. Bibliography, p. 216-221. 97 references. Chapter 10. American retirement communities and residential relocation, by Charles F. Longino, Jr., p. 239-262. Bibliography, p. 260-262. 47 references. Chapter 15. Spatial aspects of primary health care for the elderly, by James R. Bohland and Patricia Frech, p. 339-354. Bibliography, p. 353-354. 37 references. Chapter 17. Home-based mental health care for elderly, by Christopher J. Smith, p. 375-398. Bibliography, p. 395-398. 68 references.

GOLANT, Stephen M., ed. Location and environment of elderly population. New York: John Wiley, 1979. 214 p. Index. Bibliographical references. 624

PLACE, Linna F., PARKER, Linda, and BERGHORN, Forrest J. Aging and the aged: an annotated bibliography and library research guide. Boulder, Colorado: Westview Press, 1980. 128 p. Author and title indexes. 625

Includes a chapter on the environment and the elderly. Entries partly annotated.

NATIONAL Council on the Aging. Research and Evaluation Department. Fact book on aging: a profile of America's older population. Washington, D. C.: National Council on the Aging, 1978. 263 p. Bibliographical notes at end of each chapter. 626

Data on demography, income, employment, health, housing, transportation, and criminal victimization. Sources indicated.

HANDBOOK of aging and the social sciences. Editors: Robert H. Binstock and Ethel Shanas. New York: Van Nostrand Reinhold, 1976. 684 p. Author index. Subject index. Bibliographies. 627

Review of research organized by broad sections, with extensive bibliographies.

VANCE, Mary. Housing for the elderly. Monticello, Illinois: Council of Planning Librarians. Exchange bibliography, no. 27, 1963. 154 p. Geographic index. Author index. 628

1,676 entries, arranged by bibliographies; indexes; lists, reviews and abstracts; directories; background on aging and the aged; housing for the elderly; community facilities and services; economic aspects; design requirements and standards; and housing types.

c. Women

LOYD, Bonnie. Women and geography: an annotated bibliography and guide to sources of information. Monticello, Illinois: Council of Planning Librarians. Exchange bibliography, no. 1159, 1976. 18 p. About 100 references on women in the field of geography and geographic research on women in society. 629

MAZEY, Mary Ellen, and LEE, David R. Her space, her place: a geography of women. Washington, D. C.: Association of American Geographers, Resource publications in geography, 1983. 83 p. Bibliography, p. 75-83. 216 references. 629a

d. Poverty

MORRILL, Richard L., and WOHLENBERG, Ernest H. The geography of poverty in the United States. New York: McGraw-Hill, 1971. 148 p. Bibliographies at ends of chapters, p. 13-14, 48, 72, 102, 118, 139. 630

PEET, Richard, ed. Geographical perspectives on American poverty. Worcester, Massachusetts: Antipode, 1972 (Antipode monographs in social geography, v. 1). Bibliographical notes at ends of articles. 631

HAFNER, James A. Perspectives on poverty: a reference bibliography. Monticello, Illinois: Council of Planning Librarians. Exchange bibliography, no. 693, 1974. 39 p. About 600 entries. 632

e. Crime

GEORGES-ABEYIE, Daniel E., and HARRIES, Keith D., eds. Crime: a spatial perspective. New York: Columbia University Press, 1980. 301 p. Author and subject indexes. Bibliographical references. 633

ROSE, Harold M., ed. Lethal aspects of urban violence. Lexington, Massachusetts: Lexington Books, 1979. 100 p. Bibliographical references. 634

GEORGES, Daniel E. The geography of crime and violence: a spatial and ecological perspective. Washington, D. C.: Association of American Geographers, 1978. 28 p. (Resource papers for college geography, no. 78-1). Bibliography, p. 28. 635

HARRIES, Keith D., and BRUNN, Stanley D. The geography of laws and justice: spatial perspectives on the criminal justice system. New York: Praeger, 1978. 174 p. Bibliographical references. 636

HARRIES, Keith D. The geography of crime and justice. New York: McGraw-Hill, 1974. 125 p. Bibliographical references. 637

PYLE, Gerald F., and others. The spatial dynamics of crime. Chicago, Illinois: University of Chicago. Department of Geography. Research paper no. 159, 1974. 221 p. Bibliography, p. 208-221. 184 references. 638

Spatial, temporal, and urban ecological aspects of crime in an American city (Akron, Ohio).

HANSON, Perry O. III, and BOEHNKE, Barbara. The spatial analysis of crime: a bibliography. Monticello, Illinois: Council of Planning Librarians. Exchange bibliography, no. 1166, 1976. 25 p. 639

About 325 references in classed arrangement.

REED, Carl N., III, and HANSON, Perry O., III. Police information systems with special interest on geographic applications: a bibliography. Monticello, Illinois: Council of Planning Librarians. Exchange bibliography, no. 1199, 1977. 27 p. 640

About 250 references arranged by: bibliographies; general; information systems; geographic information systems; police information systems; specific applications.

f. Related Studies in Sociology

MARK, Charles. Sociology of America: a guide to information sources. Detroit, Michigan: Gale Research, 1976. 454 p. (American studies information guide series, v. 1). Author, title, subject, and periodical title indexes. 641

About 1,900 entries, mostly annotated. Chapters are devoted to bibliographies, reference works, journal titles, and to subjects.

SOCIOLOGICAL abstracts. v. 1- (1952-). San Diego, California. 6 nos. a year. 5 issues, each with subject, author, and source indexes. Annual cummulation of indexes. 642

Abstracts arranged by a classification scheme.

g. Related Studies in Psychology

(Psychological studies of perception are of particular interest to students of perceptions of the environment, hazards, communities, and facilities. Such studies are also valuable in the new field of behavioral geography).

PSYCHOLOGICAL abstracts. v. 1- (1927-). Washington, D. C.: American Psychological Association. Monthly. 643

ANNUAL review of psychology. v. 1- (1950-). Stanford, California: Annual. 644

CONTEMPORARY psychology: a journal of reviews. v. 1- (1956-). Washington, D.C.: American Psychological Association. Monthly. 645

4. STUDIES OF ETHNIC GROUPS

(See also entries 812, 816, 818)

a. General

HARVARD encyclopedia of American ethnic groups. Ed. by Stephan Thernstrom and others. Cambridge, Massachusetts: Harvard University Press, 1980. 1,076 p. 646

106 ethnic groups covered with discussion of their social, cultural, religious, linguistic, political, and economic characteristics accompanied by critical bibliographies and maps.

JAKLE, John A., with the assistance of JAKLE, Cynthia A. Ethnic and racial minorities in North America: a selected bibliography of the geographical literature. Monticello, Illinois: Council of Planning Librarians. Exchange bibliography, no. 459-460, 1973. 71 p. 647

About 900 entries, arranged by 46 minority groups. The largest number of entries are for Afro-American, Amerindian, French Canadian, German, Italian, Mexican, Mormon, and Southern White. References also by major regions of Canada and the United States.

DARDEN, Joe T. Race, housing, and residential segregation: a selected bibliography of basic references. Chicago, Illinois: Council of Planning Librarians, CPL bibliography, no. 96, 1982. 34 p. 648

About 400 references on the pattern of residential segregation in the United States (and a smaller section: outside the United States), the process of discrimination in housing, and anti-discrimination housing policies and laws.

MILLER, Wayne C., and others. A comprehensive bibliography for the study of American minorities. New York: New York University Press, 1976. 2 v. 1,380 p. Author and title indexes. 649

29,300 entries, briefly annotated. Covers all major groups arranged by broad regional source then by group.

OAKS, Priscilla. Minority studies: a selective annotated bibliography. Boston, Massachusetts: G. K. Hall, 1975. 303 p. Index of authors and titles. 650

About 1,800 entries on Native Americans, Spanish Americans, Afro-Americans, and Asian Americans.

FELLOWS, Donald K. A mosaic of America's ethnic minorities. New York: John Wiley, 1972. 219 p. Index. Bibliography, p. 198-212. 651

Chapters on Blacks, Mexicans, Indians, Chinese, Japanese, and Pureto Ricans. Does not include groups of European origin.

BUENKER, John D., and BURCKEL, Nicholas C. <u>Immigration and ethnicity: a guide to information sources</u>. Detroit, Michigan: Gale Research, 1977. 305 p. (American government and history information guide series, v. 1). Author and subject index. 652

    1,468 annotated entries arranged by ethnic group or subject.

<u>ETHNIC studies bibliography</u>. v. 1- . (1975-). Pittsburgh, Pennsylvania: University of Pittsburgh. University Center for International Studies. 1977- (In conjunction with the Pennsylvania Ethnic Heritage Studies Center). 653

THOMPSON, Bryan. <u>Ethnic groups in urban areas: community formation and growth: a selected bibliography</u>. Monticello, Illinois: Council of Planning Librarians. Exchange bibliography, no. 202, 1971. 18 p. About 175 entries. 654

WARD, David. The ethnic ghetto in the United States: past and present, <u>Transactions, Institute of British Geographers</u>, n.s. v. 7, no. 3 (1982), p. 257-276. 69 bibliographical notes. 655

WEED, Perry L. <u>American ethnic groups: a selected retrospective list of publications</u>. Monticello, Illinois: Council of Planning Librarians. Exchange bibliography, no. 1158, 1976. 22 p. About 325 references. 656

KOLM, Richard. <u>Bibliography of ethnicity and ethnic groups</u>. Rockville, Maryland: National Institute of Mental Health, Center for Studies of Metropolitan Problems; for sale by Superintendent of Documents, U. S. Government Printing Office, 1973. 250 p. (DHEW publication no. (HSM) 73-9009). Index. 657

    Entries 1-451 are annotated; entries 501-1694 are unannotated. Since the arrangement is alphabetical the index must be used to locate topics or groups. Does not include American Negroes, American Indians, or Mexican Americans. Emphasis is on psychological aspects of adjustment and social aspects of community.

U. S. Bureau of Labor Statistics. <u>Directory of data sources on racial and ethnic minorities</u>. Washington, D. C.: Government Printing Office, 1975. 83 p. (U. S. Bureau of Labor Statistics. Bulletin 1879). Subject and report series indexes. 658

    Lists recent Federal Government publications on the social and economic characteristics of minority groups for the country as a whole and for selected areas based on household surveys, the 1970 census, <u>Current Population Surveys</u>, and other sources, arranged by racial or ethnic group: Black Americans; persons of Spanish ancestry; races other than Black; ethnic groups other than Spanish ancestry.

MESSNER, Stephen D., ed. <u>Minority groups and housing: a selected bibliography, 1950-67</u>. Storrs, Connecticut: University of Connecticut. Center for Real Estate and Urban Economic Studies. General series, no. 1. 1968. 60 p. Author index. 659

    About 700 references on housing arranged by topic sections: community and group action; discrimination and integration; brokerage, development and finance; costs and values; environmental; legislation and legal action; public housing and urban renewal; and materials for further research.

BOYCE, Byrl N., and TUROFF, Sidney. <u>Minority groups and housing: a bibliography, 1950-1970</u>. Morristown, New Jersey: General Learning Press, 1972. 202 p. Author and detailed subject indexes. 66

    Arranged by topics. Continues S. D. Messner, 1968 ed. [659]

NORTH, Jeannette H., and GRODSKY, Susan J. <u>Immigration literature: abstracts of demographic, economic, and policy studies</u>. Washington, D. C.: U. S. Department of Justice, Immigration and Naturalization Service, Office of Planning, Evaluation and Budgeting; for sale by the Superintendent of Documents, 1979. 89 p. 66

88 annotated entries for demographic studies; 173, for economic studies; 79, for brain drain studies; and 141, on policy studies.

RECENT immigration to the United States: the literature of the social sciences. Prepared by Paul Meadows and others. Washington, D. C.: Smithsonian Institution Press, 1976. 112 p. (Research Institute on Immigration and Ethnic Studies, Bibliographic studies, no. 1). 662

909 entries on immigration after World War II, arranged by broad subjects.

BUTTLAR, Lois, and WYNAR, Lubomyr. Building ethnic collections: an annotated guide for school media centers and public libraries. Littleton, Colorado: Libraries Unlimited, 1977. 434 p. Author index. Title index. Audiovisual index. 663

2,286 annotated entries. Particularly strong on reference sources, history, culture, and sociology.

GAGALA, Kenneth L. The economics of minorities: a guide to information sources. Detroit, Michigan: Gale Research, 1976. 212 p. (Economics information guide series, v. 2). Author, title, and subject indexes. 664

Annotated entries arranged by chapters: education, urbanization, housing, consumption, labor, economic development and inequality, governmental law and policy of Blacks in the United States; American Indians; and Spanish Americans.

b. Indians

CARLSON, Alvar W. A bibliography of the geographical literature on the American Indian, 1920-1971, Professional geographer, v. 24, no. 3 (1972), p. 258-263. 665

95 entries, with introductory discussion.

THORNTON, Russell, and GRASMICK, Mary K. Bibliography of social science research and writings on American Indians. Minneapolis, Minnesota: University of Minnesota. Center for Urban and Regional Affairs, 1979. 160 p. 666

List of articles in scholarly journals of history, sociology, geography, political science, economics, and American and ethnic studies, arranged by subject classification and author.

THORNTON, Russell, and GRASMICK, Mary K. Sociology of American Indians: a critical bibliography. Bloomington, Indiana: Indiana University Press for the Newberry Library, 1980. 113 p. (Newberry Library. Center for the History of the American Indian. Bibliographical series). 667

331 references discussed in a bibliographic essay by fields with an alphabetical list and index.

THORNTON, Russell, SANDEFUR, Gary D., and GRASMICK, Harold G. The urbanization of American Indians: a critical bibliography. Bloomington, Indiana: Indiana University Press for the Newberry Library. 1982. 87 p. (Newberry Library. Center for the History of the American Indian. Bibliographical series). Index. 668

RAMSTEDT, Wayne C. North American Indians in towns and cities: a bibliography. Monticello, Illinois: Vance bibliographies. Public Administration series: Bibliography, P-234, 1979. 74 p. About 850 references. 669

c. European Immigrants

(The literature is enormous. Only a few samples are here included).

BRYE, David L., ed. European immigration and ethnicity in the United States and Canada: a historical bibliography. Santa Barbara, California; Oxford, England: Clio Press, 1983. 458 p. Subject and author indexes.

United States, p. 1-209. 3,012 entries arranged by resources and general studies of immigration; response to immigration; immigrants and ethnics by groups; immigrants and ethnics by topics; and contemporary ethnicity.

CORDASCO, Francesco, and ALLOWAY, David N. American ethnic groups: the European heritage: a bibliography of doctoral dissertations completed at American universities. Metuchen, New Jersey: Scarecrow Press, 1981. 366 p. Index of names. Subject index. Bibliography, p. 333-337.

1,412 dissertations, arranged regionally by place of emigration.

KERESZTESI, Michael, and COCOZZOLI, Gary. German-American history and life: a guide to information sources. Detroit, Michigan: Gale Research, 1980. 372 p. (Ethnic studies information guide series, v. 4). Author, title, and subject indexes.

1,294 entries, mostly annotated, in classified arrangement, with major sections on reference works, the German-American experience, regional and state histories, history of special groups, and economic, social, cultural, and other characteristics.

TOLZMANN, Don Heinrich. German-Americana: a bibliography. Metuchen, New Jersey: Scarecrow Press, 1975. 384 p. Indexed.

More than 5,300 entries in classed arrangement.

MEYNEN, Emil. Bibliography on German settlements in colonial North America, especially on the Pennsylvania Germans and their descendants 1683-1933. Bibliographie des Deutschtums der Kolonialzeitlichen Einwanderung in Nordamerika, insbesondere der Pennsylvanien-Deutschen und ihrer Nachkommen 1683-1933. Leipzig: Otto Harrassowitz, 1937. 636 p. Index of authors. Index of surnames.

7,858 entries.

CORDASCO, Francesco. Italian Americans: a guide to information sources. Detroit, Michigan: Gale Research Co., 1978. 222 p. (Ethnic studies information guide series, v. 2). Author, title, and subject indexes.

About 1,500 references arranged by general, reference works, social sciences, history and regional studies, applied science, and humanities. Lists of newspapers and periodicals and of fraternal, professional, and religious organizations.

CORDASCO, Francesco, and CORDASCO, Michael V. Italians in the United States: an annotated bibliography of doctoral dissertations completed at American universities, with a handlist of selected published bibliographies, related reference materials, and guide books for Italian immigrants. Fairview, New Jersey: Junius Press, 1981. 229 p.

508 doctoral dissertations and master's theses with annotations, arranged in six chapters: Italians and the American experience; interethnic and related studies; emigration/immigration (history, politics, economics, and policy); miscellanea; selected published bibliographies and related reference works; and guide books for Italian emigrants.

VELIKONJA, Joseph. Italians in the United States: bibliography. Carbondale, Illinois. Southern Illinois University. Department of Geography. Occasional paper no. 1, 1963. 90 p.

ZURAWSKI, Joseph W. Polish American history and culture: a classified bibliography. Chicago, Illinois: Polish Museum of America, 1975. 218 p. Indexes. 678

About 1,700 entries arranged by subject classification.

d. Afro-Americans

(See also entries 461-465)

LYTLE, Elizabeth E. The geography of Black America, 1949-1980: a comprehensive bibliography. Monticello, Illinois: Vance bibliographies. Public administration series: Bibliography, no. P-924, 1982. 21 p. About 240 references. 679

DAVIS, George A., and DONALDSON, O. Fred. Blacks in the United States: a geographic perspective. Boston, Massachusetts: Houghton Mifflin, 1975. 270 p. Index. Bibliographies. 680

Bibliographies at ends of chapters: Introduction: Blacks in the United States, p. 6-7 (9 references); pre-civil war Black migration, p. 26-27 (21); post-civil war migration, p. 51, 91-93 (80); migrant labor, p. 107 (8); residential segregation, p. 148-153 (114); school segregation, p. 185-187 (39); geography as expressed in the Black humanities, p. 206-207 (27); Black America: colony or soulsville? p. 245-247 (41); summary, p. 251 (3). 342 references. Maps, tables, illustrations.

ERNST, Robert T. The geographical literature of black America, 1949-1972: a selected bibliography of journal articles, serial publications, theses, and dissertations. Monticello, Illinois: Council of Planning Librarians. Exchange bibliography, no. 492, 1973. 29 p. 681

About 300 entries arranged in 8 sections: general studies; racial research in places other than the United States; economic geography of race; spatial patterns of race and education; urban racial patterns; political-electoral geography of race; black population migration trends; and rural black geographic environments.

ERNST, Robert T., and HUGG, Lawrence, ed. Black America: geographic perspectives. Garden City, New York: Doubleday-Anchor Books, 1976. 438 p. Index. Bibliography, p. 409-425. 682

About 250 references, arranged by broad categories, as in entry 681.

ROSE, Harold M., ed. Contributions to an understanding of Black America. Economic geography, v. 48, no. 1 (Jan., 1972), p. 1-134. Special issue. 683

Bibliographies at end of each article. About 230 references.

ROSE, Harold, ed. Geography of the ghetto: perceptions, problems and alternatives. DeKalb, Illinois: Northern Illinois University Press, 1972. 273 p. (Perspectives in geography, 2). 684

Bibliographic footnotes or references at ends of individual articles.

CARLSON, Alvar W. A bibliography of the geographical literature on the American negro, 1920-1971. The Virginia geographer, v. 7, no. 1 (spring-summer 1972), p. 12-19. 685

169 references arranged in six sections including general and historic studies, regional studies, migration patterns, and negroes in urban and rural environments.

DESKINS, Donald R. Geographical literature on the American Negro 1949-1968: a bibliography, Professional geographer, v. 21, no. 3 (May, 1969), p. 145-149. 686

cont.

Studies of Ethnic Groups

58 entries on geographical studies arranged under (1) articles and abstracts in major American geographical periodicals, on the American Negro, (2) articles in such journals on racial issues outside the United States, (3) theses and dissertations. A further section, "Other literature on the American Negro" includes 86 entries arranged alphabetically by author.

LEY, David. The black inner city as frontier outpost: images and behavior of a Philadelphia neighborhood. Washington, D. C.: Association of American Geographers, 1974. 282 p. (Monograph series, no. 7). Bibliography, p. 271-282. 687

ENCYCLOPEDIA of Black America. W. Augustus Low, ed. Virgil A. Clift, assoc. ed. New York: McGraw-Hill, 1981. 921 p. Index. Bibliographies. 688

    Mainly biographical entries but with about 325 articles, many with bibliographies, on subjects such as Afro-American history, banks, bibliographies, business, civil disorders, civil rights, discrimination, education, employment, family, housing, literature, music, politics, population, poverty, race, segregation, slavery, and women.

U. S. Bureau of the Census. The social and economic status of the Black population in the United States: an historical view, 1790-1978. Washington, D. C.: U. S. Bureau of the Census; for sale by the Superintendent of Documents, 1979. 271 p. (Current population reports: Special studies, series P-23, no. 80). 689

    Statistical summary of changes in distribution, and demographic, social, political, economic, and other characteristics.

DAVIS, Lenwood G. The black family in the United States: a selected bibliography of annotated books, articles, and dissertations on black families in America. Westport, Connecticut: Greenwood Press, 1978. 132 p. Author and subject indexes. 690

    385 annotated entries arranged by type of material subdivided by subject.

PORTER, Dorothy B. The Negro in the United States: a selected bibliography. Washington, D. C.: Library of Congress. For sale by the Superintendent of Documents, U. S. Government Printing Office, 1970. 313 p. Author and subject index. 691

    1,781 entries with some annotations and call numbers in the Library of Congress or identification of other library in which a copy is located.

MILLER, Elizabeth W. The Negro in America; a bibliography. 2nd ed. Compiled by Mary L. Fisher. Cambridge, Massachusetts: Harvard University Press, 1970. 351 p. Author index. (1st ed. 1966. 190 p.). 692

    Classified list of books and articles, especially for the period 1954-1969.

e. Hispanic Americans

CARLSON, Alvar W. Mexican-Americans and a bibliography of the geographical literature: 1920-1971, Revista geografica (PAIGH), no. 75 (D 1971), p. 154-161. 48 references. 693

ROBINSON, Barbara J., and ROBINSON, J. Cordell. The Mexican American: a critical guide to research aids. Greenwich, Connecticut: JAI Press, 1980. 287 p. (Foundations in library and information science, v. 1). Author, title, and subject indexes. 694

    668 annotated entries arranged by general works (general bibliographies... statistical sources...); and subject bibliographies (education...history, labor... social and behavioral sciences...).

WOODS, Richard D. Reference materials on Mexican Americans: an annotated bibliography. Metuchen, New Jersey: Scarecrow Press, 1976. 190 p. Author, title, and subject indexes. 695

    387 annotated entries.

TREJO, Arnulfo D. Bibliografia Chicana: a guide to information sources. Detroit, Michigan: Gale Research, 1975. 193 p. Author and title indexes. 696

More than 300 annotated entries in classed arrangement within major divisions: reference works, humanities, social sciences, and history.

PINO, Frank. Mexican Americans: a research bibliography. East Lansing, Michigan: Michigan State University. Latin American Studies Center, 1974. 2 v. 631 p. 728 p. Author index in v. 2. 697

Interdisciplinary bibliography arranged in 35 subject categories. Bibliography, v. 1, p. 69-135. Geography, v. 1, p. 399-405.

STANFORD University. Center for Latin American Studies. The Mexican American: a selected and annotated bibliography. Luis G. Nogales, ed. 2nd ed. Stanford, California: Stanford University, 1971. 162 p. Subject index. (1st ed., 1969, 139 p.). 698

444 entries with detailed annotations, arranged by author.

CORDASCO, Francesco; BUCCHIONI, Eugene; and CASTELLANOS, Diego. Puerto Ricans on the United States mainland: a bibliography of reports, texts, critical studies and related materials. Totowa, New Jersey: Rowman and Littlefield, 1972. 146 p. Author index. 754 entries, partly annotated, arranged by general bibliographies, the island experience, migration to the mainland, and the mainland experience (conflict and acculturation, education, health, employment, and social needs). 699

f. Asian Americans

U, Elena S. H., MURATA, Alice K., and LIN, Chien. Bibliography of Pacific/Asian American materials in the Library of Congress. Chicago, Illinois: Pacific/Asian American Mental Health Research Center, 1982. 254 p. 700

Divided in 2 parts: Roman alphabet materials and non-roman alphabet materials, each arranged by national group. About 2,000 entries in roman alphabet and about 330 in non-roman scripts (Japanese, Chinese, Korean).

FUJIMOTO, Isao, SWIFT, Micheyo Yamaguchi, and ZUCKER, Rosalie. Asians in America: a selected annotated bibliography. Davis, California: University of California. Department of Applied Behavioral Sciences. Asian American Studies Division, 1971. 295 p. Geographical index. Author index. 701

Arranged by groups: Chinese (252 references), Japanese (359), Filipinos (48), East Indians (10), Koreans and Thais (4), General (92), bibliographies (27), and addendum.

5. CULTURAL GEOGRAPHY

a. General Studies

ZLINSKY, Wilbur. The cultural geography of the United States. Englewood Cliffs, New Jersey: Prentice-Hall, 1973. 164 p. (Foundations of cultural geography series). Bibliographical footnotes. Annotated bibliography, p. 141-155, arranged by topics. 702

DUNBAR, Gary S. Illustrations of the American earth: a bibliographical essay on the cultural geography of the United States. American studies: an international newsletter, v. 12, no. 1 (Autumn 1973), p. 3-15. Supplement to American quarterly, October 1973. 703

HART, John Fraser. The look of the land. Englewood Cliffs, New Jersey: Prentice-Hall, 1975. 210 p. (Foundations of cultural geography series). Index. Bibliographical footnotes. 704

MAN and cultural heritage. Papers in honor of Fred B. Kniffen, edited by H. J. Walker and W. G. Haag. Baton Rouge, Louisiana: Louisiana State University. School of Geoscience, Geoscience and man, v. 5, 1974. 235 p. References at the end of each paper.

GASTIL, Raymond D. Cultural regions of the United States. Seattle, Washington: University of Washington Press, 1975. 366 p. Index. Bibliographical note, p. 307-331, arranged by chapters. Bibliography, p. 333-357, arranged by region.

MEINIG, Donald W., ed. The interpretation of ordinary landscapes: geographical essays. New York: Oxford University Press, 1979. 255 p. Index. Bibliographical notes at end of each article.

    b. Settlements (See also Urban Geography [390-513]

GREEN, Jerry E., and MIDDAGH, Mark. Human settlement in the perspective of geography. Monticello, Illinois: Council of Planning Librarians. Exchange bibliography, no. 1161, 1976. 34 p.

 About 475 references in regional arrangement. United States, p. 14-22. 127 references.

RURAL settlement patterns in the United States as illustrated on 100 topographic quadrangle maps. Washington, D. C.: National Research Council. Committee to Select Topographic Quadrangles illustrating Cultural Geography, 1956. 52 p. (National Academy of Sciences- National Research Council Publication 380).

 Annotated list of 100 topographic sheets illustrating patterns of settlement in the United States arranged by 34 regions.

    c. Houses and Farm Buildings

JAKLE, John A., MEYER, Douglas K., and BASTIAN, Robert W. American common houses: a selected bibliography of vernacular architectures. Monticello, Illinois: Vance bibliographies. Architecture series: Bibliography, no. A-574, 1981. 28 p.

 About 400 references on house types in the United States and Canada.

JORDAN, Terry G. Texas log buildings: a folk architecture. Austin, Texas: University of Texas Press, 1978. 230 p. Index. Bibliography, p. 211-222.

CARLSON, Alvar W. Bibliography on barns in the United States and Canada. Pioneer America: the journal of historic American material culture [Louisiana State University. Department of Geography and Anthropology. Baton Rouge, Louisiana]. v. 10, no. 1 (1978), p. 65-71. 120 references, from 1940s to 1977.

CALKINS, Charles F. The Barn as an element in the cultural landscape of North America: a bibliography. Monticello, Illinois: Vance Bibliographies. Architecture Series: Bibliography, no. A-84. 1979. About 150 references.

NOBLE, Allen G. The farm silo: an annotated bibliography. Journal of cultural geography, Bowling Green, Ohio. v. 1. no. 2 (Spring/Summer 1981), p. 118-126.

    4. Other Special Studies

CARTER, George F. Earlier than you think: a personal view of man in America. College Station, Texas: Texas A and M University Press, 1980. 348 p. Index. Bibliography, p. 327-339.

 Challenging view of date of arrival and the paleolithic culture of the earliest inhabitants of the Americas.

ROONEY, John F., Jr. A geography of American sport: from Calvin Creek to Anaheim. Reading, Massachusetts: Addison-Wesley, 1974. 306 p. Index. Bibliography, p. 290-301.

LEWIS, Peirce F., LOWENTHAL, David, and TUAN, Yi-Fu. Visual blight in America. Washington, D. C.: Association of American Geographers, 1973. 48 p. (Commission on College Geography. Resource paper no. 23). Bibliographical footnotes. 717

e. Related Studies in Anthropology

ANNUAL review of anthropology. v. 1- , 1972- . Palo Alto, California: Annual Reviews, Inc., 1972- . Annual. Author and subject indexes. 718

Successor to Biennial review of anthropology. Chapters by specialists on current work and trends in archaeology, biological anthropology, lingusitics, regional anthropology, and cultural-social anthropology. Extensive bibliographies. Cumulative indexes of authors and chapter titles, for recent volumes in each volume.

BIENNIAL review of anthropology. v. 1-7, 1959-1971. Stanford, California: Stanford, University Press. 1959-1972. 719

Superseded by Annual review of anthropology [718].

ANTHROPOLOGICAL literature: an index to periodical articticles and essays. v. 1- (1979-). South Salem, New York: Redgrave Publishing Co., 1979- . Quarterly. Indexes by author, archeological site and culture, ethnic and linguistic group, and geographic area in each issue and annually. 720

Compiled by Tozzer Library, Peabody Museum of Archaeology and Ethnology, Harvard University. Subject index to articles in about a thousand serials or collected works arranged by broad fields.

6. POPULATION GEOGRAPHY

a. General Studies

SCHNELL, George A., and MONMONIER, Mark S. The study of population: elements, patterns, processes. Columbus, Ohio: Charles E. Nerrill, 1983. 371 p. Index. Notes and bibliographies at ends of chapters. 721

Examples from the United States. Utilizes the 1980 census.

ZLINSKY, Wilbur. A bibliographic guide to population geography. Chicago, Illinois: University of Chicago. Department of Geography. Research paper no. 80, 1962. 257 p. Author index. 722

The United States, p. 38-59, entries 371-595; p. 239, entries 2561-2563.

ZLINSKY, Wilbur. Recent publications on the distribution of population in the United States, Annals of the Association of American Geographers, v. 48, no. 4 December, 1958), p. 472-481. 723

Review of 16 monographs published 1950-1958.

SOURCEBOOK on population, Population bulletin, v. 25, no. 5 (November 1969). 31 p. 724

430 annotated references arranged by some 50 categories and subcategories. Not limited to the United States with some emphasis on U. S. data, programs, and publications.

SINK, Tine, VAN DER TAK, Jean, and ZUGA, Connie S. Sourcebook on population, 1970-1976. Washington, D. C.: Population Reference Bureau. 1976. 72 p. Index. 725

More than 900 annotated entries in classed arrangement. Not limited to U. S. but with emphasis on U. S. data, programs, and publications.

U. S. Commission on Population Growth and the American Future. Research reports. Washington, D. C.: Government Printing Office, 1972-1974. 7 v.

    v. 1. Demographic and social aspects of population growth. Edited by Charles F. Westoff and Robert Parke, Jr. 1972. 674 p.
    v. 2. Economic aspects of population change. Edited by Elliott R. Morss and Ritchie H. Reed. 1973. 379 p.
    v. 3. Population, resources, and the environment. Edited by Ronald G. Ridker. 1972. 377 p.
    v. 4. Governance and population: the governmental implications of population change. Edited by A. E. Keir Nash. 1972. 342 p.
    v. 5. Population, distribution, and policy. Edited by Sara Mills Mazie. 1973. 719 p.
    v. 6. Aspects of population growth policy. Edited by Robert Parke, Jr., and Charles F. Westoff. 1972. 607 p.
    v. 7. Statements at public hearings. 1974. 230 p.

_____. Report: Population and the American Future. Washington, D. C.: Government Printing Office, 1972. 186 p.

TAEUBER, Irene B., and TAEUBER, Conrad. People of the United States in the 20th Century. Prepared in cooperation with the Social Science Research Council. Washington, D. C.: U. S. Bureau of the Census. For sale by Superintendent of Documents, U. S. Government Printing Office, 1971. 1,046 p. (A 1960 census monograph). Bibliographical references. Index.

TAEUBER, Conrad, and TAEUBER, Irene B. The changing population of the United States. New York: Wiley, 1958. 357 p. (Social Science Research Council in cooperation with the U. S. Bureau of the Census. Census monograph series). Sources for national demographic statistics, p. 327-334. Bibliographical footnotes.

BOGUE, Donald J. The population of the United States. Glencoe, Illinois: The Free Press, 1959. 873 p. (Studies in population distribution, no. 14). Index. New edition in preparation.

b. Migration

CLARK, Gordon L. Interregional migration, national policy, and social justice. Totowa, New Jersey: Rowman and Allanheld, 1983. 191 p. Bibliography, p. 175-185.

ROSEMAN, Curtis C. Changing migration patterns within the United States. Washington, D. C.: Association of American Geographers, 1977. 34 p. (Resource papers for college geography, no. 77-2). Bibliography, p. 32-34.

JOHNSON, Gary T. Mobility, residential location, and urban change: a partially annotated bibliography. Chicago, Illinois: Council of Planning Librarians, CPL Bibliography, no. 48, 1981. 28 p. Key word index. About 200 references.

GOBER, Patricia. An annotated bibliography of population growth and migration of nonmetropolitan areas of the U. S. Monticello, Illinois: Vance bibliographies. Public administration series: Bibliography, no. P-419, 1980. 31 p. About 140 annotated references.

WEISS, Joseph E. A Bibliography on migration with special emphasis on sunbelt migration. Monticello, Illinois: Vance Bibliographies. Public Administration Series: Bibliography, no. P-371. 1979. 23 p. About 200 partly annotated references.

LEX, Barbara W. From south to north: cityward migration of low income whites in the twentieth century: part I. Monticello, Illinois: Council of Planning Librarians, Exchange bibliography, no. 907-908, 1975. 84 p. Part II, nos. 909-910. 1975. 169 p.

    About 2,100 references, arranged by topics.

PRICE, Daniel O., and SIKES, Melanie M. Rural-urban migration research in the United States: annotated bibliography and synthesis. Washington, D. C.: U. S. Public Health Service, National Institutes of Health, 1975. 250 p. New Publication no. (NIH) 75-565. (Center for Population Research Monograph). Index. 736

    1,232 entries alphabetically by author, primarily for 1950-1972. The topical index provides an entry by subject and region.

GREENWOOD, Michael J. Research on internal migration in the United States: a survey, Journal of economic literature, v. 13, no. 2 (June 1975), p. 397-433. 251 references with discussion. 737

SCHWIND, Paul J. Migration and regional development in the United States 1950-1960. Chicago, Illinois: University of Chicago. Department of Geography. Research paper no. 133, 1971. 170 p. Bibliography, p. 157-170. 738

    213 references arranged by topic: regional development, growth, and spatial structure (65); migration and spatial interaction (121); regions for analysis (9); methods of analysis (8); and census data sources (10).

c. Comprehensive Bibliography

POPULATION index. v. 1- , 1935- . Quarterly. Princeton, New Jersey: Princeton University. Office of Population Research, and Population Association of America. Quarterly. 739

    Annotated bibliography of books and periodical articles, arranged by subjects. Annual cumulations of author index and country index.

PRINCETON University. Office of Population Research. Population index bibliography. Cumulated 1935-1968, by authors and geographical areas. Boston, Massachusetts: G. K. Hall, 1971. 9 v. Authors index, 4 v. 3,148 p. About 81,800 entries. Geographical index, 5 v. 3,843 p. About 91,400 entries. 740

    The United States in Geographical index, v. 4, p. 70-544. Entries by topic, p. 70-453, by regions, p. 453-462, and by state, p. 462-544.

_____. _____. _____. Cumulated 1969-1981. 1983. 2 v. About 40,000 entries. 740a

7. MEDICAL GEOGRAPHY

a. General

PYLE, Gerald F. Applied medical geography. New York: John Wiley, 1979. 282 p. Index. Bibliographical references at end of each chapter. 741

MAYER, Jonathan D. "Relations between two traditions of medical geography: health systems planning and geographical epidemiology," Progress in human geography, v. 6, no. 2 (1982), p. 216-230. 64 references with commentary. 742

PYLE, Gerald F., ed. "Human health problems: spatial perspectives," Economic geography, v. 52, no. 2 (April, 1976). p. 95-191 (Special issue). Bibliographies at ends of articles. 743

HUNTER, John Melton, ed. The geography of health and disease. Chapel Hill, North Carolina: University of North Carolina. Department of Geography, 1974. 193 p. (Papers of the First Carolina geographical symposium. Studies in geography, no. 6). Bibliographies. 744

b. Health Care Services

ROSENBERG, Mark W. Accessibility to health care: a North American perspective, Progress in human geography, v. 7, no. 2 (1983), p. 78-87. 38 references with commentary. 745

De VISE, Pierre. Misused and misplaced hospitals and doctors: a locational analysis of the urban health care crises. Washington, D. C.: Association of American Geographers, 1973. 96 p. (Commission on college geography. Resource paper no. 22). Bibliography, p. 86-93. 746

SHANNON, Gary William, and DEVER, G. E. Alan. Health care delivery: spatial perspectives. New York: McGraw-Hill, 1974. 141 p. Bibliographical references. 747

PYLE, Gerald F. Heart disease, cancer, and stroke in Chicago: a geographical analysis with facilities, plans for 1980. Chicago, Illinois: University of Chicago. Department of Geography. Research paper no. 134, 1971. 292 p. Bibliography, p. 287-292. 748

    98 references arranged by topic: health care facilities planning (21); heart disease and stroke (17); cancer (18); characteristics of the hospital supply (14); methodology (28).

TRAVIS, Richard W., and HART, L. Gary. Physician and dental manpower distribution: a bibliography. Monticello, Illinois: Council of Planning Librarians. Exchange bibliography, no. 1362, 1977. 25 p. 749

    About 350 references under the following headings: general, national, state and regional, intra-urban, rural, migration, hospitals and location, and medical schools and location.

LEE, Joel M., and others. Factors influencing the rural location of doctors and students of dentistry, medicine, and osteopathy. Monticello, Illinois: Council of Planning Librarians. Exchange bibliography no. 1073, 1976. 40 p. About 325 annotated references. 750

c. Spatial Aspects and Ecology of Disease

BISSELL, H. Preston, FOUST, J. Brady, and LOOMBA, Bodh. Spatial aspects of mortality in the United States. Monticello, Illinois: Council of Planning Librarians. Exchange bibliography, no. 439, 1973. 39 p. About 450 entries. 751

SMITH, Christopher J. Geography and mental health. Washington, D. C.: Association of American Geographers, 1976. 51 p. Bibliography, p. 47-51. (Resource papers for college geography, no. 76-4). 752

8. POLITICAL GEOGRAPHY

a. General

BRUNN, Stanley D. Geography and politics in America. New York: Harper and Row, 1974. 443 p. Index. Bibliographic footnotes at ends of chapters. 753

COX, Kevin R. Conflict, power, and politics in the city: a geographic view. New York: McGraw-Hill, 1973. 133 p. Bibliographical footnotes. Bibliography, p. 133. 754

SANGUIN, André-Louis. Géographie politique: bibliographie internationale. Montréal: Les Presses de l'Université du Québec, 1976. 232 p. Index of authors. 755

    3,138 entries in classed arrangement. International in scope but includes many works on the United States.

b. Political Areal Organization

MORRILL, Richard L. Political redistricting and geographic theory. Washington, D. C.: Association of American Geographers, 1981. 76 p. (Resource publications in geography). Bibliography, p. 66-76. 756

HOGGART, Keith. Geography and local administration: a bibliography. Monticello, Illinois: Vance bibliographies, Public administration series. Bibliography no. P-530, 1980. 84 p. 757

1,005 references on political geography, territorial needs, spatial structure of local government, particularly in the United States and the United Kingdom.

WHITE, Anthony G. Local government boundary commissions: a revision of exchange bibliography 442. Monticello, Illinois: Council of Planning Librarians. Exchange bibliography, no. 1116, 1976. 10 p. More than 120 references. 758

VAN ZANDT, Franklin K. Boundaries of the United States and the several states with miscellaneous geographic information concerning areas, altitudes, and geographic centers. Washington, D. C., Government Printing Office, 1966. 291 p. (United States Geological Survey, Bulletin no. 1212). Bibliography, p. 275-284. Index. A revision of DOUGLAS, Edward M. Boundaries, areas, geographic centers and altitudes of the United States and the several states, with a brief record of important changes in their territory and government, 2nd ed. reproduced with corrections. Washington, D. C., Government Printing Office, 1939. 265 p. (U. S. Geological Survey, Bulletin no. 817). 1st ed., 1923. 2nd ed., 1932. 759

Standard work on the boundaries of the United States and of the individual states, including their histories and changes.

WHITE, Anthony G. A selected bibliography: city-county consolidation in the United States. Monticello, Illinois: Council of Planning Librarians. Exchange bibliography, no. 294. 1972. 53 p. About 700 references. 760

WHITE, Anthony G. City-county consolidation: a supplemental source to Bibliography no. 294. Monticello, Illinois: Council of Planning Librarians. Exchange bibliography, no. 417, 1973. 11 p. 65 references. 761

NOVAK, Benjamin. Selected bibliography on special districts and authorities in the United States, annotated. Washington, D. C., Government Printing Office, 1968. 57 p. (U. S. Department of Agriculture, Miscellaneous Publication no. 1087). Subject index. 250 annotated entries. 762

STETZER, Donald F. Special districts in Cook County: toward a geography of local government. Chicago, Illinois: University of Chicago. Department of Geography. Research paper no. 169. 1975. 177 p. Bibliography, p. 163-177. 245 references. 763

c. Other Special Studies

JOHNSTON, Ronald J. MacKENZIE, Alec, and WALDO, Kay Cronkite. The geography of Federal spending in the United States of America. Chichester, England; New York: John Wiley, 1980. 179 p. (Geographical research studies series, no. 2). Bibliography, p. 173-179. 764

HAYNES, Kingsley E. The role of modernization in the spatial diffusion of public policies in the United States between 1870 and 1970. Monticello, Illinois: Council of Planning Librarians. Exchange bibliography, no. 854. 1975. 41 p. 765

About 5,000 references to material published in the United States, 1870-1970, partly annotated, organized in 8 sections: (1) introduction and overview; (2) public policy determinants: economics, environment, or politics; (3) modernization in the United States: economic, political, and regional; (4) state planning and economic development: the role of states in modernization; (5) innovation

cont.

diffusion in the United States: selected empirical case studies; (6) diffusion models: interpretive structures; (7) modernization, regional development and diffusion: the case of the Third World; and (8) data sources.

SCHIFFMAN, Irving. The politics of land use planning: a review essay and annotated bibliography. Davis, California: University of California, Davis. Institute of Governmental Affairs and Institute of Ecology. Environmental quality series, no. 28, December 1977. 110 p. Annotated bibliography, p. 24-110. 766

    272 annotated references arranged by topics: the nature of urban growth and development; participants and politics in urban development; land use planning and zoning; land use planning and zoning politics; the politics of land use planning and zoning; the administration of the zoning ordinance; and critiques of municipal zoning and proposals for reform. Introductory review essay.

d. Related Studies in Political Science

HOLLER, Frederick L. Information sources of political science. 3rd ed. Santa Barbara, California: ABC-Clio Press, 1981. 278 p. Subject, author and title indexes. 767

    1,707 annotated entries arranged in 6 parts: general reference sources; social sciences; American government, politics, and public law; international relations and organizations, comparative and area studies; political theory; and public administration. Each part organized in a detailed classification indicated at the beginning of the part.

9. HISTORICAL GEOGRAPHY

a. Bibliographies and Guides

GRIM, Ronald E. Historical geography of the United States: a guide to information sources. Detroit, Michigan: Gale Research Co., 1982. 291 p. (Geography and travel information series, v. 5). Author, title, and subject indexes. 768

    686 annotated entries arranged by three major parts: cartographic sources; archival and other historical sources; and selected literature in historical geography. These are further divided into 20 chapters covering primary cartographic sources (cartographic reference aids; temperal listings; geographical listings; urban maps; and historical atlases); archival and other historical sources (archival reference aids; narrative sources; census records; land records; and pictorial sources); and selected literature in historical geography, mainly for the period 1965-1980 (general reference aids; periodicals and collections of essays; regional synthesis; exploration and frontier settlement; native Americans; land survey and tenure; economic activities; historical urban geography; historical cultural geography; and physical environment). For the literature of historical geography of the United States before 1965 see Douglas R. McManis. Historical geography of the United States: a bibliography [769].

McMANIS, Douglas R. Historical geography of the United States: a bibliography--excluding Alaska and Hawaii. Ypsilanti, Michigan: Eastern Michigan University, Division of Field Services, 1965. 249 p. 769

    3,551 numbered entries in regional arrangement: the United States as a whole, major regions (Northeastern, Southern, Northcentral, and Western states), and within each region by component states. Within each region or state arrangement is by eight major classifications: general, exploration and settlement, population characteristics, agriculture, trade and commerce, manufacture and industry, transportation and communication, and urban developments. Covers books, monographs, and periodical articles published in the United States through 1964. Part I covers prehistoric times. Part II covers historic times to 1900 A. D. Separate list of 53 unnumbered bibliographies. For publications 1964-1980 see Ronald E. Grim, Historical geography of the United States: a guide to information sources [768].

EHRENBERG, Ralph E., ed. Pattern and process: research in historical geography. Washington, D. C.: Howard University Press, 1975. 360 p. Appendix A: Bibliography to resources on historical geography in the National Archives, p. 315-349. (National Archives Conferences, v. 9. Papers and proceedings of the Conference on the National Archives and Research in Historical Geography). 770

About 260 finding aids on textual, pictorial, and cartographic records in the National Archives potentially useful for research in historical geography of the United States.

b. Surveys of Research in the Field

CONZEN, Michael P. "Historical geography: North American progress during the 1970s," Progress in human geography, v. 4, no. 4 (1980), p. 549-559. 771

86 references.

_____. Historical geography: changing spatial structure and social patterns," Progress in human geography, v. 7, no. 1 (1983), p. 88-107. 772

98 references.

CONZEN, Michael P. New geographies of the past: a register of research interests in and recent publications on American and related historical geography. Chicago, Illinois: University of Chicago, Department of Geography, for the Historical Geography Specialty Group of the Association of American Geographers, 1981. 56 p. Index. 773

Research interests and recent publications of more than 300 geographers.

CLARK, Andrew H. "Historical geography in North America," in Alan R. H. Baker, ed. Progress in historical geography. Newton Abbot, Devon, England: David and Charles; New York: John Wiley, 1972. p. 129-143. 63 bibliographical notes, p. 242-250. 774

CLARK, Andrew H. "Historical geography," chapter 3 in American geography: inventory and prospect, ed. by Preston E. James and Clarence F. Jones. Syracuse, New York: Syracuse University Press for the Association of American Geographers, 1954, p. 70-105. Bibliography, p. 96-105. 203 references. 775

MEINIG, Donald W. "The continuous shaping of America: a prospectus for geographers and historians," American historical review, v. 83, no. 5 (December 1978), p. 1186-1217. Bibliographical footnotes. 776

JAKLE, John A. "Time, space, and the geographic past: a prospectus for historical geography," American historical review, v. 76, no. 4 (October, 1971), p. 1084-1103. Bibliographical footnotes. 777

c. General Historical Geography of the United States

BROWN, Ralph H. Historical geography of the United States. New York: Harcourt, Brace, 1948. 596 p. Bibliographical index. Subject index. Bibliography, p. 539-571. Arranged by chapters. 778

WARD, David, ed. Geographic perspectives on America's past: readings on the historical geography of the United States. New York: Oxford University Press, 1979. 364 p. Bibliographical footnotes. Bibliographies, p. 113-114. 244-246, and 361-362. 779

EUROPEAN settlement and development in North America: essays on geographical change in honour and memory of Andrew Hill Clark. Edited by James R. Gibson. Toronto and Buffalo: University of Toronto Press, 1978. 230 p. Bibliographical footnotes. 780

Historical Geography   126

d. Studies in Topical Fields

(1) Settlements and Frontiers

COLONIZATION and settlement in the Americas: a selected bibliography. Compiled by
S. C. Wiley. Ottawa: Canada. Department of Mines and Technical Surveys. Geographical Branch. Bibliographical series, no. 25, 1960. 68 p.   781

About 400 references on the conterminous United States, p. 15-31 and on Alaska, p. 4-5.

MIKESELL, Marvin W. Comparative studies in frontier history, Annals of the Association of American Geographers, v. 50, no. 1 (March, 1960), p. 62-74. 65 bibliographical footnotes.   782

EDWARDS, Everett E. References on the significance of the frontier in American history, 2nd ed. Washington, D. C. 1939. 99 p. mimeographed. (U. S. Department of Agriculture. Library. Bibliographical contributions, no. 25 [1st ed., 1935]).783

(2) Immigration and Ethnicity

(See also Studies of Ethnic Groups, entries 646-701, p. 111-117)

EUROPEAN immigration and ethnicity in the United States and Canada: a historical bibliography. David L. Brye, ed. Oxford; Santa Barbara, California: Clio Press, 1983. 458 p. Subject index. Author index. List of periodicals. List of abstracts. List of abbreviations.   784

United States, p. 1-209, entries 1-3012. 3,012 references with abstracts for 1973-1979 in classed arrangement: resources and general studies of immigration; immigrants and ethnics by groups; immigrants and ethnics by topics; and contemporary ethnicity. Emphasis is on historical materials but includes studies also in geography, sociology, political science, economics, psychology, and literature.

(3) Cities

WARD, David. Cities and immigrants: a geography of change in nineteenth-century America. New York, London, and Toronto: Oxford University Press, 1971. 164 p. Index. Bibliography, p. 151-160.   785

PRED, Allan R. Urban growth and the circulation of information: the United States system of cities, 1790-1840. Cambridge, Massachusetts: Harvard University Press, 1973. 348 p. Index. Bibliographical notes.   786

PRED, Allan R. Urban growth and city-systems in the United States, 1840-1860. Cambridge, Massachusetts: Harvard University Press, 1980. 282 p. Index. Bibliographical notes, p. 233-276, arranged by chapters.   787

PRED, Allan R. The spatial dynamics of U. S. urban-industrial growth, 1800-1914: interpretive and theoretical essays. Cambridge, Massachusetts: M.I.T. Press, 1966. 225 p. (Regional science studies series, no. 6). Index. Bibliographical footnotes.   788

Three major sections: (1) American metropolitan growth: 1860-1914, industrialization, initial advantage; (2) industrial invention, industrial innovations; some locational relationships with urban growth; and (3) the American mercantile city: 1800-1840, manufacturing, growth, and structure.

(4) Agriculture

SCHLEBECKER, John T. Bibliography and pamphlets on the history of agriculture in the United States, 1607-1967. Santa Barbara, California: ABC (American Bibliographical Center)-Clio Press, 1969. 183 p. Index.   78

cont.

2,042 occasionally annotated entries, listed alphabetically by author. Detailed index provides an entry by subject.

EDWARDS, Everett E. A bibliography of the history of agriculture in the United States. Washington, D. C.: Government Printing Office, 1930. 307 p. (U. S. Department of Agriculture. (Miscellaneous publication no. 84). Index. (Reprinted: Detroit, Michigan: Gale Research, 1967). 790

Annotated entries in classed arrangement.

(5) Land Survey

PATTISON, William D. Beginnings of the American rectangular land survey system, 1784-1800. Chicago, Illinois: University of Chicago. Department of Geography. Research paper no. 50, 1957. 248 p. Bibliography, p. 235-248. 791

226 references arranged by categories: manuscripts and manuscript collections (28); published collections (42); published journals, reports and contemporary writings (21); surveying instructions (11); reference works (7); secondary accounts: books (49); secondary accounts: articles (43); newspaper (1); miscellaneous unpublished materials (6); maps and atlases (18).

THROWER, Norman J. W. Original survey and land subdivision: a comparative study of the form and effect of contrasting cadastral surveys. Washington, D. C.: Association of American Geographers, 1966. 160 p. (Association of American Geographers. Monograph, no. 4). Index. Bibliography, p. 137-145. 792

JOHNSON, Hildegard Binder. Order upon the land: the U. S. rectangular land survey and the upper Mississippi country. New York: Oxford University Press, 1976. 268 p. Index. Bibliographical notes arranged by chapters, p. 243-261. 793

WHITE, C. Albert. A history of the rectangular survey system. Washington, D. C.: U. S. Government Printing Office, 1983. 774 p. 793a

(6) Historic Preservation

JAKLE, John A., with the assistance of Virginia Oliver. Past landscapes: a bibliography for historic preservationists. (A revised edition). Monticello, Illinois: Vance bibliographies. Architecture series: Bibliography, no. A-314, 1980. 68 p. 794

About 800 references, arranged by subject: general survey; methodology; historic preservation as landscape management; the rural scene; the village and small town scene; the urban scene; the highway roadside; environmental images.

Revision of John A. Jakle. Past landscapes: a bibliography for historic preservationists selected from the literature of historical geography. Council of Planning Librarians. Exchange bibliography, no. 651, 1974. 56 p.

CLINE, William Eric. Historic preservation literature 1969-1977: selected references. Monticello, Illinois: Council of Planning Librarians. Exchange bibliography, no. 1457, 1978. 51 p. 291 references, especially on the Southwest of the United States and Arizona. 795

MELNICK, Robert A. Cultural and historic landscapes: a selected bibliography. Monticello, Illinois: Vance bibliographies. Architecture series: Bibliography, no. A-343, 1980. 26 p. 796

About 250 references arranged by: architecture; geography; historic preservation; landscape; planning; miscellaneous; and related bibliographies. Geography, p. 5-8 includes 45 references.

e. Regional Studies

(1) The Northeast

McMANIS, Douglas R. European impressions of the New England coast 1497-1620. Chicago, Illinois: University of Chicago. Department of Geography. Research paper no. 139, 1972. 147 p. Bibliography, p. 139-147. 797

   173 references arranged by primary (77) and secondary (96).

McMANIS, Douglas R. Colonial New England: a historical geography. New York: Oxford University Press, 1975. 159 p. Index. Bibliography, p. 149-155. 798

BROWN, Ralph H. Mirror for Americans: likeness of the Eastern Seaboard, 1810. New York: American Geographical Society, 1943. 312 p. (Special publication, no. 27). Reprinted New York: Da Capo Press, 1968. Index. Bibliography, p. 248-259. Bibliographical references included in Notes, p. 260-298. 799

LEMON, James T. The best poor man's country: a geographical study of early southeastern Pennsylvania. Baltimore, Maryland: Johns Hopkins Press, 1972. New York: W. W. Norton, 1976. 295 p. Index. Bibliographical notes, p. 229-283, arranged by chapters. 800

WACKER, Peter O. Land and people, a cultural geography of preindustrial New Jersey: origins and settlement patterns. New Brunswick, New Jersey: Rutgers University Press, 1975. 499 p. Index. Bibliography, p. 451-468. Footnotes, p. 419-450. 801

WACKER, Peter O. The Musconetcong Valley of New Jersey: a historical geography. New Brunswick, New Jersey: Rutgers University Press, 1968. 207 p. Bibliography, p. 185-197. Bibliographic notes, p. 163-184. 802

MITCHELL, Robert D., and MULLER, Edward K., eds. Geographical perspectives on Maryland's past. College Park, Maryland. University of Maryland. Department of Geography. Occasional paper no. 4, 1979. 187 p. Bibliographical footnotes. 803

EARLE, Carville V. The evolution of a tidewater settlement system: All Hallow's Parish, Maryland, 1650-1783. Chicago, Illinois: University of Chicago. Department of Geography. Research paper no. 170, 1975. 239 p. Bibliography, p. 231-239. 125 references. 804

(2) The South

MITCHELL, Robert D. Commercialism and frontier: perspectives on the early Shenendoah Valley. Charlottesville, Virginia: University Press of Virginia, 1977. 251 p. Index. Bibliographical footnotes. 805

MERRENS, Harry Roy. Colonial North Carolina in the eighteenth century: a study in historical geography. Chapel Hill, North Carolina: University of North Carolina Press, 1964. 293 p. Index. Bibliography, p. 266-288. 806

HILLIARD, Sam B. Hog meat and hoecake: food supply in the Old South, 1840-1860. Carbondale, Illinois: Southern Illinois University Press, 1972. 296 p. Index. Bibliographical notes, p. 239-286. 807

(3) The Middle West

JAKLE, John A. Images of the Ohio Valley: a historical geography of travel, 1740 to 1860. New York: Oxford University Press, 1977. 217 p. Index. Bibliography, p. 199-212. 808

McMANIS, Douglas R. The initial evaluation and utilization of the Illinois prairies, 1818-1840. Chicago, Illinois: University of Chicago. Department of Geography. Research paper no. 94, 1964. 109 p. Bibliography, p. 96-109. 809

242 references, arranged by categories of material: manuscripts and manuscript collections (54); contemporary published books (81); contemporary published articles (10); contemporary published magazines and newspapers (6); contemporary published maps (1); secondary materials: books and monographs (55); secondary materials; articles (30); and secondary materials: atlases and maps (5).

BLOUET, Brian W., and LAWSON, Merlin P., eds. Images of the plains: the role of human nature in settlement. Lincoln, Nebraska: University of Nebraska Press, 1975. 214 p. Bibliographies at ends of articles. 810

BLOUET, Brian W., and LUEBKE, Frederick C., eds. The Great Plains: environment and culture. Lincoln, Nebraska: University of Nebraska Press for the Center for Great Plains Studies of the University of Nebraska-Lincoln, 1979. 256 p. Bibliographical notes at the end of each article. [May be difficult to locate in some libraries as the Library of Congress lists under Cultural Heritage of the Plains Symposium, University of Nebraska-Lincoln, 1977. The Great Plains]. 811

LUEBKE, Frederick C., ed. Ethnicity on the Great Plains. Lincoln, Nebraska: University of Nebraska Press for the Center for Great Plains Studies of the University of Nebraska-Lincoln, 1980. 237 p. Index. Bibliographical notes at ends of articles. 812

HEWES, Leslie. The suitcase farming frontier: a study in historical geography of the central Great Plains. Lincoln, Nebraska: University of Nebraska Press, 1973. 281 p. Index. Bibliography, p. 257-271. 813

MALIN, James C. The grassland of North America: prolegomena to its history, with addenda and postscript. Lawrence, Kansas: The author, 1956. Gloucester, Massachusetts: Peter Smith, 1967. 490 p. Bibliographies. (First published Lawrence, Kansas: The Author, 1947. 398 p.). Bibliography, p. 336-397. 814

(4) Texas and the Southwest

MEINIG, Donald W. Imperial Texas: an interpretive essay in cultural geography. Austin, Texas: University of Texas Press, 1969. 145 p. Index. Bibliography, p. 125-136. 815

JORDAN, Terry G. German seed in Texas soil: immigrant farmers in Nineteenth-Century Texas. Austin, Texas: University of Texas Press, 1966. 237 p. Index. Bibliography, p. 207-227. 816

JORDAN, Terry G. Trails to Texas: southern roots of Western cattle ranching. Lincoln, Nebraska: University of Nebraska Press, 1981. 220 p. Index. Bibliographic notes, p. 159-190. Bibliography, p. 191-214. 817

MEINIG, Donald W. Southwest: Three peoples in geographical change 1600-1970. New York: Oxford University Press, 1971. 151 p. Index. Bibliography, p. 135-144. 818

(5) Exploration and Fur Trade of the West (See also entry 927)

GILBERT, E. W. Exploration of the western America, 1800-1850. Cambridge, England: Cambridge University Press, 1933. Reprinted New York: Cooper Square, 1966. 233 p. Index. Bibliography, p. 203-220. 819

ALLEN, John Logan. Passage through the garden: Lewis and Clark and the image of the American Northwest. Urbana, Illinois: University of Illinois Press, 1975. 412 p. Index. Bibliography, p. 399-405. Bibliographical footnotes. 820

WISHART, David J. The fur trade of the American West, 1807-1840: a geographical synthesis. Lincoln, Nebraska: University of Nebraska Press, 1979. 237 p. Index. Bibliography, p. 219-230. 821

(6) The Pacific Northwest and Alaska (See also entry 963)

MEINIG, Donald W. The Great Columbia Plain: a historical geography. 1805-1910. Seattle, Washington: University of Washington Press, 1968. 576 p. Index. Bibliography, p. 519-551. 822

DICKEN, Samuel N., and DICKEN, Emily F. The making of Oregon: a study in historical geography. Portland, Oregon: Oregon Historical Society, 1979. 208 p. (Two centuries of Oregon geography, v. 1). Index. Bibliographical notes, p. 191-197, arranged by chapters. [See also entry 962]. 823

GIBSON, James R. Imperial Russia in frontier America: the changing geography of supply of Russian America, 1784-1867. New York: Oxford University Press, 1976. 257 p. Index. Bibliographic notes, p. 218-238. Bibliography, p. 239-248. 824

f. Related Studies in American History

AMERICA: history and life (ABC-Clio Information Service), Santa Barbara, California, 1- (1965-). In four parts. Part A. Article abstracts and citations. 3 nos. a year. Part B. Index to book reviews. 2 nos. a year. Part C. American history bibliography. Bibliography of articles cited in Part A, new books cited in Part B, and Dissertations. Part D. Annual index. Cumulative subject and author indexes to Parts A, B, and C, book review index, book title index, list of abstractors, and list of periodicals. Cumulative 5-year indexes, v. 1-5 (1964-1969); v. 6-10 (1969-1973), and v. 11-15 (1974-1978), and Supplement to volumes 1-10 (1964-1973). 825

Supplemented by America: history and life: a guide to periodical literature. Volume 0 (1972. 537 p.), which from the 51,213 abstracts which appeared in Historical abstracts, v. 1-15 (1955-1969), selected 6,154 which relate to American and Canadian history and studies, and thus expands the coverage of America: history and life to include the periodical literature abstracted from 1954 to 1963.

CASSARA, Ernest. History of the United States of America: a guide to information sources, Detroit, Michigan: Gale Research, 1977. 459 p. (American studies information guide series, v. 3). Author and short title index. Subject index. 826

1,995 annotated entries, arranged by chronological period chapters, except for chapter 1. Aids to research and chapter 2. Comprehensive histories.

HARVARD guide to American history, ed. by Frank Freidel. rev. ed. Cambridge, Massachusetts: Belknap Press of Harvard University Press, 1974. 2 v. 1,290 p. Name index. Subject index. 827

Entries in v. 1 are arranged by subjects with many subdivisions. Entries in v. 2 are chronological.

10. GEOGRAPHY OF RECREATION, LEISURE, and TOURISM

LANCASTER, Joel R., and NICHOLS, Leland J. A selected bibliography of geographical references and related research in outdoor recreation and tourism, 1930-1971. Monticello, Illinois: Council of Planning Librarians. Exchange bibliography, no. 190, 1971. 41 p. 828

About 600 entries. Books, articles in geographical journals or by geographers, geographical theses and dissertations, government publications, studies in related fields of tourism, and bibliographies.

TRAVIS, Richard W. The spatial organization of recreation: a bibliography of theses and dissertations on the geography of recreation. Monticello, Illinois: Council of Planning Librarians. Exchange bibliography, no. 350, 1972. 18 p. Activities index. Location index. 829

197 numbered entries listing master's theses and doctoral dissertation in universities of the United States and Canada on the geography of recreation, 1950-1971. Organized in sections: environmental impact; economic effects; resource inventories and potentials; travel and hinterlands; legislation; location; perception; and planning.

POST, Joyce A., and POST, Jeremiah B. Travel in the United States: a guide to information sources. Detroit, Michigan: Gale Research, 1981. 578 p. Indexes for authors, titles, subjects, places, organization, and publishers. (Geography and travel information guide series, v. 3). 830

About 2,000 annotated references for prospective travelers, arranged by areas from large to small, mostly individual states, by categories: books, atlases, and magazines; maps; specialized publishers; major tourist organizations; regional tourism; associations; other organizations; information centers and phones; outdoor recreation activities; national and state parks; forests; and individual cities or areas.

GOELDNER, Charles R., and DICKE, Karen. Bibliography of tourism and travel research studies, reports, and articles. Boulder, Colorado: University of Colorado, Graduate School of Business Administration, Business Research Division in cooperation with The Travel Research Association, 1971. 3 v. 831

v. 1. National and regional, 122 p. Index.
v. 2. State studies, 135 p. Index.
v. 3. Foreign, 114 p. Index.
Entries are annotated.

PINKERTON, James R., and PINKERTON, Marjorie J. Outdoor recreation and leisure: a reference guide and selected bibliography. Columbia, Missouri: University of Missouri, School of Business and Public Administration, Research Center, 1969. 332 p. Author index. Title index. 832

MEYERSOHN, Rolf. International selective bibliography on leisure. Part 1. USA (1966-1972). Praha: European Centre for Leisure and Education. Bibliography series, no. 7, 1973. 57 p. Author index. Index of periodicals. (Amsterdam: Swets and Zeitlinger, 1976). 833

300 entries arranged by fields.

IVY, Joy. The concept and determination of carrying capacity of recreational land in the USA. A review of relevant literature up to the end of September 1971, together with a bibliography on the ecological effects of recreational activities. Perth, Scotland: Countryside Commission for Scotland. Occasional paper no. 3, 1972. 58 p. Bibliogtaphy, p. 33-58. 834

STANKEY, George H., and LIME, David W. Recreational carrying capacity: an annotated bibliography. Ogden, Utah: U. S. Forest Service. Intermountain Forest and Range Experiment Station, Forest Service General Technical Report INT-3, 1973. 45 p. 835

INKLEY, Clark. Estimating recreation benefits: a critical review and bibliography. Monticello, Illinois: Council of Planning Librarians. Exchange bibliography, no. 1219. 1977. 35 p. About 300 references, mainly on the United States. 836

CORDELL, Harold K. The state-of-the-art in developing and operating intensive-use natural resource recreation sites. Monticello, Illinois: Council of Planning Librarians, Exchange bibliography, no. 1072, 1976. 29 p. 147 references, with discussion of definition of public-use objectives; plan site development; site construction; and operation and maintenance. 837

JOHNSON, Julia, and DUNNING, Glenna. Land planning in national parks and forests: a selective bibliography. Monticello, Illinois: Council of Planning Librarians. Exchange bibliography, no. 1291-1292, 1977. 68 p. Subject index. 297 annotated references 1970-1975, to government publications and to journal articles. 838

ORR, James F., and ROWNTREE, Rowan A. The American national park system: a selected review. Monticello, Illinois: Vance Bibliographies. Public Administration Series: Bibliography no. P-168, 1979. 64 p. 839

About 600 references organized by: general history, character, and issues; specific units and locations; and topical issues.

VOGELER, Ingolf. Bibliography of rural recreation. Monticello, Illinois: Council of Planning Librarians. Exchange bibliography, no. 1094, 1976. 9 p. 105 references. 840

BARKAUSKAS, Mary Ellen. Hiking and hiking trails: a trails and trail-based activities bibliography. Washington, D.C.: U. S. Department of the Interior. Office of Library Services, 1970. 57 p. (Bibliography series no. 20). Index. 470 entries. 841

DITTON, Robert B. Water-based recreation: access, water quality, and incompatible use considerations: an interdisciplinary bibliography. Monticello, Illinois: Council of Planning Librarians. Exchange bibliography, no. 193, 1971. 46 p. 842

About 250 references arranged by key words: access; federal grants; health guidelines; multiple use; public laws; public rights; riparian rights; shoreland and lake zoning; water quality criteria; water quality maintenance; water quality standards; water pollution; water reuse.

ANDERSON, Dorothy H., LEATHERBERRY, Earl C., and LIME, David W. An annotated bibliography on river recreation. St. Paul, Minnesota: U. S. Department of Agriculture. Forest Service. North Central Forest Experiment Station, 1978. 62 p. (USDA Forest Service general technical report NC-41. 62 p.). Author index. 843

355 entries arranged by subjects such as bibliographies, river resources, inventory, economic evaluations, environmental impacts, use and users, management, Federal legislation, and selected guidebooks.

KLAIN, Ambrose, and PHELAN, Dennis M. Second homes, vacation homes: potentials, impacts and issues: an annotated bibliography. Monticello, Illinois: Council of Planning Librarians. Exchange bibliography, no. 839. 1975. 35 p. About 200 references. 844

11. GEOGRAPHIC EDUCATION

BALL, John M. A bibliography for geographic education. Athens, Georgia: University of Georgia, 1976. 113 p. (Geography curriculum project, no. 2). (1st ed., 1969. 91 p.). 845

Curriculum and teaching methods in geography in the United States.

12. APPLIED GEOGRAPHY

FRAZIER, John W., ed. Applied geography: selected perspectives. Englewood Cliffs, New Jersey: Prentice-Hall, 1982. 333 p. Index. Bibliographical notes at the end of each article. 846

13. PLACE NAMES

SEALOCK, Richard B., SEALOCK, Margaret M., and POWELL, Margaret S. Bibliography of place-name literature, United States and Canada. 3rd ed. Chicago, Illinois: American Library Association, 1982. 435 p. Author and personal name index. Subject index. 847

4,830 numbered entries arranged by states and provinces. United States, p. 1-309, entries 1-3941.

14. GENERAL GUIDES TO THE SOCIAL SCIENCES

SHEEHY, Eugene P., with the assistance of Rita G. Keckeissen and Eileen McIlvaine. Guide to reference books. 9th ed. Chicago: American Library Association, 1976. 1,015 p. 848

    Section C. Social Sciences, p. 497-596, including CA general works, CB education, CC sociology, CD anthropology and ethnology, CG statistics, CH economics, CJ political science, CK law, and CL geography. Section DB history and area studies, especially, DB the Americas: United States, p. 611-620.

_____. _____. Supplement, 1980. 305 p. Same sections. Covers 1974-1978. 849

_____. _____. Second supplement, 1982. 243 p. Same sections. Covers 1978-1981. 850

SOCIAL sciences index. v. 1- , 1907- . New York: Wilson. Quarterly. Annual cumulations (April to March). Cumulations, v. 1-17 (1907-March 1964) covered multiple years. v. 1-18 (1907-March 1965)as International index to periodicals; v. 19-27 (April 1965-March 1974) as Social sciences and humanities index. 851

    Author and subject index to about 300 scholarly periodicals in the social sciences in the fields of anthropology, economics, environmental studies, geography, law and criminology, planning and public administration, political science, psychology, social aspects of medicine, sociology, and related subjects.

PUBLIC Affairs Information Service (PAIS). Bulletin. New York, v. 1- , 1915- . Issued in weekly bulletins; cumulations five times a year, and a fifth cumulated issue which forms the permanent annual volume. 852

    A highly useful subject index to the literature on topics of current public concern, valuable in gleaning from a wide network materials relevant to the topics included in the index.

WHITE, Carl M., and others. Sources of information in the social sciences: a guide to the literature. 2nd ed. Chicago, Illinois: American Library Association, 1973. 702 p. Index. (1st ed., Totowa, New Jersey: Bedminster Press, 1964. 498 p.). 853

    Arranged by fields: social science literature; history; geography; economics and business administration; sociology; anthropology; psychology; education; and political science. Each chapter consists of two parts: a discussion of basic works in the discipline and guides to the literature. 3rd edition in preparation edited by William H. Webb, is expected to be published in the fall of 1984.

HOSELITZ, Bert F., ed. A reader's guide to the social sciences. Rev. ed. New York: The Free Press, 1970. 425 p. General bibliography, p. 319-425. (1st ed., 1959). 854

    General bibliography, arranged by fields: sociology; anthropology; psychology; political science, economics, and geography. Textual discussion of the major fields: sociology by Peter M. Blau and Joan W. Moore, p. 1-40; anthropology by Gail M. Kelly, p. 41-90; psychology by Water R. Reitman, p. 91-127; political science, p. 129-237; economics by Bert F. Hoselitz, p. 239-291; and geography by Norton Ginsburg, p. 293-318.

McINNIS, Raymond G., and SCOTT, James W. Social science research handbook. New York: Barnes and Noble, a division of Harper and Row, 1974. 395 p. Bibliography, p. 309-395. 855

    Includes both extensive bibliography and a textual discussion of disciplinary studies: social sciences: general works, p. 1-20; anthropology, p. 21-33; demography, p. 34-42; economics, p. 43-59; geography, p. 60-80; history, p. 81-99; political science, p. 100-123; sociology, p. 124-140, and area studies, by regions, p. 141-304.

    See especially, Part O. American studies, p. 246-282.

WALFORD, Albert John, with the assistance of Joan M. Harvey and L. J. Taylor. Walford's guide to reference material. v. 2. Social and historical sciences, philosophy and religion. 4th ed. London: The Library Association, 1982. 812 p. 856

Section 3, Social Sciences, p. 80-364, including, 31, statistics, 32, political science, 33, economics, 34, law, 35, public administration, 36, social relief and welfare, insurance, 37, education, and 38, commerce.

IV. REGIONS OF THE UNITED STATES

1. REGIONS AND REGIONALISM IN GENERAL

PATERSON, John H. Writing regional geography: problems and progress in the Anglo-American realm, Progress in geography, v. 6, 1974, p. 1-26. Bibliography p. 24-26. 48 references with commentary on the problem of writing regional geography. 857

ODUM, Howard W., and MOORE, Harry E. American regionalism: a cultural-historical approach to national integration. New York: Holt, 1938. Reprinted Gloucester, Massachusetts: Peter Smith, 1966. 693 p. Index. Bibliography, p. 643-675. 858

2. THE NORTHEAST

a. General

GOTTMANN, Jean. Megalopolis: the urbanized northeastern seaboard of the United States. New York: Twentieth Century Fund, 1961. Cambridge, Massachusetts: MIT Press, 1964. 810 p. Bibliographical footnotes. 859

ALEXANDER, Lewis M. The Northeastern United States. 2nd ed. New York: Van Nostrand, 1976. 142 p. Index. Bibliography, p. 131-133. (1st ed., 1967. 123 p.). 860

WESTVIEW Press, Boulder, Colorado, has announced plans for the publication in 1984 or later, of the following volumes in the series, Geographies of the United States, edited by Ingolf K. Vogeler: 861

    NEW HAMPSHIRE, by William H. Wallace.
    CONNECTICUT, by Tom Lewis and John E. Harmon.
    NEW YORK, by Richard T. Lewis.
    PENNSYLVANIA, by Chester E. Zimolzak.
    WEST VIRGINIA, by Thomas D. Hankins.

b. New England

WRIGHT, John K., ed. New England's Prospect: 1933. New York: American Geographical Society, 1933. 502 p. (Special Publication no. 16). Index. Bibliographies at ends of articles. 862

ESTALL, Robert C. New England: a study in industrial adjustment. London: Bell, New York: Praeger, 1966. 296 p. Index. Footnotes at ends of chapters. 863

U. S. Department of Commerce. Office of Regional Economic Development. New England development bibliography. Washington, D. C. 1966. 437 p. 864

    Many references on agriculture, economic development, fisheries, forestry, geography, housing, industries, natural resources, planning, population, recreation, transportation, and other topics.

ANCTIL, Pierre. Bibliographie commentée sur les Franco-Américains de la Nouvelle-Angleterre, Les Cahiers de géographie de Québec, v. 23, no. 58 (1979), p. 179-182. 865

    23 annotated references on French Americans of New England.

CONZEN, Michael P., and LEWIS, George K. Boston: a geographical portrait. Cambridge, Massachusetts: Ballinger, 1976. 87 p. Bibliography, p. 83-86. Also in Contemporary metropolitan America [390], v. 1, p. 51-138. 866

MEYER, David R. From farm to factory to urban pastoralism: urban change in Central Connecticut. Cambridge, Massachusetts: Ballinger, 1976. 57 p. Bibliography, p. 55-56. Also in Contemporary metropolitan America [390], v. 1, p. 291-348. 867

c. The Middle Atlantic States

THOMPSON, John H., ed. Geography of New York State, 2nd ed. Syracuse, New York: Syracuse University Press, 1977. 543 p. Index. Bibliographies at end of each chapter. (1st ed. 1966). 868

O'BRIEN, Raymond J. American sublime: landscape and scenery of the lower Hudson valley. New York: Columbia University Press, 1981. 353 p. Index. Bibliography, p. 333-347. 868a

CAREY, George W. A vignette of the New York-New Jersey metropolitan region. Cambridge, Massachusetts: Ballinger, 1976. 75 p. Bibliography, p. 73-74. Also in Contemporary metropolitan America [390], v. 1, p. 139-216. 869

BERGMAN, Edward F., and POHL, Thomas W. A geography of the New York metropolitan region. Dubuque, Iowa: Kendall/Hunt, 1975. 205 p. Bibliography, p. 203-205. 870

NEW YORK metropolitan region study. Cambridge, Massachusetts: Harvard University Press. 1959-1960. 10 v. 871

STANSFIELD, Charles A., Jr. New Jersey: a geography. Boulder, Colorado: Westview Press, 1983. 245 p. Index. Bibliography, p. 231-235. 872

KELLAND, Frank A., and KELLAND, Marilyn C. New Jersey: garden or suburb? a geography of New Jersey. Dubuque, Iowa: Kenall/Hunt, 1978. 250 p. Index. Bibliography, p. 243-244. 873

BRUSH, John E. The population of New Jersey, 2nd ed. New Brunswick, New Jersey: Rutgers University Press, 1958. 123 p. (1st ed., 1956. 114 p.). Bibliographical footnotes. 874

MULLER, Peter O., MEYER, Kenneth C., and CYBRIWSKY, Roman A. Metropolitan Philadelphia: a study of conflicts and cleavages. Cambridge, Massachusetts: Ballinger, 1976. 73 p. Bibliography, p. 69-72. Also in Contemporary metropolitan America [390], v. 1, p. 217-290. 875

VERNON, Philip H., and SCHMIDT, Oswald. Metropolitan Pittsburgh: old trends and new directions, in Contemporary metropolitan America: twenty geographical vignettes [390]. Cambridge, Massachusetts: Ballinger, 1976. v. 3. p. 1-59. Bibliography, p. 59. 876

d. Border States

DILISIO, James E. Maryland: a geography. Boulder, Colorado: Westview Press, 1983. 233 p. Index. Bibliography, p. 219-224. 877

OLSON, Sherry H. Baltimore. Cambridge, Massachusetts: Ballinger, 1976. 93 p. Bibliography, p. 91-93. Also in Contemporary metropolitan America [390] v. 2, p. 1-95. 878

THOMAS, Jean-Claude Marceau. Washington, D. C., in Contemporary metropolitan America: twenty geographical vignettes [390], Cambridge, Massachusetts: Ballinger, 1976. v. 4, p. 297-344. Bibliography, p. 343-344. 879

ADKINS, Howard G., EWING, Steve, and ZIMOLZAK, Chester E. West Virginia and Appalachia: selected readings. Dubuque, Iowa: Kendall/Hunt, 1977. 199 p. Bibliographies. 880

3. THE SOUTH

a. General

HART, John Fraser. The South, 2nd ed. New York: Van Nostrand, 1976. 166 p. (New searchlight series). Index. Bibliography, p. 155-157. (1st ed. The Southeastern United States, 1967. 106 p.). 881

PARKINS, Almon E. The South: its economic-geographic development. New York: John Wiley, 1938. 528 p. Reprinted Westport, Connecticut: Greenwood Press, 1970. Index. Bibliography, p. 506-518. 882

VANCE, Rupert B. Human geography of the South: a study in regional resources and adequacy. Chapel Hill, North Carolina: University of North Carolina Press. 1932. 596 p. 2nd ed., 1935. 596 p. Index. Bibliography, p. 512-579. Reprinted New York: Russell and Russell, 1968. 883

ODUM, Howard W. Southern regions of the United States. Chapel Hill, North Carolina: University of North Carolina Press, 1936. 664 p. Index. Bibliography and source materials, p. 605-620. 884

POLOVITSKAIA, M. E. Ekonomicheskie raiony SShA: Iug (Economic regions of the USA: the South). Moskva: Geografgiz, 1956. 609 p. Bibliography, p. 478-494. About 350 references. 884a

ANDERSON, James R. A geography of agriculture in the United States' Southeast. Budapest, Hungary: Akadémiai Kiadó, 1973. 136 p. (Geography of world agriculture, 2). Bibliographical references, p. 132-136. 885

BRAND, Ulrich. Die Entwicklung der Industrie in den Südstaaten der USA. Unter besonderer Berücksichtigung der petrochemischen Industrie. Marburg: Geographisches Institut der Universität. Marburger geographische Schriften, v. 36, 1968. 236 p. Bibliography, p. 197-233. 886

WESTVIEW Press, Boulder, Colorado, has announced plans for the publication in 1984, or later, of the following volumes in the series, Geographies of the United States, edited by Ingolf K. Vogeler: 887

NORTH CAROLINA, by Ole Gade and H. Daniel Stillwell.
SOUTH CAROLINA, by Charles F. Kovacik and John J. Winberry.
MISSISSIPPI, by Jesse O. McKee.
LOUISIANA, by Henry W. Bullamore and others.

b. South Atlantic States

BUSHONG, Allen D. Research on the Southeast by geographers, 1946-1967, Southeastern geographer, v. 9, no. 1 (April 1969), p. 48-84. 888

505 references with analysis of form of publication, theses and dissertations, geographical journals, geographical areas investigated, and subject fields.

GOTTMANN, Jean. Virginia in our century. New printing with supplementary chapter. Charlottesville, Virginia: University Press of Virginia, 1969. 656 p. Index. Bibliographical suggestions, p. 625-635. Bibliographical footnotes. (1st ed., 1955. 584 p.). 889

PETTY, Julian J. A bibliography of the geography of the state of South Carolina. Columbia, South Carolina: University of South Carolina. Research Committee, 1952. 126 p. (University of South Carolina publications. Ser. 2. Physical sciences. Bulletin no. 2). 890

HARTSHORN, Truman A., and others. Metropolis in Georgia: Atlanta's rise as a major transaction center. Cambridge, Massachusetts: Ballinger, 1976. 73 p. Bibliography, p. 67-71. Also in Contemporary metropolitan America [390], v. 4, p. 151-225. 891

PÖTKE, Peter Michael. Retirement und Tourismus an der Westküste Floridas. Bochum: Geographisches Institut der Ruhr Universität. Materialien zur Raumordnung. Band 13, 1973. 225 p. Bibliography, p. 167-199. Preface and summary in English. 892

LONGBRAKE, David B., and NICHOLS, Woodrow W., Jr. Sunshine and shadows in metropolitan Miami. Cambridge, Massachusetts: Ballinger, 1976. 65 p. Bibliography, p. 63-64. Also in Contemporary metropolitan America [390], v. 4, p. 41-106. 893

c. Kentucky and Tennessee

ZIMMER, Dietrich M. Die Industrialisierung der Bluegrass Region von Kentucky. Heidelberg: Geographisches Institut der Universität. Heidelberger geographische Arbeiten, Heft 31, 1970. 196 p. Bibliography, p. 165-177. English summary, p. 161-164. 894

VOLLMAR, Rainer. Regionalplanung in den USA. Das "Appalachian Regional Development Program" am Beispiel von Ost-Kentucky. Berlin: Geographisches Institut der Freien Universität. Abhandlungen. Anthropogeographie, Heft 25, 1976. 196 p. Summary in English. 895

FULLERTON, Ralph O., Jr. and RAY, John B., eds. Tennessee: geographical patterns and regions. Dubuque, Iowa: Kendall/Hunt, 1977. 150 p. Bibliography, p. 127-129. 896

d. Louisiana

HILLIARD, Sam B., ed. Man and environment in the lower Mississippi valley. Baton Rouge, Louisiana: Louisiana State University. School of Geoscience. Geoscience and man, v. 19, 1978. 165 p. Bibliographies at ends of articles. 897

COMEAUX, Malcolm L. Atchafalaya swamp life: settlement and folk occupations. Baton Rouge, Louisiana: Louisiana State University. School of Geoscience. Geoscience and man, v. 2, 1972. 111 p. Index. Bibliography, p. 103-106. 898

LEWIS, Peirce F. New Orleans: the making of an urban landscape. Cambridge, Massachusetts: Ballinger, 1976. 115 p. Bibliography, p. 111-114. Also in Contemporary metropolitan America [390], v. 2, p. 97-216. 899

e. Texas

JORDAN, Terry G., with BEAN, John L., Jr., and HOLMES, William M. Texas. Boulder, Colorado: Westview Press, 1983. 450 p. Index. Bibliographies. 900

WRIGHT, Rita J., ARBINGAST, Stanley A., CHANDLER, Robert, and GREEN, Paul. Texas sources: a bibliography. Austin, Texas: University of Texas. Bureau of Business Research, Bibliography series no. 17, 1976. 67 p. 901

Includes sections on agriculture, area economic surveys, cities and towns, climatology, forest and forestry, industry, maps and atlases, marine resources, mines and mineral resources, periodicals, population, ports, regions, tourism, transportation, water, and other topics.

PALMER, Martha E., and RUSH, Marjorie N. Houston, in Contemporary metropolitan America: twenty geographical vignettes [390]. Cambridge, Massachusetts: Ballinger, 1976. v. 4, p. 107-149. Bibliography, p. 149. 902

CONWAY, Dennis, and others. The Dallas-Fort Worth region, in Contemporary metropolitan America: twenty geographical vignettes [390]. Cambridge, Massachusetts: Ballinger, 1976. v. 4, p. 1-39. Bibliography, p. 39. 903

WEIGAND, Karl. Stadtgeographische Studien in Südwesttexas: und ausgewählter Untersuchungen zur Mobilität der spanisch sprechenden Wanderarbeiter in dissen Raum. Wiesbaden: Steiner Verlag, 1973. 116 p. Bibliography, p. 114-116. Numerous maps. 903

4. THE MIDDLE WEST

a. General

GARLAND, John H., ed. The North American Midwest: a regional geography. New York: John Wiley, 1955. 252 p. Bibliography, p. 243-245. 99 references. 90

AKIN, Wallace E. The North Central United States. Princeton, New Jersey: Van Nostrand, 1968. 160 p. Index. Bibliography, p. 152-155. 9C

ANDREEVA, V. M., GOKHMAN, V. M., KOVALEVSKII, V. P., and POLOVITSKAIA, M. E. Ekonomicheskie raiony SShA: Sever (Economic regions of the USA: the North). Moskva: Geografgiz, 1958. 830 p. Bibliography, p. 801-807. About 150 references. 905a

WESTVIEW Press, Boulder, Colorado, has announced plans for the publication, in 1984 or later, of the following volumes in the series, Geographies of the United States, edited by Ingolf K. Vogeler: 906

    MICHIGAN, by Lawrence M. Sommers.
    WISCONSIN, by Ingolf K. Vogeler.
    ILLINOIS, by A. Doyne Horsley.
    NEBRASKA, by Brad H. Baltensperger.

    b. East North Central States

SANTER, Richard A. Michigan: heart of the Great Lakes. Dubuque, Iowa: Kendall/Hunt Publishing Co., 1977. 364 p. Index. Bibliography, p. 339-351, 320 references, arranged by chapters: general references; introduction; historical geography; political geography; geology and mining resources; glacial lakes and ice sculptured land; climate, soil, vegetation, and lumber resources; population and settlement; Michigan's fourteen planning and development regions; economic geography, transportation and communication systems; quest for quality environment. 907

MORRISON, Paul Cross. Geographers' mirror of Michigan: a bibliography of professional writings, Papers of the Michigan Academy of Science, Arts, and Letters, v. 50 (1965), p. 493-518 (1964 meeting). 908

SINCLAIR, Robert, and THOMPSON, Bryan. Metropolitan Detroit: an anatomy of social change. Cambridge, Massachusetts: Ballinger, 1977. 66 p. Bibliography, p. 65-66. Also in Contemporary metropolitan America [390], v. 3, p. 285-354. 909

MAYER, Harold M., and CORSI, Thomas M. The Northeastern Ohio urban complex, in Contemporary metropolitan America: twenty geographical vignettes [390]. Cambridge, Massachusetts: Ballinger, 1976, v. 3, p. 109-179. Bibliography, p. 179. 910

DILLON, Lowell I., and LYON, Edward E., eds. Indiana: crossroads of America. Dubuque, Iowa: Kendall/Hunt Publishing Co., 1978. 160 p. Index. Bibliography, p. 145-149. 911

    138 references arranged by chapters: geology; drainage; streams and lakes; weather and climate; vegetation; soils; transportation; agriculture; minerals; manufacturing; population; outdoor recreation.

NELSON, Ronald E., ed. Illinois: land and life in the prairie state. Dubuque, Iowa: Kendall/Hunt Publishing Co.,1978. 359 p. Index. Bibliographical references. 912

    255 references, arranged by chapters: general; physical environment; historical geography; population and social geography; farms and farming; mining and manufacturing; the Metro East Area [St. Louis]; the Chicago Metropolitan Area.

CUTLER, Irving. Chicago: metropolis of the mid-continent. 3rd ed. Dubuque, Iowa: Kendall/Hunt, 1982. 319 p. Index. Bibliography, p. 299-309. 913

    300 references arranged by topics covered by chapters: references and general readings; physical setting, evolution of Chicago; people and settlement patterns; economy of Chicago; transportation; expansion of the Chicago Metropolitan Area; planning and the future; fiction, poetry, and reflections.

BERRY, Brian J. L. and others, Chicago: transformation of an urban system. Cambridge, Massachusetts: Ballinger, 1976. 101 p. Bibliography, p. 95-99. Also in Contemporary metropolitan America [390], v. 3, p. 181-283. 914

MAYER, Harold M., and WADE, Richard. Chicago: growth of a metropolis. Chicago: University of Chicago Press, 1969. 510 p. Index. Bibliography, p. 475-493. 915

MAYER, Harold M. The port of Chicago and the St. Lawrence Seaway. Chicago, Illinois: University of Chicago. Department of Geography. Research paper no. 49, 1957. 283 p. Bibliography, p. 273-283. 202 references. 916

MATHER, E. Cotton, HART, J. Fraser, JOHNSON, Hildegard Binder, and MATROS, Ron. Upper Coulee country. Prescott, Wisconsin: Trimbelle Press, 1975. 101 p. Bibliographical references. 917

      c. West North Central States
        and the Great Plains

RAFFERTY, Milton D. Missouri: a geography. Boulder, Colorado: Westview Press, 1983. 262 p. Index. Bibliographies at ends of chapters. 918

SCHROEDER, Walter A. Bibliography of Missouri geography: a guide to written material on places and regions of Missouri. Columbia, Missouri: University of Missouri. Extension Division, 1977. 260 p. Author index. Place-name index. 919

  1,550 annotated numbered entries arranged by sections: bibliographies; atlases and gazetteers; maps and cartography; geographic education; regional geography; general physical geography and land forms; earthquakes; caves, karst, and springs; water; climate and weather; biogeography; soils geography; environmental geography; exploration and 19th century description; historical geography; cultural and population geography; geography of speech and literature; place names; political geography; medical geography; general economic geography; urban and industrial geography, transportation and trade; planning and land use; mining, mineral resources, and energy; agricultural geography; forestry; geography of recreation; additions.

EHRHARDT, Dennis K. The St. Louis daily urban system, in Contemporary metropolitan America: twenty geographical vignettes [390]. Cambridge, Massachusetts: Ballinger, 1976, v. 3, p. 61-107. Bibliography, p. 107. 920

RAFFERTY, Milton D. The Ozarks: land and life. Norman, Oklahoma: University of Oklahoma Press, 1980. 282 p. Index. Bibliographies at ends of chapters. 921

GERLACH, Russell L. Immigrants in the Ozarks: a study in ethnic geography. Columbia, Missouri: University of Missouri Press, 1976. 206 p. Index. Bibliography, p. 184-196. 922

COLLIER, James E. Geography of the northern Ozark border region in Missouri. Columbia, Missouri: University of Missouri Studies, v. 26, no. 1, 1953. 105 p. Index. Bibliography, p. 99-102. 923

SELF, Huber. Environment and man in Kansas: a geographical analysis. Lawrence, Kansas: Regents Press of Kansas, 1978. 288 p. Index. Bibliography, p. 264-273. 924

ABLER, Ronald F., ADAMS, John S., and BORCHERT, John R. The Twin Cities of St. Paul and Minneapolis. Cambridge, Massachusetts: Ballinger, 1976. 69 p. Bibliography, p. 67. Also in Contemporary metropolitan America [390], v. 3, p. 355-423. 925

SPÄTH, Hans-Joachim. Die agro-ökologische Trockengrenze in den zentralen Great Plains von Nord-Amerika. Zur Neudefinition und Dynamik der Trockengrenze des Regenfeldbaus. The agro-ecological dry boundary of non-irrigated agriculture in the Central Great Plains of North America. On the redefinition and the mobility of the dry boundary of the rain-fed agriculture. Wiesbaden: Steiner, 1980. 160 p. (Erdwissenschaftliche Forschung, Band 15). English summary, p. 143-146. Bibliography, p. 147-154. 926

LAWSON, Merlin P. The climate of the Great American Desert: reconstruction of the climate of the western interior United States, 1800-1850. Lincoln, Nebraska: University of Nebraska Press, 1974. 135 p. (University of Nebraska Studies, n.s. v. 46). Bibliography, p. 128-134. Bibliographical notes, p. 118-127. 927

5. THE WEST

HOPKINS, Stephen T., and JONES, Douglas E. With the technical assistance of John A. Rogers. Research guide to the arid lands of the world. Phoenix, Arizona: Oryx Press, 1983. 391 p. United States, p. 261-288, 417 entries. 927a

POLOVITSKAIA, M. E. Ekonomicheskie raiony SShA: Zapad (Economic regions of the USA: the West). Moskva, "Mysl'," 1966. 534 p. Bibliography, p. 509-534. 190 references. 927b

a. Mountain States

CALEF, Wesley C. Private grazing and public lands: studies of the local management of the Taylor Grazing Act. Chicago, Illinois: University of Chicago Press, 1960. 292 p. Index. Bibliographical footnotes. 928

GRIFFITHS, Thomas Mel, and RUBRIGHT, Lynnell. Colorado: a geography. Boulder, Colorado: Westview Press, 1983. 325 p. Index. Bibliographies. 929

BROWN, Robert H. Wyoming: a geography. Boulder, Colorado: Westview Press, 1980. 374 p. Index. Bibliographic notes at ends of chapters. Bibliography, p. 359-363. 930

TRAVIS, Richard W. A Wasatch chronicle: a basic bibliography of geographic literature on the State of Utah. Salt Lake City, Utah: University of Utah. Department of Geography. Research paper, no. 76-2, July 1976. 26 p. 931

STRASSER, Manfred. Die Bewässerungslandschaft der Wasatch Oase in Utah. Freiburg im Breisgau: Schulz, 1972. 246 p. Freiburger geographische Arbeiten, Heft 4. Bibliography, p. 241-244. 932

MORRIS, John W. The Southwestern United States. New York: Van Nostrand Reinhold, 1970. 142 p. Bibliography, p. 135-136. 933

BIRLE, Siegfried. Irrigation agriculture in the southwest United States. Regional variation of crop pattern. Marburg: Geographisches Institut der Universität. Marburger geographische Schriften, Heft 67, 1976. 217 p. Bibliography, p. 204-217. 934

Area extends from High Plains of West Texas through New Mexico and Arizona to Sonoran desert of extreme southeast California.

CARLSON, Alvar W. A bibliography of the geographers' contributions to understanding the American Southwest (Arizona and New Mexico), 1920-1971. Arizona quarterly, v. 28, no. 2 (1972), p. 101-141. 935

About 375 references arranged by categories: general regional and state studies; prehistoric occupation, discovery, and historic-geographic developments prior to 1850; historic-geographic developments after 1850; physical environments of the past and present; population characteristics, minorities, trends, rural settlement and agriculture; urban places and their economic functions; transportation and trade; water and mineral resources; recreation and tourism; political and military; and geography in education.

_____. An addendum to "A Bibliography of the geographers' contributions to understanding the American Southwest (Arizona and New Mexico), 1920-1971," Arizona quarterly, v. 29, no. 4 (1973), p. 352-357. 61 entries. 936

WEHMEIER, Eckhard. Die Bewässerungsoase Phoenix/Arizona. Stuttgart: Geographisches Institut der Universität. Stuttgarter geographische Studien, Heft 89, 1975. 176 p. Bibliography, p. 164-173. English summary, p. 161-163. 937

COMEAUX, Malcolm L. Arizona: a geography. Boulder, Colorado: Westview Press, 1981. 336 p. Index. Bibliography, p, 321-328, arranged by chapters. 938

WESTVIEW Press, Boulder, Colorado, has announced plans for the publication, in 1984 or later, of the following volumes in the series, Geographies of the United States, edited by Ingolf K. Vogeler: 939

    UTAH, by Clifford B. Craig.
    IDAHO, by Olen P. Matthews and others.

b. California

ZIERER, Clifford M., ed. California and the Southwest. New York: John Wiley, 1956. 376 p. Index. Bibliographies at end of chapters. 940

    Covers Nevada, Arizona, and Utah in part but emphasis is on California.

LANTIS, David W., in collaboration with STEINER, Rodney, and KARINEN, Arthur E. California: land of contrasts. 3rd ed. Dubuque, Iowa: Kendall/Hunt, 1977. 486 p. (1st ed. 1963. 509 p.). Index. Bibliography, p. 459-475. 941

    Extensive bibliography.

DURRENBERGER, Robert W., with Robert B. Johnson. California: patterns on the land. 5th ed. Palo Alto, California: Mayfield Publishing Co., 1976. 134 p. Index. (A California Council for Geographic Education Publication). (1st ed., 1957. 59 p.). 942

    Atlas maps, text, photographs, diagrams, and tables on the physical geography, history and demography, and economy of California.

DURRENBERGER, Robert W. California: the last frontier. New York: Van Nostrand Reinhold. 1969. 160 p. Index. Bibliography, p. 153-157. 943

DURRENBERGER, Robert W. A selected California bibliography: exploration and settlement--the Spanish and Mexican period, California geographer, v. 6 (1965), p. 73-85. 211 entries.

_____. _____: exploration and settlement--the American period, v. 7 (1966), p. 55-81. About 500 entries.

_____. _____: water resources, Part I, v. 8 (1967), p. 47-61; part II, v. 9 (1968), p. 65-71. 508 entries. 944

DURRENBERGER, Robert W. Sources of information about California. Northridge, California: Roberts Publishing Co. 1961. 126 p. Bibliography, p. 90-115. 945

GREGOR, Howard F. An agricultural typology of California. Budapest, Hungary: Akadémiai Kiadó, 1974. 107 p. (Geography of world agriculture, 4). Bibliography, p. 105-107. 946

LAMPRECHT, Sandra J. California: a bibliography of theses and dissertations in geography. Monticello, Illinois: Council of Planning Librarians. Exchange bibliography, no. 753, 1975. 53 p. Author index. 447 entries. 947

HUMLUM, Johannes. Water development and water planning in the Southwestern United States. Aarhus, Denmark: Aarhus Universitet. Kulturgeografisk Institut. (Munksgaard). Atlantic Highlands, New Jersey: Humanities Press, 1969. 240 p. Index. Bibliography, p. 224-232. 948

    Emphasis on California but includes Arizona and plans for water transfer in the West.

SPÄTH, Hans-Joachim. Die hydrologischen Probleme des Bewässerungsfeldbaues. Eine Fallstudie für aride Beckenlandschaften, dargestellt am Beispiel der Colorado-Wüste in Kalifornien. Frankfurt: DLG Verlag, 1975. 255 p. (Zeitschrift für Bewässerungswirtschaft, Sonderheft, 3). 949

NELSON, Howard J. The Los Angeles metropolis. Dubuque, Iowa: Kendall/Hunt Publishing Co., 1983. 344 p. Index. Bibliography, p. 325-329. About 200 references. Also suggested readings at the end of each chapter. 950

STEINER, Rodney. Los Angeles: the centrifugal city. Dubuque, Iowa: Kendall/Hunt, 1981. 218 p. Index. Bibliography, p. 205-211. 951

NELSON, Howard J., and CLARK, William A. V. The Los Angeles metropolitan experience: uniqueness, generality, and the goal of the good life. Cambridge, Massachusetts: Ballinger, 1976. 69 p. Bibliography, p. 65-67. Also in Contemporary metropolitan America [390], v. 4, p. 227-295. 952

PRYDE, Philip R., ed. San Diego: an introduction to the region: an historical geography of the natural environments and human developments of San Diego county. Prepared by the Department of Geography of San Diego State University. Dubuque, Iowa: Kendall/Hunt, 1976. 267 p. Index. Bibliographies at ends of chapters. 953

KOCH, Josef. Rentnerstädte in Kalifornien; Einen bevölkerungs- und sozialgeographische Untersuchung. Tübingen: Geographisches Institut der Universität. Tübinger geographische Studien, Heft 59, 1975. 154 p. Bibliography, p. 129-154. English summary, p. 127-128. 954

VANCE, Jean. The cities of the San Francisco Bay in Contemporary metropolitan America: twenty geographical vignettes [390]. Cambridge, Massachusetts: Ballinger, 1976, v. 2, p. 217-307. Bibliography, p. 305-307. 955

VANCE, James E. Geography and urban evolution in the San Francisco Bay area. Berkeley, California: University of California. Institute of Governmental Studies, 1964. 89 p. Bibliographical footnotes. 956

SALTER, Christopher L. San Francisco's Chinatown: how Chinese a town? San Francisco, California: R and E Research Associates, 1978. 82 p. Bibliography, p. 79-82. 957

PEASE, Robert W. Modoc county: a geographic time continuum on the California volcanic tabeland. Berkeley, California: University of California. Publications in geography, v. 17, 1965. 304 p. Index. Bibliography, p. 193-199. 958

c. Pacific Northwest

FREEMAN, Otis W., and MARTIN, Howard H., eds. The Pacific Northwest: an overall appreciation. 2nd ed. New York: John Wiley, 1954. 540 p. Index. Bibliographies at ends of chapters. (1st ed.: 1942, 542 p.). 959

Covers Washington, Oregon, Idaho, and western Montana.

BOOTH, Charles W. The Northwestern United States. New York: Van Nostrand Reinhold, 1971. 115 p. Index. Bibliography, p. 110-111. 960

APPLETON, John B. The Pacific northwest; a selected bibliography covering completed research in the natural resources and socio-economic fields, an annotated list of in-progress and contemplated research together with critical comments thereon, 1930-39. Portland, Oregon, Northwest Regional Council, 1939. 474 p. 4,635 entries. 961

DICKEN, Samuel N., and DICKEN, Emily F. Oregon divided: a regional geography. Portland, Oregon: Oregon Historical Society, 1982. 176 p. (Two centuries of Oregon geography, v. 2). 106 illustrations including 46 oblique areal photographs of representative landscapes. Index. Bibliographic notes, p. 164-167. 962

BOWEN, William A. The Willamette Valley: migration and settlement on the Oregon frontier. Seattle, Washington: University of Washington Press, 1978. 120 p. Index. Bibliography, p. 107-117. 963

KONNECKE, Bernd. Die Kulturlandschaftliche Bedeutung des primären Wirtschaftssektors im Staate Oregon, USA. Regensburg: Institut für Geographie an der Universität Regensburg. Regensburger geographische Schriften, Heft 13, 1979. 269 p. Bibliography, p. 236-269. Summary in English. 964

ANDRUS, A. Phillip, and others. Seattle. Cambridge, Massachusetts: Ballinger, 1976. 73 p. Bibliography, p. 71-72. Also in Contemporary metropolitan America [390], v. 3, p. 425-500. 965

d. Alaska

RESEARCH catalogue of the American Geographical Society [66], v. 3, p. 2023-2094. First supplement. Regional, v. 2, p. 5-21. Second supplement, v. 2. Regional, p. 4-12. 966

BIBLIOGRAPHIE géographique internationale [67]. "Alaska," v. 1-57 (1891-1947); "Etats-Unis et Alaska," v. 58 (1948); "Regions polaires: Alaska," v. 59-62 (1949-1956); v. 65 (1959); v. 67-81 (1961-1976); v. 82- (1977-). "Régions polaires: Arctique--Alaska." 967

DIETRICH, Bruno. "Nordamerika," 1916-1930. Geographisches Jahrbuch [68], v. 46 (1931), p. 332-340; 1931-1942, v. 59, part 2 (1948). 968

BARTZ, Fritz. Alaska. Stuttgart: K. F. Koehler Verlag. 1950. 384 p. (Geographische Handbücher). Subject index. Bibliography, p. 374-381. 214 references. 969

WAHRHAFTIG, Clyde. Physiographic divisions of Alaska. Washington, D. C.: Government Printing Office, 1965. 52 p. (U. S. Geological Survey. Professional paper no. 482). 6 plates in pocket. Index. Bibliography, p. 43-50. 970

Description of 60 physiographic regions of Alaska and geomorphological processes in them.

WESTVIEW Press. Boulder, Colorado, has listed the following work for publication in 1984 or later: 971

ALASKA, by Roger W. Pearson and Donald F. Lynch.

ZUBKOVA, A. N. Aleutskie ostrova: fiziko-geograficheskii ocherk (The Aleutian islands: a physical-geographic study). Moskva: Geografgiz, 1948. 288 p. Bibliography, p. 275-286. 333 references. 971

e. Hawaii

RESEARCH catalogue of the AGS [66], "Hawaii," v. 14, p. 9939-9967. 590 entries for 1923-1961. First supplement, Regional, v. 2, p. 616-621. About 150 entries for 1962-1971. Second supplement, v. 2, Regional, p. 580-582. About 70 entries for 1972-1976. 972

HUETZ-DE-LEMPS, Christian. Les Îles Hawaï depuis 1970. Les cahiers d'Outre-Mer, v. 30, no. 118 (1977), p. 193-200. 973

Annotated bibliography of principal works on the Hawaiian Islands, 1970-1976.

MORGAN, Joseph R. Hawaii: a geography. Boulder, Colorado: Westview Press, 1983. 293 p. Index. Bibliographical references. 974

INDEX OF SUBJECTS, AUTHORS, AND SHORT TITLES

Numbers refer to entries. Numbers in parentheses refer to reports issued by the National Technical Information Service; these are all listed under entry 195, on pages 37-52. The letter "n" after an entry indicates that the reference occurs in the textual annotation.

A

AAG, see also Association of American Geographers
AAG, Commission on College Geography, Resource papers, 460, 461, 746; see also Resource papers for college geography, and Resource publications in geography
AAG, Comparative metropolitan analysis project. See under title of project.
AAG, Great Plains-Rocky Mountain Division, 90
AAG, Historical Geography Speciality Group, 773
AAG, members, directory, 235
AAG, Middle States Division, 123
AAG, Southeastern Division, 104
AGS, 1, 1a, 2, 38, 53, 55, 66, 86
Abler, Ronald F., 212, 925
Accessibility to health care, 745
Acid mine drainage, 195 (151, 152)
Acid precipitation, 195 (126-133)
Adams, Gerald H., 195 (199, 224, 239)
Adams, John S., 212, 390, 391, 925
Adams, Russell B., 555
Adkins, Howard G., 880
Aerial photographs, 220
Afro-Americans, 679-692
After a hundred years, agriculture, 551
Aging and the aged, 625
Agricultural dry boundary, 926
Agricultural index, 541
Agricultural land, 538
Agricultural occupance of flood plains, 300
Agricultural regions of the United States, 533
Agricultural resources, NTIS reports, 195 (256-257)
Agricultural resources, remote sensing, 195 (256-257)
Agricultural statistics, 163
Agricultural typology of California, 535, 946
Agricultural watersheds, 195 (32)
Agriculture, 531-551
Agriculture, historical geography, 789-790
Agriculture, industrialization of, 539
Agrogeografiia kapitalisticheskikh stran (na primere S.Sh.A. i Kanady), 536
Agro-ökologische Trockengrenze in den zentralen Great Plains von Nord-Amerika, 926

Aids to geographical research, 10
Air freight, 581
Air pollution, 195 (112-137)
Air pollution, atmospheric modelling of, 195 (118-122)
Air pollution economics, 195 (112-117)
Air pollution emission factors, 195 (123)
Air pollution and urban planning, 382
Air pollution, urban, 195 (134-137)
Air quality monitoring, 195 (107-111)
Air transportation, 195 (231, 232)
Air, water, and noise pollution, NTIS reports, 195 (105-186)
Airphoto atlas of the rural U.S., 339
Airport development: social and economic effects, 195 (236)
Airport noise, 195 (166)
Akin, Wallace E., 905
Alaska, 824, 966-971
Alaska geographic, 122
Alaska Geographic Society, 122
Albaum, Melvin, 619
Albertson, F. W., 333
Aleutian islands, 971a
Aleutskie ostrova, 971a
Alexander, Ernest R., 474
Alexander, Gerard L., 41
Alexander, Lewis M., 860
Alexandersson, Gunnar, 517
All Hallow's parish, Maryland, 1650-1783, 804
Allen, John Logan, 820
Alloway, David N., 671
American agriculture, 532
American cartographer, 80
American cities, geography of, 394
American city: an urban geography, 400
American coal industry, 271
American common houses, 710
American Congress on Surveying and Mapping, 80
American Desert, 1800-1850, 927
American earth, illustrations, 703
American economic history: a guide to information sources, 614
American environment: perceptions and policies, 368
American ethnic groups, 646-701
American ethnic groups: the European heritage, doctoral dissertations, 671
American Geographical Society, 1, 1a, 2, 38, 53, 55, 66, 86

American Geographical Society Collection of the University of Wisconsin-Milwaukee Library, 2, 38a, 86
American Geographical Society of New York, 1, 38, 53, 55, 66, 77, 862, 966, 972
American geography: inventory and prospect, 249, 775
American Geological Institute, 58
American Geophysical Union, 285a
American government and history information guide series, 509, 652
American habitat: a historical perspective, 331
American history, 825-827
American Indian, Center for the History of, 667, 668
American Indian, geographic literature, 665
American Indians, 195 (196-198)
American Indians in towns and cities, 669
American Indians, social science research on, 666
American Indians, sociology of, 667
American Indians, urbanization of, 668
American Library Association Government Documents Round Table, 198
American Meteorological Society, 321
American metropolitan system, 419
American national park system, 839
American Petroleum Institute data base, 195 (160)
American quarterly, 703
American regionalism, 858
American small town: twentieth-century place images, 490
American Southwest, 818, 933-938, 940-958
American sport, 716
American statistical publications from private organizations and state government sources, 140
American statistics index, 134
American steel industry, 528
American studies: an international newsletter, 703
American studies information guide series, 641, 826
American sublime: landscape and scenery of the lower Hudson valley, 868a
American Universities Field Staff, 26, 26a
American urban system, 418
Americas, The, 53-54
America's land and its use, 342
Anaheim, Califronia, 716
Anctil, Pierre, 865
Anderson, Dorothy H., 843
Anderson, James R., 531, 534, 885
Anderson, Richard, 369
Andreeva, V. M., 905a
Andrews, Howard F., 431
Andriot, John L., 134, 154, 169, 217

Andrus, A. Phillip, 965
Anglo-America: a systematic and regional geography, 243
Anglo-American realm, 241
Anglo-American state and provincial thematic atlases, 207
Annales de géographie, 4
Annals, AAG, 77
Annotated bibliography of bibliographies on selected government publications, 171
Annotated bibliography of coastal zone management work products, 308
Annotated bibliography of geology and land use planning, 262
Annotated bibliography on Great Lakes hydrology, 293
Annotated bibliography on hydrology, 285
Annotated bibliography on hydrology and sedimentation, 285
Annotated bibliography on hydrology. United States and Canada, 285
Annotated bibliography on techniques of forecasting demand for water, 302
Annotated bibliography on water conservation, 287, 299
Annotated world list of selected current geographical serials, 15, 71
Annual report of the director, U.S.G.S., 164
Annual review of anthropology, 718
Annual review of psychology, 644
Annual survey of manufacturers, 165
Anthropological literature, 720
Anthropology, 718-720
Antipode, 81
Appalachia and West Virginia, 880
Appalachian Regional Development Program, 895
Applebaum, Richard P., 434
Appleton, John B., 961
Applied geography, 846
Applied geography: selected perspectives, 846
Applied medical geography, 741
Arbingast, Stanley A., 901
Architecture, folk, 711
Architecture, vernacular, 710
Area planning, population projections for, 195 (189-191)
Areawide environmental assessment, 195 (1)
Argonne National Laboratory, 195 (83)
Arid and semiarid areas, 195 (42), 927a
Arizona, 818, 933-938, 948
Arizona: a geography, 938
Arizona, geographers' contributions, 935, 936
Arnim, Helmuth, 13
Asian Americans, 700-701
Asians in America, 701
Aspects of population growth policy, 72

Assessment of research on natural
  hazards, 385
Association of American Geographers,
  76, 82, 90, 101, 104, 123, 212, 235,
  236, 250, 298, 357, 369, 390, 391,
  399, 460, 461, 538, 731, 746, 752,
  756; see also AAG
Association of American Geographers,
  directory of members, 235
Association of North Dakota Geographers,
  124
Association of Pacific Coast Geographers,
  83
Atchafalaya swamp life: settlement and
  folk occupations, 898
Atlanta, Georgia, 212, 390, 891
Atlas, airphoto of rural U. S., 339
Atlas, energy, U. S., 269
Atlas of industrialization of agri-
  culture, 539
Atlas of the historical geography of
  the United States, 213
Atlas of United States and Canadian
  society and culture, 214
Atlas, water, 286
Atlases and maps, 210-219
Atlases, county, 209
Atlases, cultural, 214
Atlases, historical, 213
Atlases, state, 205-208
Atmospheric modeling of air pollution,
  195 (118-122)
Austin, Morris E., 338
Author, title, and subject guide to
  books reviewed and index to reviews,
  227-228
Automobile air pollution: abatement
  through management and planning,
  195 (124, 125)
Averitt, Paul, 272

B

BB, 22
Bair, Frank E., 326
Baker, Alan R. H., 774
Baker, Simon, 339
Balachandran, M., 143, 148, 149
Balachandran, Sarojini, 270, 582, 583
Baldwin, John L., 324
Ball, John M., 407, 845
Baltensperger, Brad H., 906
Baltimore, Maryland, 212, 390, 878
Barkausaks, Mary Ellen, 841
Barns, 712, 713
Barr, Charles W., 578
Barrier islands, 317
BART-Rapid transit, San Francisco Bay
  area, 195 (242)
Bartz, Fritz, 969
Basic economic statistics, 148
Basic geographical library, 9
Basic maps of the U. S. economy, 516

Basler, Ray P., 130, 131
Bastian, Robert W., 710
Baumann, Duane D., 287, 298, 299, 302
Beach erosion, 195 (67-68), 311-312
Beach erosion and protection, 195 (68)
Beach Erosion Board, 311, 312
Beaches in coastal management, 313
Beale, Calvin L., 603
Bean, John L., Jr., 900
Beauregard, Robert A., 399
Beginnings of the American rectangular
  land survey system, 1785-1800, 791
Bell, Gwen, 511
Beltways, land use and urban develop-
  ment impacts, 566
Bercaw, Louise O., 591
Berghorn, Forrest J., 625
Bergman, Edward F., 870
Berlin, G. Lennis, 488
Berry, Brian J. L., 422, 423, 430, 433,
  437, 441, 448, 527, 553, 596, 600,
  914
Best place to live, 417
Best poor man's country: early south-
  eastern Pennsylvania, 800
Besterman, Theodore, 17, 18
Bestor, George C., 475
Betebenner, Lyle, 479
Bewässerungslandschaft der Wasatch Oase
  in Utah, 932
Bewässerungsoase Phoenix/Arizona, 937
Beyond the urban fringe, 347, 585
Bibliografia Chicana: a guide to in-
  formation sources, 696
Bibliographic data bases of the U. S.
  Geological Survey, 256
Bibliographic guide to government
  publications--foreign, 31
Bibliographic guide to government
  publications--U. S., 168
Bibliographic guide to population
  geography, 722
Bibliographic guide to the economic
  regions of the U. S., 600
Bibliographic index, 21
Bibliographical bulletin (BB), 22
Bibliographie cartographique française,
  39
Bibliographie cartographique inter-
  nationale, 39
Bibliographie commentée sur les Franco-
  Américains de la Nouvelle-Angleterre,
  865
Bibliographie des Deutschtums der
  Kolonialzeitlichen Einwanderung in
  Nordamerika, 674
Bibliographie der geographischen
  Literatur in deutscher Sprache, 13
Bibliographie géographique inter-
  nationale, 4, 54, 56, 67, 967
Bibliographie zum Geographiestudium,
  12, 72
Bibliographische Berichte, 22

Bibliography and index of geology, 58
Bibliography and index of U. S. Geological Survey publications relating to coal, 272, 273
Bibliography and pamphlets on the history of agriculture, 789
Bibliography and review of geography department discussion papers, 115
Bibliography for geographic education, 845
Bibliography of agriculture, 540
Bibliography of dissertations in geography, 229-231
Bibliography of ethnicity and ethnic groups, 657
Bibliography of geography. Part I. Introduction to general aids, 8
Bibliography of highway impact studies, 565
Bibliography...of interest to community planners, 416
Bibliography of land and natural resources information systems, 258
Bibliography of Missouri geography, 919
Bibliography of North American geology, 58
Bibliography of Pacific/Asian American materials, 700
Bibliography of place-name literature, U. S. and Canada, 847
Bibliography of publications of the Coastal Engineering Research Center and the Beach Erosion Board, 311, 312
Bibliography of regional geography in Western languages, 13a
Bibliography of scientific and industrial reports (NTIS), 195n
Bibliography of state land resources planning, 589, 590
Bibliography of technical reports (NTIS), 195n
Bibliography of the geography of the state of South Carolina, 890
Bibliography of the history of agriculture in the U. S., 790
Bibliography of tourism and travel research studies, 831
Bibliography of United States government bibliographies, 172, 173
Bibliography of urban geography, 1940-1964, 409
Bibliography of water conservation, 297
Bibliography on German settlements in colonial North America, 674
Bibliography on ground-water recharge, 195 (42)
Bibliography on land utilization, 1918-36, 591
Bibliography on regulation of development for stormwater management, 292
Bibliography on shopping centers, 451
Bibliography on soil erosion and soil and water conservation, 336

Bibliography on the urban crisis, 496
Bibliography on urban and regional information systems, 412
Biennial guide to U. S. government publications, 170
Biennial review of anthropology, 718, 719
Binkley, Clark, 836
Binstock, Robert H., 627
Biological abstracts, 542
Biological and agricultural index, 541
Birdsall, Stephen S., 247
Birle, Siegfried, 934
Bissell, H. Preston, 751
Black America, encyclopedia, 688
Black America: geographic perspectives, 682
Black family, 690
Black ghetto: a spatial behavioral perspective, 463
Black inner city as frontier outpost; Philadelphia, 687
Black population, 1790-1978, 689
Black suburbanization, 483
Black urban households, 464
Blackburn, P. S., 195 (130)
Blacks, 463, 464, 483, 679-692
Blacks in the United States: a geographic perspective, 680
Blight, visual, 717
Blotevogel, Hans H., 12, 72
Blouet, Brian W., 810, 811
Blue Grass region, Kentucky, 894
Blume, Helmut, 246
Boas, Franz, 57
Bockheim, James G., 335
Body, Alexander C., 171
Boehnke, Barbara, 639
Bogue, Donald J., 603, 729
Boland, John J., 302
Bol'shaia sovetskaia entsiklopediia, 48
Bonem, Gilbert W., 307
Books reviewed, 227-228
Booth, Charles W., 960
Borchert, John R., 925
Border states, 877-880
Boston, Massachusetts, 212, 390, 866
Boston: a geographical portrait, 866
Boundaries, areas, geographic centers and altitudes of the United States, 759
Boundaries of counties, 218
Boundaries of the U. S. and the several states, 759
Bourne, Larry S., 426
Bowen, William A., 963
Bowman, James S., 373
Boyce Byrl N., 660
Boyd, Anne Morris, 180
Boyer, Richard, 417
Brackett, Carolyn, 522
Bragdon, Clifford R., 378
Bramstedt, Wayne C., 669

Brand, Ulrich, 886
Brewer, J. Gordon, 11
Brickford, Deborah, 438
British Library, 20, 36
British Museum, 20, 36
Brockel, Harry C., 575
Brockhaus Enzyklopädie, 46
Broden, Thomas F., 440
Brown, Eric H., 245
Brown, John H., 588
Brown, Ralph H., 778, 799
Brown, Robena J., 195 (15, 19, 24, 34, 53, 61, 64, 142, 143, 153, 154, 156, 157, 217, 218)
Brown, Robert H., 930
Brownell, Blaine A., 512
Browning, Clyde E., 229, 230
Brunn, Stanley D., 351, 419, 617, 636, 753
Brush, John E., 874
Brye, David L., 670, 784
Bryson, Reid A., 59, 320
Bucchioni, Eugene, 699
Buchanan, William W., 167
Buenker, John D., 507, 652
Buetikofer, Larry B., 293
Building ethnic collections, 663
Bullamore, Henry W., 887
Bulletin, Association of North Dakota Geographers, 124
Bulletin, Illinois Geographical Society, 92
Bulletin, Special Libraries Association, Geography and Map Division, 105
Burckel, Nicholas C., 652
Bureau of the Census, 136, 137, 138, 141, 142, 145, 150, 151, 152, 153, 155, 156, 157, 158, 159, 160, 161, 162, 165, 218, 689
Bureau of the Census catalog, 136, 137
Bureau of the Census guide to programs and publications: subjects and areas, 138
Bureau of Economic Analysis, 615
Bureau of Mines, 279
Burg, Nan C., 436
Burk, Janet L., 375
Burton, Ian, 300, 301, 350, 389
Bus transportation: local studies, 195 (243, 244)
Bus transportation: national and general studies, 195 (245, 246)
Bushong, Allen D., 888
Business and economics, 604-615
Business statistics, 615
Bussink, Tine, 725
Butson, Keith D., 319
Buttel, Frederick H., 370
Buttlar, Lois, 663
Buxton, Elizabeth M., 32

C

CPL bibliographies (Council of Planning Librarians), 440, 480, 648, 732
Calef, Wesley C., 928
California, 84, 535, 940-958
California Council for Geographic Education, 84
California geographer, 84
California: land of contrasts, 941
California: patterns on the land, 942
California and the Southwest, 940
California: the last frontier, 943
California, theses and dissertations, 947
California, University. Publications in geography, 111
California volcanic tableland, 958
Calkins, Charles F., 713
Calvin Creek, 716
Capitals and central places, 430-432
Carberry, Michael, 258
Carey, George W., 869
Carlson, Alvar W., 665, 685, 693, 712, 935, 936
Carrigan, Brian, 195 (120)
Carrington, David K., 223
Carrying capacity of recreational land, 834, 835
Carter, George F., 715
Cartographic guide, regional vegetation literature, 328
Cassara, Ernest, 826
Castellanos, Diego, 699
Catalog of Government publications, 30
Catalog of United States census publications, 136, 137
Catalogue of printed maps, charts, and plans, 36
Catanese, Anthony J., 474
Cattle ranching, 817
Cavagnaro, Diane M., 195 (107-109, 113-116, 119, 139, 171, 181)
Census Library Project, 136, 144
Census of agriculture, 157
Census of business, 158
Census of housing, 156
Census of manufacturers, 159
Census of mineral industries, 161
Census of population, 155, 156, 157
Census of retail trade, 158
Census of service industries, 158
Census of transportation, 160
Census of wholesale trade, 158
Center for Latin American Studies, Stanford University, 698
Center for Natural Areas, 308
Central business district, 446, 447
Central place studies: bibliography, 430, 431
Central places, 430-432

Centre National de la Recherche
  Scientifique, 4
Chandler, Robert, 901
Changing migration patterns, 731
Changing population of the U.S., 728
Changing shape of metropolitan America,
  423
Chapin, F. Stuart, Jr., 442
Chapman, John D., 215
Chatfield, Mary, 574
Chatham, Ronald L., 243
Chicago area urban studies, 411
Chicago: growth of a metropolis, 915
Chicago, Illinois, 212, 390, 411, 579,
  913-916
Chicago: metropolis of the mid-continent,
  913
Chicago, port, 579, 916
Chicago: transformation of an urban
  system, 914
Chicago. University. Center for Urban
  Studies. Directory of theses and
  dissertations, 411
Chicago, University. Department of
  Geography, Research papers. See under
  University of Chicago. List of papers
  at end of this volume.
Childs, James B., 175
Christian, Charles M., 421, 487
Church, Martha, 9
Cities, 212, 390-513, 785-788, 859, 866,
  867, 869-871, 875, 876, 878, 879,
  891, 893, 899, 902, 903, 909, 910,
  913-915, 920, 925, 950-953, 955-957,
  965. See also names of individual
  cities or metropolitan areas.
Cities and immigrants, 785
Cities, classification, 437-438, 517
Cities, growth, 433-436
Cities, guide to the literature, 415
Cities, historical geography, 785-788
Cities in crisis, 495
Cities of the nation's historic
  metropolitan core, 390
Cities of the San Francisco Bay, 955
Cities, pension, 954
Cities, periodical literature, 413
Cities, pollution problems, 381
Cities, retirement, 954
Cities, space and behavior, 396
Cities, systems of, 418-429
City, American, how to read, 513
City classification and urban need, 438
City classification handbook, 437
City-county consolidation, 760, 761
City planning, 416, 474-480
City planning and zoning, 479
City planning bibliography, 475
City planning, history, 477
City redevelopment, 195 (222)
City and regional planning, 478
City, society, and the space economy of
  urbanism, 460

City structures in urban geography, 439
City systems in advanced economies, 428
Cityward migration, 735
Clapp, James, 491
Clark, Andrew H., 774, 775, 780
Clark, Andrew Hill, essays in honour
  of, 780
Clark, Gordon L., 730
Clark, Linda, 311
Clark University, 78
Clark, William A. V., 952
Clarke, Paul F., 255
Classification of cities, 437-438, 517
Clawson, Marion, 342, 343, 343a, 344,
  486
Clay, Grady, 513
Clay, Phillip L., 435
Cleveland, Ohio, 212, 390, 910
Clift, Virgil A., 688
Climate, 319-327, 545
Climate and man, 545
Climate of the Great American Desert,
  1800-1850, 927
Climate of the Great Lakes, 322
Climate, western interior United
  States, 1800-1850, 927
Climates of North America, 59, 320
Climates of the states, 327
Climates of the United States, 324
Climatic atlas of the United States,
  323, 325
Climatology and meteorology, NTIS
  reports, 195 (56-63)
Climatology of the United States, 327
Cline, William Eric, 795
Close-up: how to read the American
  city, 513
Coal industry, 271
Coal mine refuse disposal, 195 (149)
Coal mine wastes, 195 (150)
Coal mining, surface, 195 (79-83)
Coal surface mining reclamation, 274
Coal, U.S.G.S. publications, 272, 273
Coastal Engineering Research Center,
  311, 312
Coastal erosion protection, 314
Coastal flood hazard, 301
Coastal management, 313
Coastal Plains Center for Marine
  Development Services, 321
Coastal Plains Region, hurricanes and
  severe storms, 321
Coastal regions: geomorphology, 195 (70
Coastal resources and management,
  308-318
Coastal zone management act of 1972,
  308
Coastal zone management and planning,
  195 (64-66)
Coastal zone management work products,
  308
Coastal zone, NTIS reports, 195 (64-70)

Coastal zone, water pollution, 195 (142-144)
Cobb, David A., 208
Cochran, Anita, 384
Cocozzoli, Gary, 672
Cohen, Yehoshua S., 450, 527
Collier, James E., 923
Colonial New England, 798
Colonial North Carolina in the 18th century, 806
Colonization and settlement in the Americas, 781
Colorado: a geography, 929
Colorado desert of California, 949
Colorado. University. Institute of Behavioral Science, 386
Comeaux, Malcolm L., 898, 938
Commerce, urban, 446-453
Commercialism and frontier: the early Shenendoah valley, 805
Committee on geography, Division of Earth Sciences, National Academy of Sciences, 401
Commodity flows, urban, 571
Common houses, 710
Community planners, government publications, 416
Community response to coastal erosion, 318
Commuter rail systems, 567
Commuting patterns, 423
Comparative atlas of America's great cities, 212
Comparative metropolitan analysis project, AAG, 212, 390, 391, 866, 867, 869, 875, 876, 878, 879, 891, 893, 899, 902, 903, 909, 910, 914, 920, 925, 952, 955, 965
Comparative studies in frontier history, 782
Comprehensive bibliography for the study of American minorities, 649
Comprehensive dissertation index, 233, 234
Comprehensive general bibliographies, 16-22, 130-133
Comprehensive geographical bibliographies, 1-7, 66-69
Comptroller General, 174
Concept of carrying capacity of recreational land, 834
Conflict, power, and politics in the city, 754
Connecticut, 861, 867
Connecticut, central, metropolitan change, 867
Connecticut Valley, 212, 390
Conrad, Adam Halicki, 354
Conservation, 348-351
Conservation and resource management, readings, 350
Conservation of natural resources, 348

Conserving American resources, 349
Contemporary metropolitan America: twenty geographical vignettes, 212, 390, 866, 867, 869, 875, 876, 878, 879, 891, 893, 899, 902, 903, 909, 910, 914, 920, 925, 952, 955, 965
Contemporary psychology: a journal of reviews, 645
Contemporary suburban America, 481
Continuous shaping of America, 776
Contributions to an understanding of Black America, 683
Conway, Dennis, 903
Conzen, Michael P., 771, 772, 773, 866
Cook, Earleen H., 276, 315
Cook, Joseph L., 276, 315
Coppa, Frank J., 278
Corbin, John Boyd, 260, 261
Cordasco, Francesco, 671, 675, 676, 699
Cordasco, Michael F., 676
Cordell, Harold K., 837
Cornog, Martha, 268
Corsi, Thomas, 910
Coulee, upper, 917
Council of Planning Librarians: see Exchange bibliographies, and CPL bibliographies
County and city data book, 151
Court, Arnold, 320
Cox, Kevin R., 754
Craig, Clifford B., 939
Crime, 633-640
Crime: a spatial perspective, 633
Crime and justice, 636
Crime and violence, 635
Crime, spatial analysis of, 639
Crime, spatial dynamics of, 638
Criminal justice system, spatial perspectives on, 636
Cuff, David J., 269
Cultural geography, 702-720
Cultural geography of the U. S., 702, 703
Cultural and historic landscapes, 796
Cultural landscape, Oregon, 964
Cultural regions of the U. S., 706
Culver, Dorothy Campbell, 592, 593
Cumberland, John H., 601
Cumulative subject index to the Monthly catalog of United States government publications, 1900-1971, 167
Current geographical publications, 2, 86
Current literature in traffic and transportation, 564
Current published searches, 195n
Cutler, Irving, 913
Cybriwsky, Roman A., 875
Cyviner, Barbara, 444

D

Dallas, Texas, 212, 390, 903
Dallas-Fort Worth region, 903
Daniels, L. K., 195 (83)
Darden, Joe T., 462, 648
Darling, F. Fraser, 366
Data bases, see:
  American Petroleum Institute
  Energy Data Base
  Engineering Index
  International Aerospace Abstracts
  National Technical Information Service
  Pollution Abstracts
  Oceanic Abstracts
  Selected Water Resources Abstracts
Data bases of the U.S. Geological Survey, 256
Daubemire, Rexford, 330
Davidson, Claud M., 489
Davies, Shane, 619
Davis, Bob J., 561
Davis, Elizabeth Gould, 445
Davis, George A., 680
Davis, Lenwood G., 690
Dean, Robert D., 290
Decentralization processes, metropolitan America, 423
Deckert, Emil, 57
de Cooke, K. J., 195 (42)
de Lange, Norbert, 72
Demand for water, 302
Demographic and social aspects of population growth, 726
Dennis, Deborah Ellis, 484, 485
Department of Energy, 264-267
Department of Energy. Technical Information Center, 266, 267
Department of the Interior, 254
Departments of geography, 236
Desalination of water, 195 (44-46)
Desert and mountains, airphoto atlas, 339
Deskins, Donald R., 686
Detroit, Michigan, 212, 390, 909
Development of the U. S. urban system, 425
Development planning for water resources, 290
Dever, G. E. Alan, 747
De Vise, Pierre, 746
Dicke, Karen, 831
Dicken, Emily F., 823, 962
Dicken, Samuel N., 823, 962
Dictionary catalog of government publications, 30
Dietrich, Bruno, 57, 968
Diffusion of an innovation in an urban system, 450
DiLisio, James E., 877
Dill, Henry W., Jr., 339
Dillon, Lowell I., 911
Directories, 235-236
Directory, members of A.A.G., 235
Directory of data sources on racial and ethnic minorities, 658
Directory of federal statistics for local areas, 145
Directory of federal statistics for states, 141
Directory of information resources in the United States: geosciences and oceanography, 251
Directory of non-Federal statistics for states and local areas, 142
Directory of urban theses and dissertations, University of Chicago, 411
Discussion paper series. University of Iowa, 119
Discussion paper, Syracuse University, 121
Disease, spatial aspects and ecology, 751-752
Dissertations, 229-234
Dissertations on land use, water use, resource conflict, resource policy, and facility location, 351
Ditton, Robert B., 842
Division of Earth Sciences, National Academy of Sciences, Committee on Geography, 401
Doctors, rural location of, 750
Dohrs, Fred E., 407
Domestic air freight, 581
Donaldson, O. Fred, 680
Dry boundary, central Great Plains, 926
Dual mode transportation, 195 (235)
Dubester, Henry J., 136, 144
Dunbar, Gary S., 703
Duncan, Beverly, 403
Duncan, Otis Dudley, 403
Dunlap, Riley E., 371, 372
Dunn, Edgar S., Jr., 425
Dunning, Glenna, 838
Durrenberger, Robert W., 73, 147, 184, 942-945
Dury, George H., 240
Dworkin, Daniel, 298
Dyett, Michael F., 566
Dziegielewski, Benedyki, 302

E

EIA data index: an abstract journal, 2
EIA publications directory: a user's guide, 264
EPA bibliographies, 252, 361-363
EPA publications bibliography. Quarterly abstract bulletin, 362
ERTS, NTIS reports, 195 (3)
Earle, Carville, V., 804
Earlier than you think, 715
Early man in America, 715
Earthquake prediction, 195 (10, 11)
Earth resources: a continuing bibliography, 253
Earth Resources Technology Statellite, NTIS reports, 195 (3)
Earth sciences, 250-389
Earth-science reports, U.S.G.S., 257

East and South, airphoto atlas, 339
Eastern Seaboard, 1810, 799
East Lakes geographer, 87
East North Central states, 87, 907-917
Eastin, Roy B., 179
Ecological dry boundary, central Great Plains, 926
Ecological perspective on crime and violence, 635
Ecology of disease, 751-752
Ecology of North America, 62
Ecology, politics of, 373
Economic areas of the United States, 603
Economic aspects of population change, 726
Economic books: current selections, 612
Economic censuses, 158-161, 161a
Economic censuses: geographic reference manual, 161a
Economic development in nonmetropolitan areas, 436
Economic development of ethnic minorities, 195 (194, 195)
Economic factors in regional water supply management, 195 (19-21)
Economic geography, 514-615
Economic geography (periodical), 78
Economic geography and locational analysis, 514, 515
Economic growth, regions, and resources, 602
Economic history, 614
Economic regions and regional development, 599-603
Economics and business, 604-615
Economics: bibliographic guide to reference books and information sources, 605
Economics information guide series, 503, 563, 614, 664
Economics library selections, 608
Economics of minorities: a guide to information sources, 664
Economics of pollution, 376
Economics selections, 607, 609, 610, 611
Economy of the U. S., basic maps, 516
Ecosystems, effects of acid percipitation, 195 (131, 132)
Ecosystem models, 195 (71-73)
Ecosystems, NTIS reports, 195 (71-74)
Ecumene, 88
Education, geographic, 845
Edwards, Everett E., 783, 790
Effects of land use and urbanization on water, 195 (206-208)
Effects of offshore oil and gas development on coastal communities, 316
Egler, Frank E., 328
Ehrenberg, Ralph E., 770
Ehrhardt, Dennis K., 920
Eister, Margaret F., 257
Ekonomicheskie raiony SShA, 884a, 905a, 927b

Elderly, the, 623-628
Elderly, geographical perspectives on, 623
Elderly, housing for, 628
Eliot Hurst, Michael E., 560
Encyclopedia of American ethnic groups, 646
Encyclopedia of Black America, 688
Encyclopedia of business information sources, 604
Encyclopedias, general, 44-48, 224
Encyclopedias, geographical, 42-43, 52
Energy, 195 (75-94), 263-279, 582-583
Energy abstracts for policy analysis, 267
Energy and environment information resource guide, 268
Energy and minerals, 263-279
Energy, bibliographies, 195 (75, 76)
Energy data base, 195 (44, 88, 131-133, 148, 149, 161)
Energy Information Administration (EIA), 264, 265
Energy information guide, 263
Energy, NTIS reports, 195 (75-94)
Energy policy, 278
Energy research abstracts, 266
Energy, state-of-the art reviews, 195 (75, 76)
Energy statistics, 582, 583
Energy statistics: a guide to information sources, 270
Energy supply and demand modelling, 195 (77, 78)
Engineering Index data base, 195 (10, 46, 67, 87, 127, 168, 179, 180, 186, 252, 254)
Entwicklung der Industrie in den Südstaaten der USA, 886
Environment: a bibliography of social science and related literature, 252
Environment and environmental protection, 359-373
Environment and man in Kansas, 924
Environment as hazard, 389
Environment in general, NTIS reports, 195 (1-3)
Environment of elderly population, 624
Environmental assessment, 195 (1)
Environmental damage, control and reclamation, 530
Environmental damage from surface mined coal, 530
Environmental Data and Information Service, 319
Environmental Data Service, 309, 324
Environmental economics: a guide to information sources, 360
Environmental impact of offshore oil spills, 380
Environmental impact statements, 195 (2), 365, 369

Environmental issues, sociological and socio-psychological, perspectives, 372
Environmental movement, 370
Environmental planning: a guide to information sources, 359
Environmental politics and policy, 371
Environmental Protection Agency (EPA), 252, 361-363
Environmental Protection Agency, Bibliographies of publications, 361, 362, 363
Environmental quality, land use, and urban form, 596
Environmental Science Information Center, 309
Environmental Science Services Administration, 323
Environmental toxicology: a guide to information sources, 379
Environmental values: a guide, 352
Ernst, Robert T., 681, 682
Estall, Robert C., 242, 863
Estuaries, water pollution, 195 (142-144)
Ethnic and racial minorities, 647
Ethnic ghetto in the U.S., 655
Ethnic groups, encyclopedia, 646
Ethnic groups in urban areas, 654
Ethnic groups, NTIS reports, 195 (194-202)
Ethnic groups, studies of, 646-701
Ethnic minorities, 651
Ethnic neighborhoods, 461-465
Ethnic studies bibliography, 653
Ethnic studies information guide series, 672, 675
Ethnicity and immigration, historical geography, 784; see also studies of ethnic groups, 646-701
Ethnicity on the Great Plains, 812
Ethnographic bibliography of North America, 64
Europa yearbook, 50
European immigrants, 670-678
European immigrants, doctoral dissertations, 671
European immigration and ethnicity, 670-678, 784
European immigration and ethnicity, historical bibliography, 670
European impressions of the New England coast, 1497-1620, 797
European settlement and development in North America, 780
Evolution of the American metropolitan system, 1970-1976, 424
Evolution of a tidewater settlement system: All Hallow's parish, Maryland, 1650-1783, 804
Evolution of the unit train, 1960-1969, 573
Ewing, Steve, 880

Exchange bibliography, Council of Planning Librarians, 148, 149, 231, 258, 262, 277, 288, 289, 290, 291, 294, 313, 351, 354, 370, 371, 372, 373, 382, 383, 408, 410, 412, 414, 415, 416, 424, 435, 436, 444, 447, 452, 457, 562, 479, 485, 487, 488, 489, 491, 494, 498, 499, 519, 526, 557, 565, 567, 570, 571, 577, 578, 581, 582, 583, 588, 589, 590, 622, 628, 629, 632, 639, 640, 647, 654, 656, 681, 683, 708, 735, 749, 750, 751, 758, 760, 761, 765, 794, 828, 829, 836, 837, 838, 840, 842, 844, 947
Exploration of the West, 819-821
Exploration of the western America, 1800-1850, 819

F

Facility location, theses and dissertations, 351
Fact book on aging, 626
Factor influencing the rural location of doctors, 750
Fairchild, Wilma B., 250
Farm buildings and houses, 710-714
Farm silo, 714
Far West, airphoto atlas, 339
Federal housing assistance programs, 195 (229-230)
Federal information sources and systems, 174
Federal lands revisited, 343a
Fellmann, Jerome D., 14, 74
Fellows, Donald K., 651
Ferguson, Bruce K., 292, 335
Field, Barry C., 360
Filipovitch, Anthony J., 510
Fire insurance maps, 203, 204
Fisher, James S., 518
Fite, Gilbert C., 533
Flood control, 195 (24-27), 295
Flood damage prevention: an indexed bibliography, 296
Flood history, 195 (28)
Flood plain management, 195 (28), 291
Flood plain zoning and management, legal aspects, 291
Flood plains, 300
Floods, 306
Floods, see water resources
Florida geographer, 125
Florida Society of Geographers, 125
Florida, West coast retirement and tourism, 892
Florin, John W., 247
Fog prediction, 195 (58)
Food supply in the old South, 1840-1860, 807
Ford, Larry R., 467

Foreign commerce and navigation of the
    United States, 162
Forest watersheds, 195 (29-31)
Fort Worth, Texas, 212, 390
Foscue, Edwin J., 237
Foth, Henry D., 337
Foust, J. Brady, 751
Frawley, Margaret L., 530
Frazier, John W., 846
Freeman, Nelda S., 26
Freeman, Otis W., 959
Freidel, Frank, 827
French Americans in New England, 865
Fritschler, A. Lee, 509
From farm to factory to urban
    pastoralism: urban change in Central
    Connecticut, 867
Frontier history, comparative studies
    in, 782
Frontier in American history, 783
Fujimoto, Isao, 701
Fullerton, Ralph O., Jr., 896
Fur trade, 819-821
Fur trade of the American West, 1807-1840,
    821
Furuseth, Owen J., 538
Future environments of North America, 366

G

Gade, Ole, 887
Gagala, Kenneth L., 664
Gaines, Stanley H., 336
Gale, Stephen, 404
Galneder, Mary, 207
Galveston, Texas, subsidence in, 387
Gamma Theta Upsilon, 108
Garland, John H., 904
Garner, Barry J., 393
Garrison, William L., 568
Gastil, Raymond D., 706
Gauthier, Howard L., 559
Gazetteers, 225-226
Gehr, Marilyn, 383
General aids, United States, 66-249
Gereral aids, world-wide, 1-52
General economic geography of the U. S.,
    514-517
General urban geography of the U. S.,
    390-417
Geo abstracts, 3, 195n
Geo-Center, Internationales
    Landkartenhaus, 35
GeoCenter Verlagsbetrieb, 35
Geo-Data: the world almanac gazetteer,
    226
Geographers' mirror of Michigan: a
    bibliography, 908
Geographic education, 845
Geographic literature on Black America,
    681
Geographic monograph series, Indiana
    University, 118

Geographic Names Data Base, 225
Geographic perspectives on America's
    past, 779
Geographic perspectives on urban
    systems, 422
Geographic reference manual, economic
    censuses, 161a
Geographic research in the U. S.
    Geological Survey: Bibliography--
    1966-1980, 221
Geographical abstracts, 3
Geographical bibliography for American
    college libraries, 9, 71
Geographical bulletin, 108
Geographical epidemiology and health
    systems planning, 742
Geographical literature on the American
    Indian, 665
Geographical literature on the American
    Negro, 685, 686
Geographical perspectives, 89
Geographical perspectives and urban
    problems, 401
Geographical perspectives on American
    poverty, 631
Geographical perspectives on the
    elderly, 623
Geographical perspectives on Maryland's
    past, 803
Geographical research and writing, 73,
    147, 184
Geographical review, 77
Geographical serials, 14-15, 74-129
Geographical vignettes, metropolitan
    America, 390
Géographie politique, 755
Geographies, atlases, and special
    references on states and provinces,
    206
Geographies of U. S. (general), 237-249
Geographies of the United States, by
    states (series), 861, 887, 906, 939,
    971
Geographisches Jahrbuch, 5, 57, 68, 968
Geography and contemporary issues, 619
Geography and earth science publica-
    tions, 227-228
Geography and local administration, 757
Geography and mental health, 752
Geography and politics in America, 753
Geography and travel information series,
    768, 830
Geography and urban evolution in the
    San Francisco Bay area, 956
Geography, applied, 846
Geography, graduate departments, 236
Geography of agriculture in the South-
    east, 534, 885
Geography of American cities, 394
Geography of American sport, 716
Geography of Black America, 679
Geography of crime and justice, 637
Geography of crime and violence, 635

Geography of Federal spending, 764
Geography of health and disease, 744
Geography of laws and justice, 636
Geography of manufacturing, 523
Geography of market centers and retail distribution, 448, 553
Geography of marketing, 552
Geography of New York State, 868
Geography of poverty in the United States, 630
Geography of recreation, leisure, and tourism, 828-844
Geography of social well-being in the United States, 618
Geography of the ghetto, 684
Geography of the New York metropolitan region, 870
Geography of the northern Ozark border region in Missouri, 923
Geography of transportation, 559
Geography of wholesaling, 449
Geography of world agriculture, 534, 535, 885, 946
Geo-Katalog, 35
Geolit, 6
Geological Society of America, 58
Geology and geomorphology, 259-262
Geology and geomorphology, NTIS reports, 195 (4-11)
Geology, remote sensing applied to, 195 (4-5)
Geomorphological abstracts, 3
Geomorphology and geography, NTIS reports, 195 (4-11)
Geomorphology and geology, 259-262
Geomorphology, coastal regions, 195 (70)
Geomorphology of the United States, 259
Georges, Daniel E., 633, 635
Georges-Abeyie, Daniel E., 633, 635
Geoscience and man, 112
Geraghty, James J., 286
Gerlach, Linda, 444
Gerlach, Russell L., 922
German-American history and life: a guide to information sources, 672
German-Americana, 673
German seed in Texas soil, 816
Gerrard, Michael B., 376
Geyer, Mark C., 555
Ghetto sociodynamics, 195 (201)
Ghetto, the, 462
Ghettos, 461-465
Gibson, James R., 780, 824
Gieffer, Gerald J., 282, 283, 284
Gilbert, E. W., 819
Gillard, Quentin, 423
Gober, Patricia, 733
Goddard, Stephen, 70
Goehlert, Robert, 478
Goeldner, Charles R., 831
Gokhman, V. M., 905a
Golant, Stephen M., 624
Goldfield, David R., 512

Goldstein, Gerald S., 504
Golledge, Reginald G., 396
Gottmann, Jean, 429, 482, 859, 889
Governance and population: the governmental implications of population change, 726
Governance and services, 468-473
Government Affairs Foundation, 468
Government document bibliography, 175
Government publications, 30-32, 166-194
Government publications.
 Inventories, 166-174
 Selective guides, 175-184
 NTIS, 195
 State and municipal governments, 196-198
Government publications: a guide to bibliographic tools, 175
Government publications and their use, 179
Government reference books, 170
Government reports announcements (NTIS), 195n
Government reports. Announcements and index (NTIS), 195
Government, urban, 468-473
Goyer, Doreen S., 27a
Graber, Linda H., 357
Graduate departments of geography, 236
Graff, Thomas O., 412, 457
Grasmick, Mary K., 666, 667, 668
Grass: yearbook of agriculture, 1948, 546
Grassland of North America: prolegomena to its history, 814
Grasslands of the Great Plains, 333
Graziani, Mary E., 221
Great American Desert, 1800-1850, 927
Great Columbia Plain, 1805-1910, 822
Great Lakes, climate, 322
Great Lakes hydrology, 293
Great Lakes region, 575
Great Lakes transportation system, 575
Great Plains and West North Central states, 918-929
Great Plains, central, 926
Great Plains, central, suitcase farming frontier, 813
Great Plains, ethnicity on, 812
Great Plains-Rocky Mountain geographical journal, 90
Great Soviet encyclopedia, 48
Green, Jerry E., 708
Green, Paul, 901
Greenberg, Michael, 369
Greenfield, Gerald Michael, 507
Greenwood, Michael J., 737
Gregor, Howard F., 535, 539, 946
Gregory, Janet E., 26a
Griffin, Paul F., 243
Grim, Ronald E., 768
Griffiths, Thomas Mel, 929
Grodsky, Susan J., 661

Grondahl, Teg C., 26a
Ground water pollution: general studies, 195 (153-155, 160)
Ground water pollution from irrigation and fertilization, 195 (156, 157)
Ground water pollution monitoring, 195 (161)
Ground-water pollution: saline ground water, 195 (158, 159)
Ground-water recharge, 195 (42)
Growth centers in the American urban systems, 433
Growth, size, and U. S. cities, 434
Growth, urban, 433-436
Guide to atlases, 41
Guide to cartographic records in the National Archives, 202
Guide to government and other official publications for social and economic geography, 32
Guide to graduate department of geography in the United States and Canada, 236
Guide to information sources in the geographical sciences, 70
Guide to obtaining information from the USGS, 255
Guide to reference books, 9th ed., 23, 23a, 23b, 848-850
Guide to reference material, 4th ed., 24, 856
Guide to the literature of cities, 415
Guide to the study of the United States of America, 130, 131
Guide to U. S. government publications, 169
Guide to U. S. government serials and periodicals, 169
Guide to U. S. government statistics, 135
Guides, general, 23-26
Guides, geographical, 8-15, 70-73
Guides to maps and atlases, 33-41, 199-209
Gulf Coast, environmental impact of offshore oil spills, 380
Gulf South Research Institute, 317

H

Haag, W. G., 705
Haas, J. Eugene, 385
Habercom, Guy E., Jr., 195 (7, 84)
Hacia, Henry, 322
Hafner, James A., 632
Hagevik, George H., 382
Hail: meteorology, damage, prevention, and forecasting, 195 (61, 62)
Hamilton, Michael S., 277
Hammond, Kenneth A., 250
Handbook of aging and the social sciences, 627
Handbook of North American Indians, 65
Handbooks, 49-52
Hanink, Dean M., 518
Hankins, Thomas D., 600, 861
Hannay, Annie M., 591
Hanson, Perry O., III, 639, 640
Hare, F. Kenneth, 59, 320
Haren, Claude C., 445
Harmon, John E., 861
Harnly, Caroline D., 388
Harper, Robert A., 421, 482
Harries, Keith D., 633, 636, 637
Harris, Chauncy D., 8, 14, 15, 74, 75
Harrison, Elizabeth A., 195 (71)
Hart, John Fraser, 248, 704, 881, 917
Hart, L. Gary, 749
Hartford, Connecticut, 212, 390, 867
Hartshorn, Truman A., 395, 891
Harvard encyclopedia of American ethnic groups, 646
Harvard guide to American history, 827
Harvey, David W., 460, 621
Harvey, Joan M., 24, 856
Hassert, Kurt, 57
Hatch, Warren L., 319
Hauptstädte und die führenden Städte der USA, 432
Hauser, Philip M., 405
Hawaii, 972-974
Hawaii: a geography, 974
Hawley, Amos H., 500
Hayes, Charles R., 443
Haynes, Kingsley E., 765
Haystead, Ladd, 533
Hazard, coastal flood, 301
Hazardous materials transportation, 195 (184-186)
Hazardous materials waste disposal, 195 (181-183)
Hazards, 384-389
Health care delivery, 747
Health care services, 745-750
Health planning systems and geographical epidemiology, 742
Heart disease, cancer, and stroke in Chicago, 748
Heikoff, Joseph M., 313
Heineberg, Heinz, 12, 72
Heizer, Robert F., 65
Helm, June, 65
Hendee, John C., 353
Her space, her place, 629a
Hernon, Peter, 198
Herstein, Sheila, 133
Hess, David, 589, 590
Hewes, Leslie, 813
Higbee, Edward C., 532
Highway and freeway planning: social and economic effects, 195 (247)
Highway beautification, 195 (248)
Highway development and geographic change, 568
Highway traffic noise, 195 (165)

Highways, socio-economic impact, 567
Hiking and hiking trails, 841
Hilding, Sabine C., 387
Hilliard, Sam B., 807, 897
Hispanic Americans, 693-699
Historic preservation literature, 795
Historical abstracts, 825
Historical geography, 91, 768-827, 868a, 882, 915, 919, 927, 935, 936, 944, 953, 963
Historical geography, agriculture, 789-790
Historical geography, bibliographies and guides, 768-770
Historical geography, by Andrew H. Clark, 775
Historical geography: changing spatial structure and social patterns, 772
Historical geography, cities, 785-788
Historical geography, immigration, 784
Historical geography in North America, 774
Historical geography, land survey, 791-793
Historical geography: 19th century county maps, 209
Historical geography: North American progress during the 1970s, 771
Historical geography of the U.S., 778
Historical geography of the U.S.: bibliography, 768, 769
Historical geography of the U.S.: a guide to information sources, 769
Historical geography, railroad maps, 19th century, 572
Historical geography, regional studies, 797-824
Historical geography, San Diego, 953
Historical geography, settlements and frontiers, 781-783
Historical geography, steel, 1850-1970, 528
Historical geography, surveys of research, 768-770
Historical geography: Texas and the Southwest, 815-818
Historical geography, the Middle West, 808-814
Historical geography: the Northeast, 797-804
Historical geography: the Pacific Northwest and Alaska, 822-824
Historical geography: the South, 805-807
Historical geography: the West, 818-824
Historical geography, topical studies, 781-798
Historical geography, U.S., general, 778-780
Historical geography, Willamette valley, 963
Historical statistics of the United States, 153
History, American, 825-827

History, economic, 614
History of city planning in the United States, 477
History of the rectangular survey system, 793a
History of the United States of America: a guide to information sources, 826
Hodgson, Helen E., 255
Hodson, Dean R., 231
Hoehn, R. Philip, 204
Hofmeister, Burkhard, 402
Hog meat and hoecake: food supply in the Old South, 1840-1860, 807
Hoggart, Keith, 757
Holcomb, H. Briavel, 399
Holleb, Doris B., 476
Holler, Frederick L., 767
Holmes, Jack D. L., 453
Holmes, William M., 900
Hoover, Dwight W., 508
Hopkins, Stephen T., 927a
Hornback, Kenneth E., 252
Horsley, A. Doyne, 906
Horton, Frank E., 422
Hoselitz, Bert F., 854
Houses and farm buildings, 710-714
Houses, common, 710
Housing, 134, 195 (224-230), 355, 455-460, 598, 628, 648, 659-660
Housing: a bibliography, 1960-1972, 598
Housing and minority groups, 659, 660
Housing and planning references, 355
Housing: Federal housing assistance programs, 195 (229, 230)
Housing for the elderly, 628
Housing, NTIS reports, 195 (224-230)
Housing, public and private, 456
Housing: public housing, 195 (228)
Housing, quality, and environment, 457
Housing, race, and residential segregation, 648
Housing, urban 455-460
Houston, Texas, 212, 390, 902
Houston, Texas, subsidence in, 387
How to read the American city, 513
Hsu, Ann Yi-rong, 565
Hudson, Barbara, 469-472
Hudson valley, 868a
Huetz-de-Lemps, Christian, 973
Hugg, Lawrence, 161a, 682
Huke, Robert E., 9
Human adjustment to floods, 306
Human behavior and urban environments, 511
Human ecology, 500, 501
Human ecology of coastal flood hazard in Megalopolis, 301
Human geography, 390-856
Human geography of the South, 883
Human health problems: spatial perspectives, 743
Human settlements, 708

Human spatial behavior: a social geography, 617
Humlum, Johannes, 948
Hundemann, Audrey S., 195 (2, 63, 79, 92, 177)
Hunt, Charles B., 356
Hunter, John Melton, 744
Hurricanes and severe storms, 321
Hurricanes forecasting, modification and research, 195 (63)
Hutchinson, William K., 614
Hydrological and limnological systems, water quality modeling, 195 (48-52)
Hydrological problem of irrigated crops 949
Hydrologische Probleme des Bewässerungsfeldbaues, 949
Hydrology, 195 (12-55), 280-307
Hydrology, remote sensing, 195 (23)
Hydrology, water resources, floods, and snow, NTIS reports, 195 (12-55)

I

Ice and fog: detection and warning systems, 195 (60)
Icebreakers and icebreaking, 195 (102-104)
Ice fog, 195 (59)
Idaho, 939
Identifying urban neighborhoods, 440
Îles Hawaï, depuis 1970, 973
Illinois, 92, 906, 912
Illinois Geographical Society, 92
Illinois: land and life in the prairie state, 912
Illinois prairie, 1818-1840, 809
Illinois, University at Urbana-Champaign, Dept. of geography, 116
Illinois. University, Water Resources Center, 293
Illustrations of the American earth, 703
Images of the Ohio Valley, 1740 to 1860, 808
Images of the plains: the role of human nature in settlement, 810
Immigrants, European, 670-678
Immigrants, European, doctoral dissertations, 671
Immigrants in the Ozarks, 922
Immigration and ethnicity: a guide to information sources, 652
Immigration and ethnicity, historical geography, 784; see also studies of ethnic groups, 646-701
Immigration literature: abstracts of demographic, economic, and policy studies, 661
Immigration, recent, 662
Impact of industry upon rural areas, 526
Imperial Russia in frontier America, 1784-1867, 824
Imperial Texas, 815

Index of economic articles, 613
Index of economic journals, 613
Index of state geological survey publications, 260, 261
Index of U.S. Geological Survey publications relating to coal, 272, 273
Index to maps in books and periodicals, 38, 38a
Index to publications of the U.S. Department of Agriculture, 194
Indiana: crossroads of America, 911
Indiana State University, Terre Haute, 117
Indiana University, 118
Indians, American, 665-669
Indians, geographic literature, 665
Industrial location, 518-522, 524
Industrial plant location, 520, 521
Industrial structure of American cities, 517
Industrial suburbanization, 488
Industrialisierung der Bluegrass Region von Kentucky, 894
Industrialization, Blue Grass region, Kentucky, 894
Industrialization, nonmetropolitan, 525
Industrialization of U.S. agriculture, 539
Industry, impact on rural areas, 526
Industry in the South, 886
Information bulletin, 107
Information sources and service directory, Department of the Interior, 254
Information sources in transportation, 561
Information sources of political science, 767
Information sources, physical geography, 250-258
Initial evaluation and utilization of the Illinois prairies, 1818-1840, 809
Inland waterways, 577
Inland waterways transportation, 574
Institute of Behavioral Science, University of Colorado, 386
Inter-Agency Committee on Water Resources, Subcommittee on Hydrology (and Sedimentation), 285
Intergéo, 4
Internal migration in the U.S., 737
Internal structure of cities, 439
International aerospace abstracts, 195 (5), 253
International Aerospace Abstracts data base, NTIS reports, 195 (5, 106, 128, 257)
International Association of Agricultural Economists, 531

International bibliography of vegetation maps, 60
International index to periodicals, 851
International list of geographical serials, 14, 74
International maps and atlases in print, 34
International population census bibliography, 27, 27a
International selective bibliography on leisure: Part 1. USA, 833
Interpretation of ordinary landscapes, 707
Interpreting the city: an urban geography, 395
Interregional migration, national policy, and social justice, 730
Introduction to library research in geography, 146, 183
Introduction to United States public documents, 177
Iowa. University, 119
Irrigated crops, 949
Irrigation agriculture in the southwest United States, 934
Irrigation oasis, Phoenix, 937
Italian Americans: a guide to information sources, 675
Italians in the United States, 676, 677
Itogi nauki i tekhniki, 536
Ives, Peter B., 208

J

Jackson, Richard H., 341, 584
Jakle, Cynthia A., 647
Jakle, John A., 490, 617, 622, 647, 710, 777, 794, 808
James, Preston E., 249, 775
Johnson, Gary T., 732
Johnson, Hildegard Binder, 793, 917
Johnson, Hugh A., 445
Johnson, Julia, 838
Johnson, Robert B., 942
Johnston, Ronald J., 418, 764
Jones, Clarence F., 249, 775
Jones, Douglas E., 927a
Jones, Holway R., 475
Jones, Victor, 468-469
Jopp, Werner, 52
Jordan, Terry G., 711, 816, 817, 900
Journal of cultural geography, 93
Journal of economic abstracts, 606
Journal of economic literature, 504, 606, 613, 737
Journal of geography, 94
Journal of historical geography, 95
Job-providing organizations and systems of cities, 427

K

Kaiser, Edward J., 442
Kale, Steven, 526
Kansas, 126, 924
Kansas Council for Geographic Education, 126
Kansas geographer, 126
Kansas State University, 126
Kanely, Edna M., 167
Karinen, Arthur E., 941
Kasarda, John D., 441
Kates, Robert W., 301, 350, 389
Keckeissen, Rita G., 23, 848
Keiffer, F. V., 262
Keith, Susan J., 195 (42)
Kelland, Frank A., 873
Kelland, Marilyn C., 873
Kenton, Edith, 195 (204, 222, 235, 247)
Kentucky, 894-895
Kentucky, Blue Grass region, 894
Kentucky, East, regional planning, 895
Keresztesi, Michael, 672
Kessler, Mary Z., 452
Key word identifiers of theses and dissertations on land use, water use, resource conflict, 351
Kharitonov, V. M., 405a
King, Leslie J., 396
King, Ruth Reece, 57
Kiraldi, Louis, 375
Klain, Ambrose, 844
Knapp, Rüdiger, 61
Kniffen, Fred B., papers in honor of, 705
Knight, Allen W., 377
Knowles, Richard, 219
Koch, Josef, 954
Koelsch, William A., 331
Kohn, Clyde F., 406
Kolm, Richard, 657
Konnecke, Bernd., 964
Kovacik, Charles F., 887
Kovalevskii, V. P., 905a
Kratkaia geograficheskaia entisklopediia, 43
Küchler, A. William, 60
Kudrna, Frank L., Jr., 289
Kulturlandschaftliche Bedeutung des primären Wirtschaftssektors im Staate Oregon USA, 964
Kurian, George Thomas, 226
Kuzina, Irina Mikhailovna, 536

L

Laboratoire d'Information et de Documentation en Géographie, 4, 54, 56, 67, 967
Lacy, Mary G., 591
La Grande encyclopédie, 45
Lake, Robert W., 465
Lamprecht, Sandra J., 947
Lancaster, Joel R., 488, 828
Land: yearbook of agriculture, 1958, 550
Land and natural resources information systems, 258
Land and people: preindustrial New Jersey, 801
Land ownership maps, 209
Land planning and information systems, 587
Land planning in national parks and forests, 838
Land reclamation, revegetation, 195 (74)
Land resource areas, 338
Land-resource planning, 257
Land resource regions, 338
Land resource regions and major land resource areas of the U.S., 338
Land resources and land use, 584-597
Land resources planning, state, 589, 590
Land survey, historical geography, 791-793
Land use, 338-347
Land use and its patterns in the U.S., 340
Land use and land resources, 584-597
Land use and urban development impacts of beltways, 566
Land use and urbanization, effects on water, 195 (206-208)
Land use and zoning, 442-445
Land use control: interface of law and geography, 346
Land use, impact of highways and commuter rail systems, 567
Land use impacts of rapid transit, 570
Land use in America, 341, 584
Land use in American cities, 443
Land use in nonmetropolitan America, 585
Land use in urban areas, 195 (203-205)
Land use issues in nonmetropolitan America, 347
Land use planning and soils, 335
Land use planning information, 588
Land use planning, politics of, 766
Land use, theses and dissertations, 351
Land use, urban form and environmental quality, 596
Land use, urban, planning, 442
Land utilization, bibliography, 591-593
Landfills, sanitary, 195 (177-180)
Landman, Georgina B., 291
Landsat, NTIS reports, 195 (3)
Landsberg, H. E., 59, 320
Landscape, 96

Landslides, 195 (6)
Landwirtschaft der Vereinigten Staaten, 537
Lange, Norbert de, 72
Lantis, David W., 941
Law of the sea: maritime boundaries and jurisdictions, 195 (95)
Lawson, Merlin P., 810, 927
Leatherberry, Earl E., 843
Lee, David R., 629a
Lee, Joel M., 750
Legal aspects of flood plain zoning and management, 291
LeGear, Clara Egli, 201
Lehmann, Edward J., 195 (47, 107, 112, 118, 124, 138, 206, 217)
Leidy, William Philip, 181
Leisure, recreation, and tourism, 828-844
Lemon, James T., 800
Lethal aspects of urban violence, 634
Lewis and Clark and the image of American Northwest, 820
Lewis, George K., 866
Lewis, Peirce F., 717, 899
Lewis, Richard T., 861
Lewis, Tom, 861
Lewthwaite, Gordon R., 9, 71
Lex, Barbara W., 735
Ley, David, 687
Library of Congress, 19, 25, 28, 40, 130, 131, 132, 136, 144, 197, 201, 203, 209, 251, 572
Library of Congress. Census Library Project, 28, 136, 144
Library of Congress. Geography and Map Division, 40, 201, 203, 209, 572
Library of Congress main reading room reference collection subject catalog, 25, 132
Library of Congress, Map Division; see Geography and Map Division
Library of Congress publications in print, 193
Lieberson, Stanley, 403
Likeness of the Eastern Seaboard, 1810, 799
Lime, David W., 835, 843
Lin, Chien, 700
List of geographical atlases, 40
List of published soil surveys, 334
Listokin, David, 444
Literature of geography, 11
Local administration, 757
Local government boundary commissions, 758
Location and environment of elderly population, 624
Location, industrial, 518-522, 524
Location of facilities, theses and dissertations, 351
Locational analysis and economic geography, 514, 515

Locational analysis of the urban health
  care crisis, 746
Log buildings, 711
Longbrake, David D., 893
Lonsdale, Richard E., 525
Look of our land, 339
Look of the land, 704
Loomba, Bodh, 751
Lopez, Lorreda, 272
Los Angeles, California, 212, 390, 950-952
Los Angeles: the centrifugal city, 951
Los Angeles metropolis, 950
Los Angeles metropolitan experience: uniqueness, generality, and the goal of the good life, 952
Louder, Dean R., 214
Louisiana, 887, 897-899
Louisiana State University, 112
Low, W. Augustus, 688
Lowenthal, David, 717
Loyd, Bonnie, 629
Lucas, Robert C., 353
Luebke, Frederick C., 811, 812
Lynch, Donald F., 971
Lyon, Edward E., 911
Lytle, Elizabeth E., 679

M

Macinko, George, 250, 347, 585
MacKenzie, Alec, 764
Mahnke, Hans-Peter, 432
Major geographical periodicals, 76-79
Major job-providing organizations and system of cities, 427
Making of Oregon, 823
Making of urban America, 477
Malin, James C., 814
Man and cultural heritage, 705
Man and environment in the lower Mississippi valley, 897
Man and environment information guide series, 359, 360, 377, 378, 379
Man and land in the U.S., 343
Man, early, in America, 715
Management information guide, 562
Manipulated city, 404
Manners, Ian R., 367
Manpower statistics, 149
Manufacturing, 523-528
Manufacturing: a study of industrial location, 524
Map collections, a directory, 223
Maps and atlases, 33-41, 199-223
Maps for America, 200
Maps illustrating rural settlement patterns, 709
Maps, marketing, 554a
Maps of the U.S. economy, 516
Maps, railroads, 19th century, 572
Maps relating to land-resource planning, U.S.G.S., 257

Marine Science Library, Pell, 310
Maritime boundaries and jurisdictions, 195 (95)
Mark, Charles, 641
Market centers, 448, 553
Marketing, geography of, 552
Marketing maps, 554a
Marschner, Francis J., 340
Martin, Howard H., 959
Martinson, Tom L., 146, 183
Maryland: a geography, 877
Maryland, All Hallow's parish, 1650-1783 804
Maryland, geographical perspectives on its past, 803
Mason, John Brown, 178
Masotti, Louis H., 485
Mass transportation, urban, 569
Master's theses in geography, 232
Mather, E. Cotton, 917
Mathieson, Raymond S., 240
Matros, Ron, 917
Matthews, Olen P., 939
Matty, Paul, 480
May, Edward E., 588
Mayer, Harold M., 406, 443, 575, 579, 910, 915, 916
Mayer, Jonathan D., 742
Mazey, Mary Ellen, 629a
Mazie, Sara Mills, 726
McAlvin, Margaret J., 335
McCormick, Jack 60
McCrum, Blanche P., 130
McDonald, Robert H., 470-472
McGaugh, Maurice E., 206
McIlvaine, Eileen, 23, 848
McInnis, Raymond G., 855
McKee, Jesse O., 887
McKnight, Tom L., 237
McManis, Douglas R., 768, 769, 797, 798, 809
Mead, William R., 245
Medical geography, 741-752
Megalapolis, 429, 859
Meinig, Donald W., 707, 776, 815, 818, 822
Melnick, Robert A., 796
Melnyk, Peter, 605
Melosi, Martin V., 381
Merchant's world, 449, 554
Meredith, Dale D., 293
Merrens, Harry Roy, 806
Meshenberg, Michael J., 359
Messner, Stephen D., 659
Metcalf, Kenneth N., 562
Meteorology and climatology, NTIS reports, 195 (56-63)
Metropolis and region, 403
Metropolis in Georgia: Atlanta, 891
Metropolis on the move, 482
Metropolitan America, 390

Metropolitan America: commuting patterns urban fields, and decentralization processes, 423
Metropolitan America: geographic perspectives and teaching strategies, 407
Metropolitan analysis projecs, comparative, AAG, 212, 390, 391. See also Metropolitan areas: geographical vignettes.
Metropolitan areas: geographical vignettes, 390, 866, 867, 869, 875, 876, 878, 879, 891, 893, 899, 902, 903, 909, 910, 914, 920, 925, 952, 955, 965
Metropolitan communities: government and politics, 468-472
Metropolitan Detroit: an anatomy of social change, 909
Metropolitan governance, 473
Metropolitan growth and change, 435
Metropolitan Philadelphia: a study of conflicts and cleavages, 875
Metropolitan Pittsburgh: old trends and new directions, 876
Metropolitan system, American, evolution, 1970-1976, 424
METRO-rapid transit, Washington, D.C., 195 (241)
Mexican American: guide to research aids, 694
Mexican Americans, 693-698
Mexican Americans: a research bibliography, 697
Mexican-Americans, geographical literature, 1920-1971, 693
Mexican Americans, reference materials, 695
Meyer, David R., 464, 867
Meyer, Douglas K., 710
Meyer, Jon K., 496
Meyer, Kenneth C., 875
Meyers Enzyklopädisches Lexikon, 47
Meyers Kontinent und Meere, 52
Meyersohn, Rolf, 833
Meynen, Emil, 674
Miami, Florida, 212, 390, 893
Michigan, 906
Michigan geographical publications, 113
Michigan: heart of the Great Lakes, 907
Michigan. University, 113
Middagh, Mark, 708
Middle Atlantic States, 868-876
Middle West, 904-927; see also historical geography, 808-814
Midwest, American: a regional geography, 904
Migrant workers, 195 (202)
Migration, 730-738
Migration and regional development in the U.S., 738
Migration, cityward, 735
Migration, internal, in the U.S., 737
Migration, low income whites, 735
Migration, south to north, 735

Migration, sunbelt, 734
Mikesell, Marvin W., 367, 782
Miller, Crane S., 241
Miller, David W., 286
Miller, E. Willard, 205, 271, 523, 524
Miller, Elizabeth W., 692
Miller, Ruby M., 271
Miller, Wayne C., 649
Mills, Barbara, 498
Milton, John P., 366
Minerals and energy, 263-279
Mineral facts and problems, 279
Mineral resources of the United States, 164
Minerals yearbook, 164
Mini-guide to the 1977 economic censuses, 161a
Mining, 529-530
Minneapolis, Minnesota, 212, 390, 925
Minorities, 665-669, 679-692, 700-701
Minorities, comprehensive bibliography, 649
Minority groups and housing, 659, 660
Minority studies: a selective annotated bibliography, 650
Mirror for Americans: likeness of the Eastern Seaboard, 1810, 799
Mississippi (state), 887
Mississippi Council for Geographic Education, 127
Mississippi geographer, 127
Mississippi valley, lower, 897
Missouri: a geography, 918
Misused and misplaced hospitals and doctors, 746
Mitchell, James K., 314, 318
Mitchell, Robert D., 803, 805
Mladenoff, David J., 587
Mobility, residential location, and urban change, 732
Modelski, Andrew W., 572
Modern geography of the United States, 242
Modern metropolitan systems, 421
Modoc county, California, 958
Moe, Christine, 295, 316, 380, 492
Monmonier, Mark S., 721
Monthly catalog of U.S. Government publications, 166, 167
Monthly checklist of state publications, 197
Moore, Eric G., 404
Moore, Harry E., 858
Morehead, Joe, 177
Morgan, Joseph R., 974
Morrill, Richard L., 630, 756
Morris, John W., 933
Morrison, Denton E., 252, 370
Morrison, Paul Cross, 908
Morss, Elliott R., 726
Mortality, spatial aspects, 751
Mosaic of America's ethnic minorities, 651

Moses, Leon N., 504
Moskovskii Gosudarstvennyi Universitet, 405a
Mount St. Helens, 388
Mountain states, 928-939
Mountains and desert, airphoto atlas, 339
Mugridge, Donald H., 130
Muller, Edward K., 803
Muller, Peter O., 481, 514, 515, 875
Multimodal transportation planning, 195 (237)
Municipal government reference sources, 198
Municipal Yearbook, 392
Murata, Alice K., 700
Murdock, George P., 64
Murin, William J., 507
Murphy, Raymond E., 400, 446
Murphy, Thomas P., 502, 505
Musconetcong Valley of New Jersey, 802

N

NASA, 253
NOAA, see U.S. National Oceanic and Atmospheric Administration
NTIS, 195
NTIS data base, 195
Nash, A. E. Keir, 726
National Academy of Sciences, Committee on geography, 401
National Aeronautics and Space Administration, 253
National Agricultural Library, 540
National assessment of water resources, 303, 304
National atlas of the United States of America, 210
National Cartographic Information Center, 199
National Climatic Center, Asheville, N.C., 319
National Council for Geographic Education, 94, 407
National Council on the Aging, 626
National Environmental Policy Act, 364
National forests and parks, land planning, 838
National gazetteer of the United States of America, 225
National Oceanic and Atmospheric Administration, 308, 309, 319, 322, 324, 327
National parks, 358, 839
National parks and forests, land planning, 838
National Planning Association, 516
National Referral Center, 251
National Sea Grant Depository, 310
National Technical Information Service, 195 (1-262)
Nation's water resources, 303, 304
Natural conditions, 250-389

Natural gas: supply, demand, and utilization, 195 (89)
Natural hazard research, 314, 384, 385
Natural hazards, 384-389
Natural landscapes, 352-358
Natural regions of the U.S. and Canada, 356
Natural resource recreation sites, 837
Natural vegetation of North America, 329
Natural world information guide series, 270
Nebraska, 906
Negro in America, 692
Negro in the United States, 691
Negroes, 463, 464, 483, 679-692
Negroes in the U.S.: social, industrial, and behavioral interactions, 195 (199-200)
Neighborhoods and urban ecology, 440-441
Neighborhoods, identifying urban, 440
Nelson, Howard J., 950, 952
Nelson, Ronald E., 912
Neufeld, M. Lynne, 268
New communities, 493
New Encyclopaedia britannica, 44
New England, 862-867
New England: a study in industrial adjustment, 863
New England development bibliography, 864
New England, francophones, 865
New England's Prospect, 1933, 862
New geographies of the past, 773
New Hampshire, 861
New Jersey: a geography, 872
New Jersey: garden or suburb, 873
New Jersey, Musconetcong valley, 802
New Jersey, population, 874
New Jersey, preindustrial, 801
New Mexico, geographers' contributions, 935, 936
New Orleans, Louisiana, 212, 390, 899
New Orleans: the making of an urban landscape, 899
New publications of the Geological Survey, 188
New suburbanites: race and housing in the suburbs, 465
New towns, 195 (223), 491-494
New towns, American experience, 491
New towns and utopias, 492
New York (state), 861
New York metropolitan region study, 871
New York-Newark air freight system, 580
New York-Northern New Jersey metropolitan areas, 212, 390, 869-871

New York Public Library, 30, 37
New York state, geography of, 868
New York. State University, Binghampton, 109
Newsome, Walter L., 170
Ng, Wing-cheung, 499
Nichols, Leland J., 828
Nichols, Woodrow W., Jr., 893
Nickles, John M., 58
Niemann, Bernard J., Jr., 587
Nilsen, Kirsti, 416
Nineteenth century inland centers and ports, 390
Nineteenth century ports, 390
No growth and the evolution of the American metropolitan system, 1970-1976, 424
Noble, Allen G., 714
Nogales, Luis G., 698
Noh, Toshio, 13a
Noise control for motor vehicles, 195 (167, 168)
Noise pollution, 195 (162-168)
Noise pollution: a guide to information sources, 378
Noise pollution economics, 195 (164)
Nonmetropolitan America, 347
Nonmetropolitan areas, land use, 585
Nonmetropolitan areas, population growth and migration, 733
Nonmetropolitan industrialization, 525
North America, 55-65
North America: a geography of Canada and the United States, 238
North America in maps, 219
North America: its countries and regions, 244
North American city, 393
North American Indians in towns and cities, 669
North American Midwest: a regional geography, 904
North American prairie, 332
North American urban patterns, 420
North Carolina, 887
North Carolina. University, 97
North Central States, 905
North Central States, airphoto atlas, 339
North Dakota Geographers, Association of, 124
North, Gary W., 255
North, Jeannette H., 661
Northam, Ray M., 398
Northeast, 859-880: see also historical geography, 797-804
Northeastern Ohio urban complex, 910
Northeastern U.S., 860
Northeastern U.S., plant communities, 328
Northwestern United States, 960
Northwestern University studies in geography, 114
Novak, Benjamin, 762
Nuclear electric power generation: economic analysis, 195 (90, 91)

O

Oakland, California, 212, 390, 955
Oaks, Priscilla, 650
Oasis, Phoenix, 937
Oasis, Wasatch, 932
O'Brien, Raymond J., 868a
Occasional publication, University of Illinois, 116
Ocean, remote sensing, 195 (96-99)
Ocean wave sensing, 195 (99)
Oceanic abstracts, 195 (68, 69, 95, 255)
Oceanography, NTIS reports, 195 (95-104)
Odum, Howard W., 858, 884
Office of Coastal Zone Management, 308
Office of Population Research, Princeton University, 740
Office of Water Research and Technology, 280, 281
Official publications, U.S. Government, 178
Offshore drilling, 195 (84-88)
Offshore drilling: environmental effects, 195 (87, 88)
Offshore oil and gas development, 316
Offshore oil spills, environmental impacts, 380
Ohio geographers: recent research themes, 128
Ohio, northeastern, urban complex, 910
Ohio valley, 1740 to 1860, 808
Oil pollution detection and sensing, 195 (145, 146)
Oil shale as a possible fossil fuel resource, 276
Oil shale waste disposal, 195 (148)
Oil spills: environmental effects, 195 (147), 380
Old South, food supply in, 1840-1860, 807
O'Leary, Timothy J., 64
Oliver, Virginia, 794
Olson, Sherry H., 878
Onibokum, Adepoju G., 567
Open space decision process, 597
Open space land, planning and taxation, 355
Open spaces, 352-358
Order upon the land: the U.S. rectangular land survey and the Upper Mississippi country, 793
Oregon, cultural landscape, 964
Oregon divided: a regional geography, 962
Oregon, historical geography, 823
Original survey and land subdivision, 792
O'Riordan, Timothy, 368
Orr, James F., 839

Orr, Oliver H., Jr., 131
Ortiz, Alfonso, 65
Our landed heritage: the public domain, 345
Outdoor recreation, 195 (259, 260), 828, 832
Outlook for water, 307
Owings, Loren C., 352
Oxford regional economic atlas: United States and Canada, 215
Ozarks, 921, 922, 923
Ozarks: land and life, 921

P

PAIS Bulletin, 852
Pacific Northwest, 822-823, 959-965
Pacific Northwest: overall appreciation, 959
Pacific northwest: select bibliography, 1930-1939, 961
Page, G. William, 369
Paleoclimatology, 195 (56)
Palic, Vladimir M., 175
Palm, Risa, 394, 439
Palmer, Martha E., 902
Palumbo, Dennis J., 506
Papers in geography, Pennsylvania State University, 120
Parish, David W., 196
Parke, Robert, Jr., 726
Parker, Linda, 625
Parkins, Almon E., 882
Parson, Ruben L., 349
Passage through the garden: Lewis and Clark, 820
Past landscapes, 794
Paterson, John H., 238, 857
Patricoski, M. L., 195 (83)
Pattern and process: research in historical geography, 770
Pattison, William D., 791
Paullin, Charles O., 213
Paulus, Virginia, 598
Paylore, Patricia, 195 (42)
Pearson, Roger W., 971
Pease, Robert W., 958
Peet, Richard, 620, 631
Pell Marine Science Library, 310
Pennsylvania, 98, 861
Pennsylvania geographer, 98
Pennsylvania Geographical Society, 98
Pennsylvania Germans, 674
Pennsylvania State University, 120
Pension cities, 954
People of the U.S. in the 20th Century, 727
Periodical literature on United States cities, 413
Perloff, Harvey S., 602
Perspectives on environment, 367
Petrochemical industry, 886
Petrochemische Industrie, 886

Petty, Julian J., 890
Phelan, Dennis M., 844
Philadelphia, black neighborhood, 687
Philadelphia, Pennsylvania, 212, 390, 875
Phillips, Phillip D., 424
Phoenix, Arizona, oasis, 937
Photo-atlas of the U.S., 222
Photo-Geographic international, 222
Physical geography of U.S., 250-389
Physical resources, 250-389
Physician and dental manpower distribution, 749
Physiographic divisions of Alaska, 970
Pickard, Jerome P., 355
Pierce, John T., 538
Pinkerton, James R., 832
Pinkerton, Marjorie J., 832
Pino, Frank, 697
Pioneer America: the journal of historic American material culture, 712
Pittsburgh, Pennsylvania, 212, 390, 876
Place, Linna F., 625
Place names, 847
Place-rated almanac, 417
Plains and prairies, airphoto atlas, 339
Planned regional shopping centers, 450
Planned suburban shopping center, 453
Planning and Management Consultants, Ltd., Carbondale, Ill., 287, 299
Planning and management of water resources programs, 195 (15, 16, 17, 18)
Planning, city, 474-480
Planning publications, 480
Plant communities, 328
Plant geography, 330
Plant location, 520, 521
Plants and people: vegetation change in North America, 63
Platt, Elizabeth T., 10
Platt, Rutherford H., 346, 347, 585, 597
Pohl, Thomas W., 870
Police information systems, 640
Polish American history and culture, 678
Political areal organization, 756-763
Political geography, 753-767
Political geography quarterly, 100
Political redistricting and geographic theory, 756
Political science, 767
Politics of ecology, 373
Politics of land use planning, 766
Pollution, 195 (105-186), 374-383
Pollution: a selected bibliography of U.S. government publications on air, water, and land pollution, 37?
Pollution abstracts, 195 (126)

Pollution abstracts with indexes, 374
Pollution, air, 195 (107-137)
Pollution, air, water, and noise, NTIS reports, 195 (105-186)
Pollution, economics, 376
Pollution, government publications, 1965-1970, 375
Pollution, noise, 195 (162-168)
Pollution, urban, 381
Pollution, water, 195 (138-161)
Polovitskaia, M. E., 884a, 905a, 927b
Popular guide to government publications, 181
Population abstract of the United States, 154
Population and the American future, 726
Population bulletin, 724
Population, distribution, and policy, 726
Population geography, 721-740
Population growth and migration, nonmetropolitan areas of U.S., 733
Population index, 739
Population index bibliography, 740
Population mobility, 195 (192, 193)
Population, NTIS reports, 195 (189-193)
Population, New Jersey, 874
Population of the United States, 729
Population projections for area planning, 195 (189-191)
Population, resources, and the environment, 726
Port development, 576
Port of Chicago and the St. Lawrence Seaway, 579, 916
Porteous, J. Douglas, 494
Porter, Dorothy B., 691
Ports and supertankers, 195 (253-255)
Post, Jeremiah B., 830
Post, Joyce A., 830
Pötke, Peter Michael, 892
Poverty, 630-632
Powell, Margaret S., 847
Power plant siting, 195 (92-94), 277
Prairies and plains, airphoto atlas, 339
Precipitation washout, 195 (57)
Pred, Allan R., 427, 428, 430, 786-788
Preparation and evaluation of environmental impact statements, 195 (2)
Preservation, urban, 467
Price, Daniel O., 736
Price, Edward T., Jr., 9, 71
Princeton University, Office of Population Research, 740
Private grazing and public lands, 928
Proceedings, AAG, Middle States Division, 123
Professional geographer, 101
Professional paper, Indiana State University, Terre Haute, 117
Profile of America's older population, 626
Progress in geography, 857

Progress in historical geography, 774
Progress in human geography, 102, 426, 439, 467, 742, 745, 771, 772
Progress in physical geography, 103
Program of Technology, Environment, and Man, 386
Pryde, Philip R., 953
Public Affairs Information Service (PAIS) Bulletin, 852
Public domain, 345
Public housing, 195 (228)
Public lands and private grazing, 928
Public lands bibliography, 594, 595
Public opinion and sociology of water resource development, 195 (22)
Publications, Bureau of Mines, 189-190
Publications, Department of Agriculture, 194
Publications, Department of Commerce, 191-192
Publications, Geological Survey, 186-188
Publications in geography, University of California, 111
Publications, Library of Congress, 193
Publications, U.S.G.S., 186-188
Puerto Ricans on the U.S. mainland, 699
Psychological abstracts, 643
Psychology, 643-645
Pyle, Gerald F., 638, 743, 748

Q

Quality of housing and its environment, 457
Quality of life in the urban environment, 195 (209-211)

R

RV-Katalog, 35
Race and housing in the suburbs, 465
Race and urban residential choice, 461
Race, housing, and residential segregation, 648
Radical geography, 620
Radical journal of geography, 81
Rafferty, Milton D., 918, 921
Railroad freight transportation, 195 (249, 250)
Railroad maps of the U.S., 19th century, 572
Rakitnikov, A. N., 536
Rakowski, James P., 563
Rand McNally and Co., 211, 216
Rand McNally commercial atlas and marketing guide, 211
Rand McNally road atlas, 216
Randall, Edwina, 511
Rapid-growth communities, 436
Rapid transit, 195 (241, 242)
Rapid transit, land use impacts, 570

Ray, John B., 896
Ray, William W., 410
Reader's guide to the social sciences, 854
Readings in resource management and conservation, 350
Readings in urban geography, 406
Recent immigration to the U.S., 662
Recent publications on distribution of population, 723
Reclamation of coal surface mining, 274
Reclamation of surface mined areas, 530
Recreation, 195 (258-262), 828-844
Recreation and tourism, NTIS reports, 195 (258-262)
Recreation and water resources, 195 (261-262)
Recreation, natural resource sites, 837
Recreation, outdoor, 195 (259-260), 828, 832
Recreation, river, 843
Recreation, rural 840
Recreation sites, intensive use, 837
Recreation, spatial organization, theses and dissertations, 829
Recreation, water based, 842
Recreational benefits, 836
Recreational carrying capacity, 835
Recreational land, carrying capacity, 834
Rectangular survey system, 793a
Reed, Carl N., III, 640
Reed, Ritchie H., 726
Rees, Philip H., 459
Reeves, Earl J., 510
Referativnyi zhurnal: geografiia, 7, 69
Reference materials on Mexican Americans, 695
References on the significance of the frontier, 783
Regional and city planning, 478
Regional and local economic development, 195 (187, 188)
Regional and urban solid waste disposal, 195 (174-176)
Regional development, 599-603
Regional economics, NTIS reports, 195 (187-188)
Regional geomorphology of the United States, 259
Regional geography of Anglo-America, 237
Regional landscapes, 247
Regional shopping centers, 450
Regional statistics, 143
Regional vegetation literature, 328
Regional water supply, 195 (19-21)
Regionalism, 857-858
Regionalplanung in den USA, Ost-Kentucky, 895
Regionen der USA, 246
Regions of the United States, 248, 857-974; see also historical geography, 797-824

Regions, resources, and economic growth, 602
Regnell, John B., 495
Regulation of stormwater, 292
Remarkable continent, atlas, 214
Remote sensing, 195 (3-5, 23, 96-99, 105-106, 212, 256-257), 221
Remote sensing applied to agricultural resources, 195 (257)
Remote sensing applied to environmental pollution detection and management, 195 (105)
Remote sensing applied to geology, 195 (5)
Remote sensing applied to geology and mineralogy, 195 (4)
Remote sensing applied to hydrology, 195 (23)
Remote sensing applied to pollution monitoring, 195 (106)
Remote sensing applied to urban and regional planning, 195 (212)
Remote sensing for natural resources, environmental, and regional planning, 195 (3)
Remote sensing of agricultural resources, 195 (256)
Remote sensing of the ocean, 195 (96-99)
Remote sensing of the ocean dynamics, 195 (98)
Renewal, urban, 466
Rentnerstädte in Kalifornien, 954
Reps, John W., 477
Research catalogue of the American Geographical Society, 1-2, 53, 55, 66, 86, 972, 996
Research directions in urban transportation geography, 558
Research guide to arid lands, 927a
Research in contemporary and applied geography, 109
Research Papers, University of Chicago, Department of Geography, 85. For individual titles see list at end of this volume.
Research resources: annotated guide to the social sciences, 178
Reservoir and lake sedimentation, 195 (33)
Residential, see Housing
Residential choice, and race, 461
Residential patterns in American cities: 1960, 459
Residential segregation, race, and housing, 648
Resource conflict, theses and dissertations, 351
Resource management and conservation, readings, 350

Resource papers for college geography, AAG, 298, 369, 399, 731, 752. See also Resource publications in geography, and AAG, Commission on College Geography, Resource papers.
Resource policy, theses and dissertations, 351
Resource publications in geography, AAG, 63, 82, 538, 756. See also Resource papers for college geography, and AAG, Commission on College Geography, Resource papers.
Resources, regions, and economic growth, 602
Retail distribution, 448, 553
Retirement cities, 892, 954
Retirement und Tourismus an der Westküste Floridas, 892
Retirement, west coast of Florida, 892
Revegetation, land reclamation, 195 (74)
Reviews, 227-228
Revitalizing cities, 399
Revzan, David A., 552
Reynolds, David R., 473
Rhode Island, University of, 310
Rickert, John E., 355
Ridd, Merrill K., 407
Ridker, Ronald G., 726
Rio Grande flood control and drainage, 295
Rips, Rae Elizabeth, 180
River basin development, 195 (43)
River recreation, 843
Ristow, Walter W., 554a
Robbins, Naomi C., 133
Robbins, Roy M., 345
Robinson, Barbara J., 694
Robinson, J. Cordell, 694
Robinson, J. Lewis, 241
Roeder, Judith E. R., 511
Rogers, John A., 927a
Rogoff, Marc Jay, 294
Role of modernization in spatial diffusion of public policies in U.S., 1870-1970, 765
Rooney, John F., Jr., 214, 716
Rose, Harold M., 461, 463, 483, 634, 683, 684
Roseman, Curtis C., 617, 731
Rosenberg, Mark W., 745
Rosenkrantz, Barbara Gutmann, 331
Ross, Bernard H., 509
Rouse, John E., Jr., 456
Rowe, James E., 274, 520, 521
Rowntree, Rowan A., 839
Rubright, Lynnell, 929
Rudd, Robert L., 379
Ruffner, James A., 326, 327
Rugg, Dean S., 397
Ruhr Universität, 892
Runte, Alfred, 358
Rural and suburban towns, 489
Rural areas, impact of industry upon, 526
Rural location of doctors, 750
Rural recreation, 840
Rural settlement patterns in the U.S. as illustrated on 100 topographic quadrangle maps, 709
Rural-urban migration research in the U.S., 736
Rush, Marjorie N., 902
Russian America, 1784-1867, 824

S

SUNY, Binghamton, 109
Sachs, Moshe Y., 51, 224
Sage urban studies abstracts, 497
St. Lawrence seaway, 579, 916
St. Louis daily urban system, 920
St. Louis, Missouri, 212, 390, 920
St. Paul, Minnesota, 212, 390, 925
Salter, Christopher L., 957
Sandefur, Gary D., 668
San Diego, historical geography, 953
San Diego, introduction to the region, 953
San Francisco bay area, 955, 956
San Francisco, California 212, 390, 955
San Francisco's Chinatown, 957
Sanguin, André-Louis, 755
Sanitary landfills, 195 (177-180)
Santer, Richard A., 907
Savageau, David, 417
Sawicki, David S., 474
Schafer, John W., 337
Schenker, Eric, 575
Schiffman, Irving, 766
Schlebecker, John T., 789
Schmeckebier, Laurence F., 179
Schmidt, Oswald, 876
Schnell, George A., 721
Schnore, Leo F., 405, 501
Schorr, Alan Edward, 170
Schroeder, Walter A., 919
Schwind, Paul J., 738
Scientific and technical aerospace reports, 253
Scientific and technical, spatial and bibliographical data base of the U.S. Geological Survey, 256
Scott, James W., 855
Scott, W. Richard, 403
Scull, Roberta A., 172, 173
Sea Grant publications index, 309, 310
Sea ice, 195 (101)
Sealock, Margaret M., 847
Sealock, Richard B., 847
Seattle, Washington, 212, 390, 965
Second homes, 844
Sediment transport and erosion in waterways, 195 (36)
Sediment transport in rivers, 195 (34, 35)

Sediment water interaction, 195 (37, 38)
Sedimentation, annotated bibliography, 285
Select bibliography, Asia, Africa, Eastern Europe, Latin America, 26, 26a
Selected and annotated bibliography of the planned suburban shopping centers, 453
Selected annotated bibliography of the climate of the Great Lakes, 322
Selected bibliography and index of earth science reports, 257
Selected bibliography of coastal erosion protection, 314
Selected bibliography on regional development, 599
Selected California bibliography, 944
Selected water resources abstracts, 280, 281
Selected Water Resources Abstracts data base, 195 (9, 12, 13, 14, 28, 31, 32, 43, 45, 52, 74, 82, 129, 147, 150, 151, 221)
Selective bibliography of surface coal mining, 195 (83)
Selective general guides, 23-26
Selective guide to climatic data sources, 319
Selective guides to geographical literature, 8-13, 70-73
Self, Huber, 924
Serials, 14-15, 74-129
Serials, guides, 14-15, 74-75
Services, urban, 468-473
Settlements and frontiers, historical geography, 781-783
Settlement geography, 708-709. See also urban geography, 390-513
Sewage treatment costs and economics, 195 (169, 170)
Seyler, H. L., 525
Sgourakis, Alice, 570
Shackelford, Jean A., 503
Shanas, Ethel, 627
Shannon, Gary William, 747
Sharma, Prakash C., 288
Shearer, Barbara Smith, 413
Shearer, Benjamin F., 413
Sheehy, Eugene P., 23, 23a, 23b, 848, 849, 850
Shelford, Victor E., 62
Shenendoah valley, early, commercialism and frontier, 805
Sherman, John C., 215
Shonyo, Carolyn, 195 (203)
Shopping center, planned suburban, 453
Shopping centers, 450-453
Shopping centers, regional, 450
Shore erosion: a survey of the literature, 315
Shoreline erosion, 195 (69)
Shorelines and beaches in coastal management, 313

Siddall, William R., 556
Sikes, Melanie M., 736
Silo, 714
Simmons, James W., 426
Simmons, Mary Ann, 377
Sinclair, Robert, 909
Single-enterprise communities, 494
Size, growth, and U.S. cities, 434
Small towns, 490
Smith, Christopher J., 752
Smith, David M., 618
Smith, Guy-Harold, 348
Smith, Mona F., 195 (145
Snead, Rodman, 301
Snipe's index, 79
Snow studies, 195 (53-55)
Sobek, A. A., 195 (83)
Social and economic information for urban planning, 476
Social and economic status of the Black Population, historical, 689
Social and historical sciences, Walford's guide to reference material, 4th ed., 856
Social geography, 616-645
Social geography of the United States, 616
Social justice and the city, 621
Social processes in the city, 461
Social processes, urban, 451-465
Social science research handbook, 855
Social sciences, general guides, 848-856
Social sciences and humanities index, 851
Social sciences index, 851
Social sciences with special emphasis on urban studies, 498
Social well-being, 618
Society, the city, and the space economy of urbanism, 460
Socio-economic impact of highways and commuter rail systems, 567
Sociological abstracts, 642
Sociology, 641-642
Sociology of America: a guide to information sources, 641
Sociology of American Indians, 667
Soil Conservation Service, 334
Soil erosion control, 195 (7, 8, 9)
Soil geography and land use, 337
Soil surveys, 334
Soil surveys, applications to land use planning, 335
Soil: yearbook of agriculture, 1957, 549
Soils, 334-337
Soils and men: yearbook of agriculture, 1938, 544
Solid waste, 195 (171-180), 383
Solid waste disposal economics, 195 (171-173)
Solid waste management, 383

Sommer, John W., 409
Sommers, Lawrence M., 906
Source list for the beginner in urban research, 414
Sourcebook on population, 724, 725
Sourcebook on the environment: a guide to the literature, 250
Sources of information about California, 945
Sources of information in the social sciences: a guide to the literature, 853
Sources of information in water resources: annotated guide, 282
South, 881-903; see also historical geography, 805-807, 815-817
South and East, airphoto atlas, 339
South Atlantic states, 888-893
South Carolina, 887, 890
South: its economic-geographic development, 882
South to north: cityward migration, 735
Southeast, 534, 881, 888
Southeast, research by geographers, 888
Southeastern geographer, 104
Southeastern United States, 881
Southeastern U.S., plant communities, 328
Southern region, 884
Southwest (Arizona and New Mexico); geographers' contributions, 935, 936
Southwest: Three peoples in geographical change, 1600-1970, 818
Southwest, water development and water planning, 948
Southwestern United States, 933
Späth, Hans-Joachim, 926, 949
Spatial allocation of costs and benefits in the open space decision process, 597
Spatial analysis of crime, 639
Spatial aspects of disease, 751-752
Spatial aspects of mortality, 751
Spatial components of manufacturing change, 1950-1960, 527
Spatial data bases of the U.S. Geological Survey, 256
Spatial dimensions of social organization, 622
Spatial dynamics of crime, 638
Spatial dynamics of U.S. urban-industrial growth, 1800-1860, 788
Spatial foundations of urbanism, 397
Spatial perspective on crime, 633
Spatial perspective on crime and violence, 635
Spatial perspectives on the criminal justice system, 636
Spatial studies in transportation, 557
Spatial structure and social issues in urban America, 405
Spatial structure and social patterns, changing, 772
Spatial variation of black urban households, 464

Special districts and authorities in the U.S., 762
Special districts in Cook County, 763
Special Libraries Association, 105
Spitzer, Manon, 26a
Sport, American, 716
Staatsbibliothek Preussischer Kulturbesitz, 22
Stadt und Kulturraum Angloamerika, 402
Stadterneuerung in den USA, 466
Stadtgeographische Studien in Südwesttexas, 903a
Stanford, Quentin H., 215
Stanford University, Center for Latin American Studies, 698
Stankey, George H., 353, 835
Stansfield, Charles A., Jr., 872
Starkey, Otis P., 241
Starr, John T., Jr., 573
State and metropolitan area data book, 152
State atlases, 205-208
State atlases: an annotated bibliography, 208
State atlases: major sources of spatial information, 205
State censuses, 144
State government reference publications, 196
State land resources planning, 589, 590
State-of-the-art reviews and bibliographies on energy, 195 (75, 76)
Statesman's year-book, 49
Statistical abstracts of the United States, 150-153
Statistical compilations, 150-165
Statistical publications of the U.S. government, 134
Statistical reference index, 140
Statistical services of the U.S. government, 135
Statistical sources: a subject guide, 139
Statistical yearbooks, 28
Statistics, 30-32, 134-165
Statistics, guides and catalogues, 134-149
Statistics sources, 29
Status of world topographic mapping, 33
Steel industry, 528
Steiner, Rodney, 941, 951
Stephenson, Richard W., 207, 209, 223
Stetzer, Donald F., 763
Stevens, Benjamin H., 522
Stevenson, Arthur J., 580
Stillwell, H. Daniel, 887
Stormwater management, 292
Stowe, Peter W. E., 219
Strand, Sverre, 408
Strässer, Manfred, 932
Strategies of American water management, 305

Stream erosion and scouring processes, 195 (39)
Strip mining, 195 (79-81), 275
Strip mining--environmental aspects, 275
Strip mining for coal, 529
Strip mining: impact on water resources, 195 (82)
Stuart, Merrill M., 232
Studies in geography. University of North Carolina, 97
Studies of highway development and geographic change, 568
Study of population, 721
Study of urbanization, 405
Subject bibliographies, U.S. Government publications, 185
Subject catalog. Library of Congress, 19
Subject catalog, Library of Congress main reading room, 132
Subject guide to books in print, 16
Subject guide to government reference books, 176
Subject index of the modern works added to the British Library, 20
Subsidence in the Houston-Galveston area, 387
Suburban America, 481
Suburban land conversion in the U.S., 344, 486
Suburban shopping center, 453
Suburban towns, 489
Suburbia: a guide to information sources, 484
Suburbanization, industrial, 488
Suburbanization of industrial firms, 487
Suburbs, 481-489
Suburbs, suburbia, and suburbanization, 485
Suitcase farming frontier, 813
Sunbelt migration, 734
Sunshine and shadows in metropolitan Miami, 893
Superports, 195 (253-255)
Supertankers, 195 (253-255)
Surface mined areas, 530
Surface transportation: demands and needs, 195 (233, 234)
Survey of current business, 615
Survey of urban economics, 504
Surveys of research, historical geography, 771-777
Swartz, Robert D., 407
Swift, Micheyo Yamaguchi, 701
Syracuse University, 121
Systems of cities and major job-providing organizations, 427
Szuwalski, Andre, 311

T

Taaffe, Edward J., 559
Taeuber, Conrad, 727, 728
Taeuber, Irene B., 727, 728
Talbot, Phillips, 26
Tankers and ports, 195 (253-255)
Taylor, George A., 506
Taylor grazing act, 928
Taylor L. J., 24, 856
Technical Information Center, U.S. Department of Energy 266, 267
Techniques of forecasting demand for water, 302
Tennessee: geographical patterns and regions, 896
Tennessee, University of, Water Resources Research Center, 296
Territorial social indicators, 618
Texas, 815-817, 900-903
Texas, historical geography, 815-817
Texas log buildings: a folk architecture, 711
Texas sources: a bibliography, 901
Texas, southwest, 903a
Texas. University. Population Research Center, 27
Theory of industrial location, 521
Thernstrom, Stephen, 646
Theses, 229-234, 351, 410-411, 829, 947
Theses and dissertations, California, 947
Theses and dissertations, land use, water use, resource conflict, 351
Theses and dissertations, recreation, 829
Theses and dissertations, urban geography, 1960-1970, 410
Theses and dissertations, urban studies, University of Chicago, 411
Thiloff, T. W., 291
Thom, Emma Mertins, 58
Thoman, Richard S., 239, 599
Thomas, Jean-Claude Marceau, 879
Thompson, Morris M., 200
Thornbury, William D., 259
Thornton, Russell, 666-668
Thrower, Norman J. W., 792
Tietze, Wolf, 42
Tiggesbäumker, Günter, 72
Time, space, and the geographic past, 777
Tivy, Joy, 834
Thompson, Bryan, 654, 909
Thompson, John H., 868
Thornton, Russell, 666-668
Todd, David K., 283, 284
Tompkins, Dorothy Campbell, 529
Topographic maps illustrating rural settlement patterns, 709
Tolzmann, Don Heinrich, 673
Toomey, Alice F., 18
Tourism, 195 (258-262), 828-844, 892
Tourism and recreation, NTIS reports, 195 (258-262)
Tourism and vacation travel: state and local government planning, 195 (258)

Tourism, recreation, and leisure, 828-844
Tourism, west coast of Florida, 892
Towns, new, 491-493
Towns, rural and suburban, 489
Towns, small, 490
Township atlas of the U.S., 217
Trade, 552-554
Trails to Texas, 317
Train, unit, evolution, 573
Transition, 110
Transportation, 195 (231-255), 454, 555-581
Transportation: a geographical bibliography, 555
Transportation economics: a guide to information sources, 563
Transportation geography: a bibliography, 556
Transportation geography: comments and readings, 560
Transportation, geography of, 559
Transportation: information sources, 562
Transportation Library, Northwestern University, 564
Transportation, NTIS reports, 195 (231-255)
Transportation, spatial studies, 557
Transportation, urban, 454, 558
Transportation, urban mass, 569
Transportation users: demands and need, 195 (238)
Transportation, water, 577
Travel habits and patterns, 195 (239, 240)
Travel in the United States: a guide to information sources, 830
Travis, Richard W., 749, 829, 931
Trees: a yearbook of agriculture, 1949, 547
Trejo, Arnulfo D., 696
Trigger, Bruce G., 65
Troise, Fred L., 286
Trygg, Lisa, 570
Tsunamis, 195 (100)
Tuan, Yi-Fu, 717
Turoff, Sidney, 660
Twentieth century cities, 390
Twenty geographical vignettes, contemporary metropolitan America, 390
Twin Cities of St. Paul and Minneapolis, 925
Tyckoson, David A., 388
Types of agricultural occupance of flood plains in the U.S., 300

U

USA: Der Grossraum in strukturellem Wandel, 246
USA. Die Regionen, 246
USA. Eine geographische Landeskunde, 246
U.S. Army, Corps of Engineers, 311, 312

U.S. Board on Geographic Names, 225
U.S. Bureau of Labor Statistics, 658
U.S. Bureau of Land Management, 594, 595
U.S. Bureau of Mines, 164, 189-190, 279
U.S. Bureau of Reclamation, 280, 285
U.S. Bureau of the Census, 136, 137, 138, 141, 142, 145, 150, 151, 152, 153, 155, 156, 157, 158, 159, 160, 161, 162, 165, 218, 689
U.S. Commission on Population Growth and the American Future, 726
U.S. Comptroller General, 174
U.S. Dept. of Agriculture, 163, 194, 543-551
U.S. Dept. of Agriculture. See also U.S. Soil Conservation Service.
U.S. Dept. of Commerce, 191, 192, 615, 864
U.S. Dept. of Commerce. Bureau of Economic Analysis, 615
U.S. Dept. of Commerce. Office of Regional Economic Development, 864
U.S. Dept. of Commerce. See also U.S. Bureau of the Census, U.S. Environmental Data and Information Service, U.S. Environmental Data Service, U.S. Environmental Science Information Center, U.S. Environmental Science Services Administration, U.S. National Oceanic and Atmospheric Administration, U.S. National Technical Information Service
U.S. Dept. of Commerce publications, 191-192
U.S. Dept. of Energy, 264, 265, 266, 267
U.S. Dept. of Energy. Technical Information Center, 266, 267
U.S. Dept. of Housing and Urban Development, 455, 493
U.S. Dept. of Justice. Immigration and Naturalization Service, 661
U.S. Dept. of Labor. See U.S. Bureau of Labor Statistics
U.S. Dept. of the Interior, 254
U.S. Dept. of the Interior. See also U.S. Board on Geographic Names, U.S. Bureau of Land Management, U.S. Bureau of Mines, U.S. Bureau of Reclamation, U.S. Geological Survey, U.S. Office of Water Research and Technology, U.S. Water Resources Scientific Information Center
U.S. Environmental Data and Information Service [now NOAA], 319
U.S. Environmental Data Service [now NOAA], 309, 324
U.S. Environmental Protection Agency, 252, 361-363

U.S. Environmental Protection Agency.
  Bibliographies of reports, 361, 363,
  363
U.S. Environmental Science Information
  Center [now NOAA], 309
U.S. Environmental Science Services
  Administration [now NOAA], 323
U.S.G.S., see U.S. Geological Survey
U.S. General Accounting Office. See
  U.S. Comptroller General
U.S. General Service Administration.
  See U.S. National Archives
U.S. Geological Survey, 58, 164, 186-188,
  199, 200, 210, 221, 225, 255, 256,
  257, 272, 273
U.S. Government Printing Office. See
  U.S. Superintendent of Documents
U.S. government publications for research
  and teaching in geography, 182
U.S. government research and development
  reports (NTIS), 195n
U.S. government research reports (NTIS),
  195n
U.S. Housing and Home Finance Agency
  [functions now in U.S. Dept. of
  Housing and Urban Development], 455
U.S. Library of Congress, 19, 25, 28,
  40, 130, 131, 132, 136, 144, 197, 201,
  203, 209, 251, 572
U.S. Library of Congress. Census Library
  Project, 28, 136, 144
U.S. Library of Congress. Geography and
  Map Division, 40, 201, 203, 209, 572
U.S. Library of Congress, Map Division.
  See Geography and Map Division
U.S. National Archives, 202
U.S. National Oceanic and Atmospheric
  Administration, 308, 309, 319, 322,
  324, 327
U.S. National Technical Information
  Service, 195
U.S. Office of Water Research and
  Technology, 280, 281
U.S. Soil Conservation Service, 334
U.S. Superintendent of Documents, 166,
  185
U.S. Water Resources Council [inactive
  as of October 1, 1982], 285, 297,
  303, 304
U.S. Water Resources Scientific Information
  Center, 281
Uhlig, Klaus R., 466
Union list of Sanborn fire insurance
  maps, 204
Unit train, evolution, 1960-1969, 573
United States, 66-974
United States and Canada, 240
United States and Canada: a regional
  geography, 245
United States and Canada: present and
  future, 239
United States atlases, 201

United States energy atlas, 269
United States Government publications, 180
United States of America (World bibliographical series), 133
United States urban revolution, 495
Universität, Freie, Berlin, 895
Universität Heidelberg, 894
Universität Marburg, 886, 934
Universität Regensburg, 964
Universität, Ruhr, 892
Universität Stuttgart, 432, 937
Universität Tübingen, 954
Université de Montréal, 328
Université du Québec, 755
Universitet, Aarhus, 948
Universitet, Moskovskii, 405a
University, American, 509
University, Bowling Green State, 93
University, Clark, 78
University, East Texas State, 88
University, Eastern Michigan, 769
University, Florida Atlantic, 125
University, George Mason, 129
University, Harvard, 574, 646, 827, 871
University, Indiana, 118
University, Indiana State, Terre Haute, 117
University, John Hopkins, 621
University, Kansas State, 126, 556
University, Louisiana State, 112, 712, 897, 898
University, New York State, at Binghamton, 109
University, Northwestern, 114, 564
University, Pennsylvania State, 120
University, Princeton, 739, 740
University, Ruhr, 892
University, Rutgers, 465, 801, 802, 874
University, San Diego State, 953
University, Southern Illinois, 677
University, Stanford, 698
University, Syracuse, 121, 868
University, Temple, 514-515
University, Texas A and M, 715
University, Western Michigan, 171, 375
University, Wilfrid Laurier, 115
University of Aarhus, 948
University of Akron, 128
University of Berlin, Free, 895
University of California, 111, 529, 552, 956, 958
University of California, Davis, 701, 766
University of Chicago, 8, 14, 15, 74, 75, 85, 300, 301, 306, 318, 411, 450, 459, 464, 476, 527, 573, 579, 580, 596, 597, 600, 638, 722, 738, 748, 763, 773, 791, 797, 804, 809, 915, 916, 928. See complete list of Research Papers at end of volume.
University of Colorado, 386, 831
University of Connecticut, 659

University of Georgia, 518, 845
University of Heidelberg, 894
University of Illinois, 116, 293
University of Iowa, 119
University of Kansas, 60
University of Marburg, 886, 934
University of Maryland, 803
University of Michigan, 113
University of Minnesota, 555, 666
University of Missouri, 832, 919, 923
University of Montreal, 328
University of Moscow, 405a
University of Nebraska, 810-813, 821, 927
University of Nevada, 495
University of North Carolina 97, 744, 883, 884
University of Northern Iowa, 39
University of Pittsburgh, 608, 612, 653
University of Quebec, 755
University of Regensburg, 964
University of Rhode Island, 310
University of South Carolina, 890
University of Southern Mississippi, 127
University of Stuttgart, 432, 937
University of Tennessee, 296
University of Texas, 27, 453, 816, 901
University of Tübingen, 954
University of Utah, 931
University of Washington, 568
University of Wisconsin, 575
University of Wisconsin-Milwaukee, 1a, 2, 38a, 86
University series, 85, 89, 93, 97, 109, 116-121
Upper Coulee country, 917
Urban affairs bibliography, 509
Urban air pollution, 195 (134-137)
Urban America: from downtown to no town, 512
Urban and regional economics: a guide to information sources, 503
Urban and regional information systems, 412
Urban and regional systems, 426
Urban areas, ethnic groups in, 654
Urban areas, NTIS reports, 195 (202-223)
Urban circulation noose, 454
Urban commerce, 446-453
Urban commodity flows, 571
Urban community: a guide to information sources, 510
Urban crisis: behavioral, psychological, and social aspects, 496
Urban development impacts of beltways, 566
Urban development in the USA and Hungary, 473
Urban ecology and neighborhoods, 440-441
Urban economics, survey of, 504
Urban environment and quality of life, 195 (209-211)

Urban environments and human behavior, 511
Urban fields, metropolitan America, 423
Urban form, land use, and environmental quality, 596
Urban geography, 106, 390-513
Urban geography, bibliography, 1940-1964, 409
Urban geography: city structures, 439
Urban geography, 1950-70: a comprehensive bibliography, 408
Urban geography, readings in, 406
Urban geography, southwest Texas, 903a
Urban governance and services, 468-473
Urban growth, 433-436
Urban growth and city systems in the U.S., 1840-1860, 787
Urban growth and the circulation of information: U.S. system of cities, 1790-1840, 786
Urban history: a guide to information sources, 507
Urban housing, 455-460
Urban housing: public and private: a guide to information sources, 456
Urban indicators: a guide to information sources, 502
Urban information systems, 195 (213-215)
Urban land use and zoning, 442-445
Urban land use planning, 442
Urban mass transportation, 195 (241-244), 454, 558, 567, 569, 570
Urban noise pollution, 195 (162, 163)
Urban parking, 195 (216)
Urban planning, 468-473
Urban planning: a guide to information sources, 474
Urban planning and air pollution, 382
Urban policy: a guide to information sources, 506
Urban policymaking and metropolitan dynamics, 391
Urban politics: a guide to information sources, 505
Urban pollution problems, 381
Urban preservation, 467
Urban preservation and the geography of the city in the USA, 467
Urban problems, 495-496
Urban problems, geographical perspectives on, 401
Urban renewal, 466
Urban residential choice and race, 461
Urban research, source list for the beginner, 414
Urban scene: human ecology and demography, 501
Urban services, 468-473
Urban social geography, 616-645
Urban social processes, 461-465
Urban society: an ecological approach, 500

Urban sociology, 499
Urban sprawl, 482
Urban storm sewers and water runoff, 134, 195 (217-221)
Urban Studies, Center for, University of Chicago, 411
Urban studies in geography: theses and dissertations, 410
Urban studies in related disciplines, 497-513
Urban studies information guide series, 456, 474, 484, 502-505, 506, 510
Urban studies, social sciences, 498
Urban surface runoff, 195 (47)
Urban system, American, growth centers, 433
Urban system, U. S., development of, 425
Urban systems, 418-429
Urban transportation, 195 (241-244), 454, 558, 567, 569, 570. See also Transportation, 555-581
Urban update to Directory of federal statistics for local areas, 145a
Urban violence, 634
Urbanism, space economy of, 460
Urbanization and changing land uses, 445
Urbanization and land use, effects on water, 195 (206-208)
Urbanization of American Indians, 668
Urbanization, study of, 405
Urbanizatsiia v S.Sh.A., 405a
Utah, 931, 932, 939
Utopias, 492

V

VINITI, 7, 69, 536
Vacation homes, 844
Vale, Thomas R., 63
Van Balen, John, 227, 228
Van der Leeden, Frits, 286
Van der Tak, Jean, 725
Van Nest, William J., 382
Van Zandt, Franklin K., 759
Vance bibliographies, 271, 274, 275, 276, 278, 292, 295, 315, 316, 335, 364, 365, 376, 380, 381, 387, 388, 438, 451, 478, 492, 520, 521, 566, 576, 577, 587, 669, 679, 710, 713, 733, 734, 757, 794, 796, 839
Vance, James E., Jr., 449, 554, 956
Vance, Jean, 955
Vance, Mary, 447, 451, 628
Vance, Rupert B., 883
Vankat, John L., 329
Vegetation, 60-63, 328-333
Vegetation change in North America, 63
Vegetation maps of North America, 60
Vegetation of North and Central America and of the Hawaiian Islands, 61
Vegetation von Nord- und Mittelamerika und der Hawaii-Inseln, 61

Vegetationsmonographie der einzelnen Grossräume, 61
Velikonja, Joseph, 677
Vernacular architecture, 710
Vernon, Philip H., 876
Vignette of the New York-New Jersey metropolitan region, 869
Vinge, Ada G., 182
Vinge, Clarence L., 182
Violence and crime, geography of, 635
Virginia geographer, 129
Virginia Geographical Society, 129
Virginia in our century, 889
Visher, Stephen S., 325
Visual blight in America, 717
Vogeler, Ingolf K., 840, 861, 887, 906, 939
Vollmar, Rainer, 895
Vseseoiuznyi Institut Nauchnoi i Tekhnicheskoi Informatsii, 7, 69, 536

W

Wacker, Peter O., 801, 802
Wade, Richard, 915
Wahrhaftig, Clyde, 970
Waldo, Kay Cronkite, 764
Walford, Albert John, 24, 856
Walford's guide to reference material, 856
Walker, Flora K., 273
Walker, H. J., 705
Wallace, William H., 861
Ward, David, 655, 779, 785
Warner, W. Keith, 252
Warnes, Anthony M., 623
Warren, Kenneth, 528
Wasatch chronicle, 931
Wasatch oasis, 932
Washington, D. C., 212, 390, 879
Wasserman, Paul, 29, 139
Waste disposal and pollution, NTIS reports, 195 (105-186)
Water, 195 (12-55, 82, 138-144, 153-161), 280-307, 377, 948
Water atlas of the U.S., 286
Water-based recreation, 842
Water conservation, 287, 299
Water demand, 302
Water development and water planning in the Southwestern U.S., 948
Water Information Center, Port Washington, N.Y., 282, 283, 284, 286
Water management, 305
Water planning, Southwestern U.S., 948
Water pollution: a guide to information sources, 377
Water pollution economics, 195 (138-141)
Water pollution in estuaries and coastal zones, 195 (142-144)
Water publications of state agencies, 283

Water quality modeling: hydrological and limnological systems, 195 (48-52)
Water Research and Technology, Office of, 280, 281
Water resource development, a bibliography, 288
Water resource development in the Great Lakes Basin, 294
Water resource development, public opinion, 195 (22)
Water resource programs, planning and management, 195 (15-18)
Water resources, 280-307
Water Resources Center, University of Illinois, 293
Water Resources Council, 285, 297, 303, 304
Water resources, development planning, 290
Water resources for our cities, 298
Water resources, hydrology, floods, and snow, NTIS reports, 195 (12-55)
Water resources, impact of strip mining on, 195 (82)
Water resources in arid and semiarid regions, 195 (40, 41)
Water resources planning, 195 (14)
Water resources, recreation, 195 (261-262)
Water Resources Research Center, University of Tennessee, 296
Water Resources Scientific Information Center, 281
Water supplies: potential, 195 (13)
Water supply, regional, 195 (19-21)
Water transportation, 577
Water use, theses and dissertations, 351
Water: yearbook of agriculture, 1955, 548
Waterfront development, 578
Watershed planning, 289
Watersheds, agricultural, 195 (32)
Watersheds, forest, 195 (29-31)
Waterway transportation, 195 (251, 252)
Waterways, inland, transportation, 574
Watson, J. Wreford, 244, 368, 616
Weather almanac: a reference guide, 326
Weather atlas of the U.S., 323
Weathers, John W., 296
Weaver, John E., 332, 333
Weber, R. David, 263
Weed, Perry L., 656
Wehmeier, Eckhard, 937
Weigand, B., 57
Weigand, Kral, 903a
Weis, Ina J., 275
Weiss, Joseph E., 734
Wellar, Barry S., 412, 457
West, 928-974; see also historical geography, 818-824
West North Central states and the Great Plains, 918-929
West Virginia, 861

West Virginia and Appalachia: selected readings, 880
Westermann Lexikon der Geographie, 42
Western America, exploration, 1800-1850, 819
Western Association of Map Libraries, 107
Western cattle ranching, 817
Western interior of United States, climate, 1800-1850, 927
Westoff, Charles F., 726
Westview Press, 861, 887, 906, 939, 971
Wheeler, James O., 419, 454, 518, 519, 557, 558, 565, 571
Wheeler, Jesse H., 70
White, Anthony G., 414, 758, 760, 761
White, C. Albert, 793a
White, C. Langdon, 237
White, Carl M., 853
White, Gilbert F., 305, 306, 385, 389
Whitelaw, Jim, 426
Wholesaling, 449, 554
Wilderness as sacred space, 357
Wilderness management, 353
Wilderness preservation, 354
Wiley, S. C., 781
Willamette Valley, 963
Williams, Connie L., 487
Willis, Cleve E., 360
Willis, Dawn E., 569
Wilson, Carolyn, 290
Wilson, L. G., 195 (42)
Winberry, John J., 887
Winch, Kenneth L., 34
Windhorst, Hans-Wilhelm, 537
Winsborough, Hal H., 403
Winters, Harold A., 9, 71
Wisconsin, 906
Wisconsin. University, Milwaukee, 1a, 38a, 86
Wishart, David J., 821
Wohlenberg, Ernest H., 630
Wolf, Harry P., 581
Wollman, Nathaniel, 307
Women, 629, 629a
Wood, James L., 499
Wood, Patricia A., 499
Woods, Richard D., 695
World almanac gazetteer, 226
World atlas of agriculture, 531
World bibliography of bibliographies, 17
World bibliography of bibliographies 1964-1974, 18
World cartography, 33
World survey of climatology, 59, 320
Worldmark encyclopedia of the nations, 51
Worldmark encyclopedia of the states, 224
World-wide bibliographies, 1-52
Worsham, John P., Jr., 364, 365, 576, 577, 588

Wright, John K., 10, 213, 862
Wright, Rita J., 901
Writing regional geography: Anglo-American realm, 857
Wynar, Lubomyr, 663
Wynkoop, Sally, 170, 176
Wyoming: a geography, 930

Y

Yearbook, Association of Pacific Coast Geographers, 83
Yearbook of agriculture, 543-551
Yeates, Maurice H., 393, 420
Young, Bruce, 115
Young, Mary E., 195 (189, 192, 209, 213, 259, 260)
Young, Robert N., 243
Young, William J., 269
Yu, Elena S. H., 700

Z

Zeitlin, Morris, 415
Zelinsky, Wilbur, 9, 214, 702, 722, 723
Zierer, Clifford M., 940
Zikmund, Joseph, II, 484
Zimmer, Dietrich M., 894
Zimolzak, Chester E., 861, 880
Zollars, Gerald F., 195 (5, 106, 257)
Zoning and city planning, 479
Zoning and land use, 442-445
Zoning--exclusionary zoning, 444
Zubkova, A. N., 971a
Zucker, Rosalie, 701
Zuga, Connie S., 725
Zumstein-Katalog, 35
Zurawski, Joseph W., 678

Total number of entries in this volume: 1,257

974 sequentially numbered entries, minus 2 numbers suppressed (458, 586), plus 23 added entries (1a, 13a, 23a, 23b, 26a, 27a, 36a, 38a, 145a, 161a, 343a, 405a, 554a, 629a, 740a, 793a, 868a, 884a, 903a, 905a, 927a, 927b, 971a), plus 262 separate entries for NTIS reports grouped under entry 195.

THE UNIVERSITY OF CHICAGO
DEPARTMENT OF GEOGRAPHY
RESEARCH PAPERS (Lithographed, 6×9 inches)

Titles in print are available from Department of Geography, The University of Chicago, 5828 S. University Avenue, Chicago, Illinois 60637, U.S.A. Price: $8.00 each; by series subscription, $6.00 each.

COMPLETE LIST, 1948–February 1984

1. GROSS, HERBERT HENRY. *Educational Land Use in the River Forest-Oak Park Community (Illinois).* 1948. 123 p.
2. EISEN, EDNA E. *Educational Land Use in Lake County, Ohio.* 1948. 161 p.
3. WEIGEND, GUIDO GUSTAV. *The Cultural Pattern of South Tyrol (Italy).* 1949. 198 p.
4. NELSON, HOWARD JOSEPH. *The Livelihood Structure of Des Moines, Iowa.* 1949. 140 p.
5. MATTHEWS, JAMES SWINTON. *Expressions of Urbanism in the Sequent Occupance of Northeastern Ohio.* 1949. 179 p.
6. GINSBURG, NORTON SYDNEY. *Japanese Prewar Trade and Shipping in the Oriental Triangle.* 1949. 308 p.
7. KEMLER, JOHN H. *The Struggle for Wolfram in the Iberian Peninsula, June, 1942—June, 1944: A Study in Political and Economic Geography in Wartime.* 1949. 151 p.
8. PHILBRICK, ALLEN K. *The Geography of Education in the Winnetka and Bridgeport Communities of Metropolitan Chicago.* 1949. 165 p.
9. BRADLEY, VIRGINIA. *Functional Patterns in the Guadalupe Counties of the Edwards Plateau.* 1949. 153 p.
10. HARRIS, CHAUNCY D., and FELLMANN, JEROME D. *A Union List of Geographical Serials.* 1950. 124 p.
11. DE MEIRLEIR, MARCEL J. *Manufactural Occupance in the West Central Area of Chicago.* 1950. 251 p.
12. FELLMANN, JEROME DONALD. *Truck Transportation Patterns of Chicago.* 1950. 109 p.
13. HOTCHKISS, WESLEY AKIN. *Areal Pattern of Religious Institutions in Cincinnati.* 1950. 103 p.
14. HARPER, ROBERT ALEXANDER. *Recreational Occupance of the Moraine Lake Region of Northeastern Illinois and Southeastern Wisconsin.* 1950. 176 p.
15. WHEELER, JESSE HARRISON, JR. *Land Use in Greenbrier County, West Virginia.* 1950. 180 p.
16. MCGAUGH, MAURICE EDRON. *The Settlement of the Saginaw Basin.* 1950. 407 p.
17. WATTERSON, ARTHUR WELDON. *Economy and Land Use Patterns of McLean County, Illinois.* 1950. 154 p.
18. HORBALY, WILLIAM. *Agricultural Conditions in Czechoslovakia, 1950.* 1951. 104 p.
19. GUEST, BUDDY ROSS. *Resource Use and Associated Problems in the Upper Cimarron Area.* 1951. 127 p.
20. SORENSEN, CLARENCE WOODROW. *The Internal Structure of the Springfield, Illinois, Urbanized Area.* 1951. 190 p.
21. MUNGER, EDWIN S. *Relational Patterns of Kampala, Uganda.* 1951. 165 p.
22. KHALAF, JASSIM M. *The Water Resources of the Lower Colorado River Basin.* 1951. Volume I, 234 p.; Volume II, 15 maps in pocket.
23. GULICK, LUTHER H., JR. *Rural Occupance in Utuado and Jayuya Municipios, Puerto Rico.* 1952. 254 p.
24. TAAFFE, EDWARD JAMES. *The Air Passenger Hinterland of Chicago.* 1952. 161 p.
25. KRAUSE, ANNEMARIE ELISABETH. *Mennonite Settlement in the Paraguayan Chaco.* 1952. 143 p.
26. HAMMING, EDWARD. *The Port of Milwaukee.* 1952. 162 p.
27. CRAMER, ROBERT ELI. *Manufacturing Structure of the Cicero District, Metropolitan Chicago.* 1952. 176 p.
28. PIERSON, WILLIAM H. *The Geography of the Bellingham Lowland, Washington.* 1953. 159 p.
29. WHITE, GILBERT F. *Human Adjustment to Floods: A Geographical Approach to the Flood Problem in the United States.* 1942. 225 p. Reprinted 1953.
30. OSBORN, DAVID G. *Geographical Features of the Automation of Industry.* 1953. 106 p.
31. THOMAN, RICHARD S. *The Changing Occupance Pattern of the Tri-State Area, Missouri, Kansas, and Oklahoma.* 1953. 139 p.
32. ERICKSEN, SHELDON D. *Occupance in the Upper Deschutes Basin, Oregon.* 1953. 139 p.
33. KENYON, JAMES B. *The Industrialization of the Skokie Area.* 1954. 124 p.
34. PHILLIPS, PAUL GROUNDS. *The Hashemite Kingdom of Jordan: Prolegomena to a Technical Assistance Program.* 1954. 191 p.
35. CARMIN, ROBERT LEIGHTON. *Anápolis, Brazil: Regional Capital of an Agricultural Frontier.* 1953. 172 p.

36. GOLD, ROBERT N. *Manufacturing Structure and Pattern of the South Bend-Mishawaka Area.* 1954. 224 p.
37. SISCO, PAUL HARDEMAN. *The Retail Function of Memphis.* 1954. 160 p.
38. VAN DONGEN, IRENE S. *The British East African Transport Complex.* 1954. 172 p.
39. FRIEDMANN, JOHN R. P. *The Spatial Structure of Economic Development in the Tennessee Valley.* 1955. 187 p.
40. GROTEWOLD, ANDREAS. *Regional Changes in Corn Production in the United States from 1909 to 1949.* 1955. 78 p.
41. BJORKLUND, ELAINE M. *Focus on Adelaide—Functional Organization of the Adelaide Region, Australia.* 1955. 133 p.
42. FORD, ROBERT N. *A Resource Use Analysis and Evaluation of the Everglades Agricultural Area.* 1956. 127 p.
43. CHRISTENSEN, DAVID E. *Rural Occupance in Transition: Sumter and Lee Counties, Georgia.* 1956. 160 p.
44. GUZMÁN, LOUIS E. *Farming and Farmlands in Panama.* 1956. 137 p.
45. ZADROZNY, MITCHELL G. *Water Utilization in the Middle Mississippi Valley.* 1956. 119 p.
46. AHMED, G. MUNIR. *Manufacturing Structure and Pattern of Waukegan-North Chicago.* 1957. 117 p.
47. RANDALL, DARRELL. *Factors of Economic Development and the Okovango Delta.* 1957. 268 p.
48. BOXER, BARUCH. *Israeli Shipping and Foreign Trade.* 1957. 162 p.
49. MAYER, HAROLD M. *The Port of Chicago and the St. Lawrence Seaway.* 1957. 283 p.
50. PATTISON, WILLIAM D. *Beginning of the American Rectangular Land Survey System, 1784-1800.* 1957. 248 p.
51. BROWN, ROBERT HAROLD. *Political Areal-Functional Organization: With Special Reference to St. Cloud, Minnesota.* 1957. 123 p.
52. BEYER, JACQUELYN L. *Integration of Grazing and Crop Agriculture: Resources Management Problems in the Uncompahgre Valley Irrigation Project.* 1957. 125 p.
53. ACKERMAN, EDWARD A. *Geography as a Fundamental Research Discipline.* 1958. 37 p.
54. AL-KHASHAB, WAFIQ HUSSAIN. *The Water Budget of the Tigris and Euphrates Basin.* 1958. 105 p.
55. LARIMORE, ANN EVANS. *The Alien Town: Patterns of Settlement in Busoga, Uganda.* 1958. 208 p.
56. MURPHY, FRANCIS C. *Regulating Flood-Plain Development.* 1958. 204 p.
57. WHITE, GILBERT F., et al. *Changes in Urban Occupance of Flood Plains in the United States.* 1958, 235 p.
58. COLBY, MARY MCRAE. *The Geographic Structure of Southeastern North Carolina.* 1958. 226 p.
59. MEGEE, MARY CATHERINE. *Monterrey, Mexico: Internal Patterns and External Relations.* 1958. 118 p.
60. WEBER, DICKINSON. *A Comparison of Two Oil City Business Centers (Odessa-Midland, Texas).* 1958. 239 p.
61. PLATT, ROBERT S. *Field Study in American Geography.* 1959. 405 p.
62. GINSBURG, NORTON, editor. *Essays on Geography and Economic Development.* 1960. 173 p.
63. HARRIS, CHAUNCY D., and FELLMANN, JEROME D. *International List of Geographical Serials.* 1960. 189 p.
64. TAAFFE, ROBERT N. *Rail Transportation and the Economic Development of Soviet Central Asia.* 1960. 186 p.
65. SHEAFFER, JOHN R. *Flood Proofing: An Element in a Flood Damage Reduction Program.* 1960. 198 p
66. RODGERS, ALLAN L. *The Industrial Geography of the Port of Genova.* 1960. 144 p.
67. KENYON, JAMES B. *Industrial Localization and Metropolitan Growth: The Paterson-Passaic District.* 1960. 224 p.
68. GINSBURG, NORTON. *Atlas of Economic Development.* 1961. 119 p. 14 × 9¼". Cloth. University of Chicago Press.
69. CHURCH, MARTHA. *Spatial Organization of Electric Power Territories in Massachusetts.* 1960. 187 p
70. WHITE, GILBERT F., et al. *Papers on Flood Problems.* 1961. 228 p.
71. GILBERT, EDMUND WILLIAM *The University Town in England and West Germany.* 1961. 74 p.
72. BOXER, BARUCH. *Ocean Shipping in the Evolution of Hong Kong.* 1961. 95 p.
73. ROBINSON, IRA M. *New Industrial Towns of Canada's Resource Frontier.* 1962. 190 p.
74. TROTTER, JOHN E. *State Park System in Illinois.* 1962. 152 p.
75. BURTON, IAN. *Types of Agricultural Occupance of Flood Plains in the United States.* 1962. 167 p
76. PRED, ALLAN R. *The External Relations of Cities during 'Industrial Revolution'.* 1962. 113 p.
77. BARROWS, HARLAN H. *Lectures on the Historical Geography of the United States as Given in 1933.* Edited by WILLIAM A. KOELSCH. 1962. 248 p.

78. KATES, ROBERT WILLIAM. *Hazard and Choice Perception in Flood Plain Management.* 1962. 157 p.
79. HUDSON, JAMES W. *Irrigation Water Use in the Utah Valley, Utah.* 1962. 249 p.
80. ZELINSKY, WILBUR. *A Bibliographic Guide to Population Geography.* 1962. 257 p.
81. DRAINE, EDWIN H. *Import Traffic of Chicago and Its Hinterland.* 1963. 138 p.
82. KOLARS, JOHN F. *Tradition, Season, and Change in a Turkish Village.* 1963. 205 p.
83. WIKKRAMATILEKE, RUDOLPH. *Southeast Ceylon: Trends and Problems in Agricultural Settlement.* 1963. 163 p.
84. KANSKY, KAREL J. *Structure of Transportation Networks: Relationships between Network Geometry and Regional Characteristics.* 1963. 155 p.
85. BERRY, BRIAN J. L. *Commercial Structure and Commercial Blight.* 1963. 235 p.
86. BERRY, BRIAN J. L., and TENNANT, ROBERT J. *Chicago Commercial Reference Handbook.* 1963. 278 p.
87. BERRY, BRIAN J. L., and HANKINS, THOMAS D. *A Bibliographic Guide to the Economic Regions of the United States.* 1963. 101 p.
88. MARCUS, MELVIN G. *Climate-Glacier Studies in the Juneau Ice Field Region, Alaska.* 1964. 128 p.
89. SMOLE, WILLIAM J. *Owner-Cultivatorship in Middle Chile.* 1963. 176 p.
90. HELVIG, MAGNE. *Chicago's External Truck Movements: Spatial Interactions between the Chicago Area and Its Hinterland.* 1964. 132 p.
91. HILL, A. DAVID. *The Changing Landscape of a Mexican Municipio, Villa Las Rosas, Chiapas.* 1964. 121 p.
92. SIMMONS, JAMES W. *The Changing Pattern of Retail Location.* 1964. 200 p.
93. WHITE, GILBERT F. *Choice of Adjustment to Floods.* 1964. 150 p.
94. MCMANIS, DOUGLAS R. *The Initial Evaluation and Utilization of the Illinois Prairies, 1815–1840.* 1964. 109 p.
95. PERLE, EUGENE D. *The Demand for Transportation: Regional and Commodity Studies in the United States.* 1964. 130 p.
96. HARRIS, CHAUNCY D. *Annotated World List of Selected Current Geographical Serials in English.* 1964. 32 p.
97. BOWDEN, LEONARD W. *Diffusion of the Decision To Irrigate: Simulation of the Spread of a New Resource Management Practice in the Colorado Northern High Plains.* 1965. 146 p.
98. KATES, ROBERT W. *Industrial Flood Losses: Damage Estimation in the Lehigh Valley.* 1965. 76 p.
99. RODER, WOLF. *The Sabi Valley Irrigation Projects.* 1965. 213 p.
100. SEWELL, W. R. DERRICK. *Water Management and Floods in the Fraser River Basin.* 1965. 163 p.
101. RAY, D. MICHAEL. *Market Potential and Economic Shadow: A Quantitative Analysis of Industrial Location in Southern Ontario.* 1965. 164 p.
102. AHMAD, QAZI. *Indian Cities: Characteristics and Correlates.* 1965. 184 p.
103. BARNUM, H. GARDINER. *Market Centers and Hinterlands in Baden-Württemberg.* 1966. 173 p.
104. SIMMONS, JAMES W. *Toronto's Changing Retail Complex.* 1966. 126 p.
105. SEWELL, W. R. DERRICK, et al. *Human Dimensions of Weather Modification.* 1966. 423 p.
106. SAARINEN, THOMAS FREDERICK. *Perception of the Drought Hazard on the Great Plains.* 1966. 183 p.
107. SOLZMAN, DAVID M. *Waterway Industrial Sites: A Chicago Case Study.* 1966. 138 p.
108. KASPERSON, ROGER E. *The Dodecanese: Diversity and Unity in Island Politics.* 1966. 184 p.
109. LOWENTHAL, DAVID, editor, *Environmental Perception and Behavior.* 1967. 88 p.
110. REED, WALLACE E., *Areal Interaction in India: Commodity Flows of the Bengal-Bihar Industrial Area.* 1967. 209 p.
111. BERRY, BRIAN J. L. *Essays on Commodity Flows and the Spatial Structure of the Indian Economy.* 1966. 334 p.
112. BOURNE, LARRY S. *Private Redevelopment of the Central City, Spatial Processes of Structural Change in the City of Toronto.* 1967. 199 p.
113. BRUSH, JOHN E., and GAUTHIER, HOWARD L., JR., *Service Centers and Consumer Trips: Studies on the Philadelphia Metropolitan Fringe.* 1968. 182 p.
114. CLARKSON, JAMES D., *The Cultural Ecology of a Chinese Village: Cameron Highlands, Malaysia.* 1968. 174 p.
115. BURTON, IAN, KATES, ROBERT W., and SNEAD, RODMAN E. *The Human Ecology of Coastal Flood Hazard in Megalopolis.* 1969. 196 p.
116. MURDIE, ROBERT A., *Factorial Ecology of Metropolitan Toronto, 1951–1961.* 1969. 212 p.
117. WONG, SHUE TUCK, *Perception of Choice and Factors Affecting Industrial Water Supply Decisions in Northeastern Illinois.* 1969. 93 p.
118. JOHNSON, DOUGLAS L.. *The Nature of Nomadism: A Comparative Study of Pastoral Migrations in Southwestern Asia and Northern Africa.* 1969. 200 p.

119. DIENES, LESLIE. *Locational Factors and Locational Developments in the Soviet Chemical Industry.* 1969. 262 p.
120. MIHELIĆ, DUŠAN. *The Political Element in the Port Geography of Trieste.* 1969. 104 p.
121. BAUMANN, DUANE D. *The Recreational Use of Domestic Water Supply Reservoirs: Perception and Choice.* 1969. 125 p.
122. LIND, AULIS O. *Coastal Landforms of Cat Island, Bahamas: A Study of Holocene Accretionary Topography and Sea-Level Change.* 1969. 156 p.
123. WHITNEY, JOSEPH B. R. *China: Area, Administration and Nation Building.* 1970. 198 p.
124. EARICKSON, ROBERT. *The Spatial Behavior of Hospital Patients: A Behavioral Approach to Spatial Interaction in Metropolitan Chicago.* 1970. 138 p.
125. DAY, JOHN C. *Managing the Lower Rio Grande: An Experience in International River Development.* 1970. 274 p.
126. MAC IVER, IAN. *Urban Water Supply Alternatives: Perception and Choice in the Grand Basin Ontario.* 1970. 178 p.
127. GOHEEN, PETER G. *Victorian Toronto, 1850 to 1900: Pattern and Process of Growth.* 1970. 278 p.
128. GOOD, CHARLES M. *Rural Markets and Trade in East Africa.* 1970. 252 p.
129. MEYER, DAVID R. *Spatial Variation of Black Urban Households.* 1970. 127 p.
130. GLADFELTER, BRUCE G. *Meseta and Campiña Landforms in Central Spain: A Geomorphology of the Alto Henares Basin.* 1971. 204 p.
131. NEILS, ELAINE M. *Reservation to City: Indian Migration and Federal Relocation.* 1971. 198 p.
132. MOLINE, NORMAN T. *Mobility and the Small Town, 1900–1930.* 1971. 169 p.
133. SCHWIND, PAUL J. *Migration and Regional Development in the United States.* 1971. 170 p.
134. PYLE, GERALD F. *Heart Disease, Cancer and Stroke in Chicago: A Geographical Analysis with Facilities, Plans for 1980.* 1971. 292 p.
135. JOHNSON, JAMES F. *Renovated Waste Water: An Alternative Source of Municipal Water Supply in the United States.* 1971. 155 p.
136. BUTZER, KARL W. *Recent History of an Ethiopian Delta: The Omo River and the level of Lake Rudolf.* 1971. 184 p.
137. HARRIS, CHAUNCY D. *Annotated World List of Selected Current Geographical Serials in English, French, and German* 3rd edition. 1971. 77 p.
138. HARRIS, CHAUNCY D., and FELLMANN, JEROME D. *International List of Geographical Serials* 2nd edition. 1971. 267 p.
139. MCMANIS, DOUGLAS R. *European Impressions of the New England Coast, 1497–1620.* 1972. 147 p.
140. COHEN, YEHOSHUA S. *Diffusion of an Innovation in an Urban System: The Spread of Planned Regional Shopping Centers in the United States, 1949–1968*, 1972. 136 p.
141. MITCHELL, NORA. *The Indian Hill-Station: Kodaikanal.* 1972. 199 p.
142. PLATT, RUTHERFORD H. *The Open Space Decision Process: Spatial Allocation of Costs and Benefits.* 1972. 189 p.
143. GOLANT, STEPHEN M. *The Residential Location and Spatial Behavior of the Elderly: A Canadian Example.* 1972 226 p.
144. PANNELL, CLIFTON W. *T'ai-chung, T'ai-wan: Structure and Function.* 1973. 200 p.
145. LANKFORD, PHILIP M. *Regional Incomes in the United States, 1929–1967: Level, Distribution Stability, and Growth.* 1972. 137 p.
146. FREEMAN, DONALD B. *International Trade, Migration, and Capital Flows: A Quantitative Analysis of Spatial Economic Interaction.* 1973. 201 p.
147. MYERS, SARAH K. *Language Shift Among Migrants to Lima, Peru.* 1973. 203 p.
148. JOHNSON, DOUGLAS L. *Jabal al-Akhḍar, Cyrenaica: An Historical Geography of Settlement and Livelihood.* 1973. 240 p.
149. YEUNG, YUE-MAN. *National Development Policy and Urban Transformation in Singapore: A Study of Public Housing and the Marketing System.* 1973. 204 p.
150. HALL, FRED L. *Location Criteria for High Schools: Student Transportation and Racial Integration.* 1973. 156 p.
151. ROSENBERG, TERRY J. *Residence, Employment, and Mobility of Puerto Ricans in New York City* 1974. 230 p.
152. MIKESELL, MARVIN W., editor. *Geographers Abroad: Essays on the Problems and Prospects Research in Foreign Areas.* 1973. 296 p.
153. OSBORN, JAMES F. *Area, Development Policy, and the Middle City in Malaysia.* 1974. 291 p.
154. WACHT, WALTER F. *The Domestic Air Transportation Network of the United States.* 1974. 98 p.
155. BERRY, BRIAN J. L., et al. *Land Use, Urban Form and Environmental Quality.* 1974. 440 p.
156. MITCHELL, JAMES K. *Community Response to Coastal Erosion: Individual and Collective Adjustments to Hazard on the Atlantic Shore.* 1974. 209 p.

157. COOK, GILLIAN P. *Spatial Dynamics of Business Growth in the Witwatersrand.* 1975. 144 p.
158. STARR, JOHN T., JR. *The Evolution of Unit Train, 1960–1969.* 1976. 233 p.
159. PYLE, GERALD F. et al. *The Spatial Dynamics of Crime.* 1974. 221 p.
160. MEYER, JUDITH W. *Diffusion of an American Montessori Education.* 1975. 97 p.
161. SCHMID, JAMES A. *Urban Vegetation: A Review and Chicago Case Study.* 1975. 266 p.
162. LAMB, RICHARD F. *Metropolitan Impacts on Rural America.* 1975. 196 p.
163. FEDOR, THOMAS STANLEY. *Patterns of Urban Growth in the Russian Empire during the Nineteenth Century.* 1975. 245 p.
164. HARRIS, CHAUNCY D. *Guide to Geographical Bibliographies and Reference Works in Russian or on the Soviet Union.* 1975. 478 p.
165. JONES, DONALD W. *Migration and Urban Unemployment in Dualistic Economic Development.* 1975. 174 p.
166. BEDNARZ, ROBERT S. *The Effect of Air Pollution on Property Value in Chicago.* 1975. 111 p.
167. HANNEMANN, MANFRED. *The Diffusion of the Reformation in Southwestern Germany, 1518–1534.* 1975. 235 p.
168. SUBLETT, MICHAEL D. *Farmers on the Road. Interfarm Migration and the Farming of Noncontiguous Lands in Three Midwestern Townships, 1939–1969.* 1975. 214 p.
169. STETZER, DONALD FOSTER. *Special Districts in Cook County: Toward a Geography of Local Government.* 1975. 177 p.
170. EARLE, CARVILLE V. *The Evolution of a Tidewater Settlement System: All Hallow's Parish, Maryland, 1650–1783,* 1975. 239 p.
171. SPODEK, HOWARD. *Urban-Rural Integration in Regional Development: A Case Study of Saurashtra, India, 1800–1960.* 1976. 144 p.
172. COHEN, YEHOSHUA S. and BERRY, BRIAN J. L. *Spatial Components of Manufacturing Change, 1950–1960.* 1975. 262 p.
173. HAYES, CHARLES R. *The Dispersed City: The Case of Piedmont, North Carolina.* 1976. 157 p.
174. CARGO, DOUGLAS B. *Solid Wastes: Factors Influencing Generation Rates.* 1978. 100 p.
175. GILLARD, QUENTIN. *Incomes and Accessibility. Metropolitan Labor Force Participation, Commuting, and Income Differentials in the United States, 1960–1970.* 1977. 106 p.
176. MORGAN, DAVID J. *Patterns of Population Distribution: A Residential Preference Model and Its Dynamic.* 1978. 200 p.
177. STOKES, HOUSTON H.; JONES, DONALD W. and NEUBURGER, HUGH M. *Unemployment and Adjustment in the Labor Market: A Comparison between the Regional and National Responses.* 1975. 125 p.
179. HARRIS, CHAUNCY D. *Bibliography of Geography. Part I. Introduction to General Aids.* 1976. 276 p.
180. CARR, CLAUDIA J. *Pastoralism in Crisis. The Dasanetch and their Ethiopian Lands.* 1977. 319 p.
181. GOODWIN, GARY C. *Cherokees in Transition: A Study of Changing Culture and Environment Prior to 1775.* 1977. 207 p.
182. KNIGHT, DAVID B. *A Capital for Canada: Conflict and Compromise in the Nineteenth Century.* 1977. 341 p.
183. HAIGH, MARTIN J. *The Evolution of Slopes on Artificial Landforms—Blaenavon, U.K.* 1978. 293 p.
184. FINK, L. DEE. *Listening to the Learner. An Exploratory Study of Personal Meaning in College Geography Courses.* 1977. 186 p.
185. HELGREN, DAVID M. *Rivers of Diamonds: An Alluvial History of the Lower Vaal Basin, South Africa.* 1979. 389 p.
186. BUTZER, KARL W., editor. *Dimensions of Human Geography: Essays on Some Familiar and Neglected Themes.* 1978. 190 p.
187. MITSUHASHI, SETSUKO. *Japanese Commodity Flows,* 1978. 172 p.
188. CARIS, SUSAN L. *Community Attitudes toward Pollution.* 1978. 211 p.
189. REES, PHILIP H. *Residential Patterns in American Cities, 1960.* 1979. 405 p.
190. KANNE, EDWARD A. *Fresh Food for Nicosia.* 1979. 106 p.
191. WIXMAN, RONALD. *Language Aspects of Ethnic Patterns and Processes in the North Caucasus.* 1980. 243 p.
192. KIRCHNER, JOHN A. *Sugar and Seasonal Labor Migration: The Case of Tucumán, Argentina.* 1980. 174 p.
193. HARRIS, CHAUNCY D. and FELLMANN, JEROME D. *International List of Geographical Serials, Third Edition, 1980.* 1980. 457 p.
194. HARRIS, CHAUNCY D. *Annotated World List of Selected Current Geographical Serials, Fourth, Edition, 1980.* 1980. 165 p.
. LEUNG, CHI-KEUNG. *China: Railway Patterns and National Goals.* 1980. 233 p.

196. LEUNG, CHI-KEUNG and NORTON S. GINSBURG, eds. *China: Urbanization and National Development*. 1980. 280 p.
197. DAICHES, SOL. *People in Distress: A Geographical Perspective on Psychological Well-being*. 1981. 199 p.
198. JOHNSON, JOSEPH T. *Location and Trade Theory: Industrial Location, Comparative Advantage, and the Geographic Pattern of Production in the United States*. 1981. 107 p.
199-200. STEVENSON, ARTHUR J. *The New York-Newark Air Freight System*. 1982. 440 p.
(Double number, price: $16.00)
201. LICATE, JACK A. *Creation of a Mexican Landscape: Territorial Organization and Settlement in the Eastern Puebla Basin, 1520–1605*. 1981. 143 p.
202. RUDZITIS, GUNDARS. *Residential Location Determinants of the Older Population*. 1982. 117 p.
203. LIANG, ERNEST P. *China: Railways and Agricultural Development, 1875–1935*. 1982. 186 p.
204. DAHMANN, DONALD C. *Locals and Cosmopolitans: Patterns of Spatial Mobility during the Transition from Youth to Early Adulthood*. 1982. 146 p.
205. FOOTE, KENNETH E. *Color in Public Spaces: Toward a Communication-Based Theory of the Urban Built Environment*. 1983. 153 p.
206. HARRIS, CHAUNCY D. *Bibliography of Geography. Part II: Regional. Vol. 1. The United States of America*. 1984. 178 p.
207-208. WHEATLEY, PAUL. *Nāgara and Commandery: Origins of the Southeast Asian Urban Traditions*. 1983. 473 p.
(Double number, price: $16.00)
210. WESCOAT, JAMES L., JR. *Integrated Water Development: Water Use and Conservation Practice in Western Colorado*. 1984. 239 p.